# HR Policies and Procedures

## MANUAL FOR MEDICAL PRACTICES

**5th EDITION**

# HR Policies
# and Procedures

## MANUAL FOR MEDICAL PRACTICES

COURTNEY PRICE, PHD

MGMA
104 Inverness Terrace East
Englewood CO 80112-5306
877.275.6462
mgma.org

**Library of Congress Cataloging-in-Publication Data**

Price, Courtney H., author.
 [MGMA HR policies & procedures manual for medical practices]
 HR policies and procedures manual for medical practices / Courtney Price. -- 5th edition.
     p. ; cm.
 Includes index.
 Preceded by MGMA HR policies & procedures manual for medical practices / Courtney Price, Alys Novak. 4th ed. c2007.
 ISBN 978-1-56829-393-6
 I. Medical Group Management Association, issuing body. II. Title.
 [DNLM: 1.  Practice Management, Medical--organization & administration.
 2.  Employment--manpower. 3.  Personnel Management--methods.  W 80]
 R728
 610.68'3--dc23
                                    2014010549

Item # 8538
ISBN-13: 978-1-56829-393-6

Printed in the United States of America

10 9 8 7 6 5 4 3 2

# Contents

# Contents

# Preface

Without effective management of its human assets, no medical practice can be successful. As a result, the Medical Group Management Association (MGMA) has emphasized human resource management (HRM) as a key domain in its Body of Knowledge for Medical Practice Management efforts, its conferences, and publications.

For example, in 1984, MGMA published *The Management Guide for Developing Policies, Procedures, and Employee Handbooks*. In 1991, that volume was revised and published as *The Group Practice Personnel Policies Manual*. A revised edition was then published in 1997. In 2007, a fourth edition was revised and published as the *HR Policies and Procedures Manual for Medical Practices*.

This newly revised and updated volume continues to demonstrate MGMA's ongoing commitment to provide the most current HRM information for its members. So it is time again for a new edition of the manual. This fifth edition includes:

- Revised and updated policies;
- New policies reflecting today's healthcare and business landscape;
- Checklists to ensure that your practice is in compliance;
- Easy-to-use forms to modify for your practice; and
- Human Resources Policy templates your practice can adopt.

This manual provides an overview of employment practices and procedures. It also provides template policies and forms designed to give you an idea about the types of policies and forms practices may consider adopting. However, much of the information covered and the template policies and forms provided are governed by various federal, state, and local laws that cannot be thoroughly discussed or addressed here. Further, employment laws and court and agency interpretations of these laws are constantly changing. Medical practices should consult with legal counsel to tailor these policies and forms to their practice's needs and to ensure compliance with all current applicable laws.

Keep in mind as you use this manual that it does not represent an interpretation of laws applicable to the various policies and procedures and should not be used as a substitute for professional legal counsel. It is strongly advised that legal counsel review the final versions and regular updates of your practice manuals and employee handbooks to ensure compliance with applicable laws.

Before initiating the development of policies and procedures, take time to review the mission, vision, and values of your practice. This forethought helps ensure that the implementation of new policies and procedures reflects your practice's core values. To meet your practice's mission, vision, and values, one simple template is not enough. I recommend you use the series of policies and procedures in this book as a guide to define and reflect the goals and objectives of your practice.

When developing or updating your human resources (HR) policies and procedures manual, try to involve managers and supervisors from all departments of your practice by soliciting their input. A team effort will help create sound policies and procedures to ensure that your patients, staff, and providers' preferences and needs will be met.

Next, collect all current policies and procedures, and be sure to put into writing any unwritten or unpublished information currently used to guide staff performance. When all of this information is gathered, the development and revision process can begin. Upon completion of the manual's development phase, ask key managers to review and approve each policy and procedure for content and presentation style.

Following the best practices listed below ensures the successful development of an HR policies and procedures manual for your practice:

- Format all policies consistently;
- Keep it simple;
- Number each policy and procedure for quick reference;
- Date each policy when developed and at each revision;
- Specify the purpose of each policy;
- Identify the procedure(s) for enacting or implementing each policy;
- Be as specific as possible without being overly restrictive;
- Include position titles rather than employee names;
- Use concise statements;
- Use action verbs;
- Use clear language;
- Review and update policies and procedures at least annually to ensure compliance with changing regulations; and
- Appoint one individual to keep the manual current and ensure that updates are communicated and distributed to all staff members.

Policies and procedures are not the same as contracts and should not replace management decision making. Medical groups cannot ignore dilemmas simply because they have a policies and procedures manual to address the problems. This manual should be used as a guide for developing and revising your practice's policies and procedures, not as a static alternative to taking appropriate management actions.

The policies and procedures provided in this manual encompass many administrative processes. Because of the wide variation in which different practices operate and their diverse communication needs, I recommend that you use this book as a resource and not an end product.

The continually changing healthcare environment periodically dictates new rules and regulations. Although this book was current at the date of publication, many of the policies and procedures are considered a work in progress and need to be frequently updated to keep pace with internal changes, new legislation, changing economic conditions, and other external forces affecting your practice.

The user should maintain a database of policies and procedures and a schedule for updates. A policies and procedures database helps to manage the updating and maintenance process. Conventions for numbering and naming policies should be designed to match your practice's preferences.

Since this manual is designed for a national audience, the authors and MGMA cannot ensure that this manual adheres to the legal requirements of each locality or state. Rather, an attempt has been made to consider the impact of federal laws and nationwide legal trends. Have your legal counsel review and approve your specific employment policies to ensure that you are following the legal requirements of your state and locality.

# Acknowledgments

The author has been a long-time author for the Medical Group Management Association (MGMA) and has written many of their human resource management books over the years, including this fifth edition of the *HR Policies and Procedures Manual for Medical Practices*. I offer special appreciation to Marilee Aust, former senior manager, knowledge management, who has worked with me since the very first edition in 1984. I also thank the Information Center and especially Marti Cox, knowledge advisor, who has been a tremendous resource, helped collect various materials, and offered fantastic support for this publication and numerous others. Lastly on the MGMA team, I thank Betsy Holt, senior manager in the Innovation and Product Design Department, who provided great guidance and assistance taking the original manuscript through the publishing process to MGMA members.

I also express appreciation to Janet McIntyre, Director of Care Management-Ambulatory Care Services at Denver Health and Hospital Authority, for her insights into medical practice management and guidance on the new and changing healthcare landscape. I also extend my gratitude to Elizabeth A. MacDonald of counsel at Faegre Baker Daniels LLC for completing the legal review of the manual.

Last, but not least, I recognize my associate Jill Hansen from VentureQuest, who worked very closely with me to redesign, update, and include all the latest trends so it is a state-of-the-art publication representing best human resources practices.

# Introduction

Medical practices epitomize service-based businesses – they depend on people. Human resources (HR) departments provide not only patient care but also handle all business-related tasks such as answering the phones, paying the bills, scheduling patients, and processing claims. Without employees with diverse talents and the motivation to help others, your practice cannot exist. It is important to understand the foundation of your HR policies and procedures – successfully managing human resources.

To ensure business success, a medical practice's manager must effectively manage people. An HR policies and procedures manual and an employee handbook help those in your practice involved in human resource management (HRM) deal appropriately and effectively with staff. Published documents specify consistent methods for selecting employees, compensating staff, and handling performance-related matters that also facilitate long-term strategic and day-to-day management.

In the past, particularly in small businesses, informalities regarding policies and procedures were fairly common and created an atmosphere based on the idea that "this is the way we do things here." This approach often leads to vagueness and misunderstandings that can cause problems between supervisors and employees, as well as accusations of favoritism or bias. To avoid such charges, the person responsible for HRM should promote the development, documentation, and implementation of policies as a consistent way to deal with specific issues.

## Managing Human Resources

To conduct business, medical practices, like any organization, need several types of resources, including space, equipment and supplies, financial capital, and, most of all, human capital. As a general rule, once an organization has two people on staff, it needs policies to guide the behavior of those people and to ensure that they are treated appropriately and consistently. On average, each physician needs six support staff. In a practice with two or more physicians, the need for HR policies is critical to ensure smooth functioning.

Since the 1990s, HRM has been considered a strategic business function. Those fulfilling this role typically operate at the senior management level and participate in such top-level decisions as the expansion of your practice and related people considerations. *Personnel*, which is an antiquated term for *human resources* as a whole, is the administrative arm of human resources and includes such roles as record-keeping and government reporting.

Decades ago, 80 percent of a company's value could be seen on their balance sheet as tangible assets, that is, facilities and equipment. The other 20 percent was referred to as intangible assets, which included brand, staff, and intellectual property. Today, the figures have reversed and intangible assets now represent most of an organization's book value. Topics such as mentoring, training and professional development, and performance management are recognized as keys to success of an organization. In short, no organization, particularly a medical practice, can afford to downplay HRM and relegate it as just another administrative duty.

### HR Functions and Roles

An HR department is generally responsible for the following functions in a medical practice:

- Strategic planning activities;
- Job analysis and descriptions;
- Recruitment and selection;
- Wage and salary administration;
- Benefits administration;
- Training and professional development;
- Leadership development;
- Labor and employee relations;
- Workplace safety and risk management;
- Personnel record-keeping and reporting;
- Employee privacy and confidentiality;
- Equal employment and affirmative action matters;
- Emergency and disaster planning;
- Employee assistance programs; and
- Wellness and fitness programs.

In some medical practices, the HR department may be responsible for payroll and perhaps some aspects of facilities management. If your medical practice has a large staff, it is typically better to delegate these duties that require specialized skill sets to other departments. For example, the Accounting Department could be responsible for payroll.

Whether you are a one-person operation or part of a large department, your medical practice may also outsource some of these functions or utilize consultants to limit your in-house responsibilities and possibly legal risks from specific HR functions. In small practices, the administrator or designee, with some outsourcing help, performs most HR tasks.

The chief person in the HR department may be titled director, manager, or administrator. In large groups, the job position of vice president of human resources may exist at the senior management level. Whatever the title, the emphasis should be on the professionalism of the person in charge and the perspective he or she can bring to the vital issues of employee relations, morale, and performance. Some various titles or roles and associated responsibilities in an HR department include the following:

- **HR manager.** Oversees all HR functions and staff, handles complex issues, makes annual and long-term plans, and represents the department at the senior management level.
- **HR specialist.** Handles legal and regulatory matters such as workers' compensation and administers the human resources information system (HRIS) and production of reports.
- **HR specialist.** Handles recruitment and selection of new employees.
- **HR specialist.** Handles benefits administration.
- **HR specialist.** Handles employee relations matters.

Depending on the size of your medical practice, a few or several people will be responsible for these HR functions. Just make sure that there are enough staff members to handle all of the tasks. A general rule is to have one HR staff member for every 100 employees if all functions are handled in-house rather than being outsourced. It may make sense to outsource some HR functions, even the ones your practice can handle. Payroll is the classic example, as well as benefits administration.

To summarize, there are five key activities that dominate most of HRM:

1. Developing departmental goals consistent with your practice's overall strategic plan, goals, and objectives;
2. Developing, maintaining, and updating HR policies and procedures with top management support;
3. Assisting managers and supervisors in policy and procedure implementation;
4. Developing and implementing internal audit and control measures to ensure appropriate policy compliance; and
5. Researching and initiating new or revised HR programs, policies, and procedures.

As you ensure that these activities and all the HR responsibilities are carried out, remember that HRM can never be just the responsibility of the HR department. The entire senior management team is responsible for ensuring that HR policy-making and implementation is fair, consistent, and current. HRM responsibilities have grown over the last few decades. Today, HR departments use their specialized knowledge and skills to increase employee productivity, improve morale, and help guide a medical practice into the future. It's a never-ending challenge, and up-to-date policies and procedures will help navigate the path to future success.

## What Is a Policy?

A policy is a definite course of action adopted for the sake of expediency and reflecting prudence and practical wisdom. Published policies provide directions for manager and employee decisions and behaviors. They also save considerable time because of the common understanding communicated to everyone by the same methods. Policies are guides to the philosophy behind an organization's goals and expectations for its human resources.

Policies provide a framework for consistent actions and decisions by supervisors and managers. Their intent is for equality and fairness for all employees in various circumstances. Sound policies help the medical practice communicate to staff members:

- The medical practice's philosophies,
- What they can expect from the medical practice,
- What the medical practice expects from them,
- What is acceptable behavior, and
- The consequences of unacceptable behavior.

Policies should be updated often to reflect changes in laws and regulations, and shifts in trends. They should also include operating procedures, which bring the policy to life. Procedures are the chronological action steps for implementing and executing a policy.

## Developing Policies and Procedures

The sample policies in this manual contain the necessary elements useful for policy development in your medical practice. You can use these samples to formulate your own policies by modifying them to fit your practice's preferred format and style. All policies should be reviewed by legal counsel before implementation.

Medical practices should have a defined process for developing new and revising existing policies and procedures. The process should be matched to your practice's size, philosophy, and needs. The process used to develop the policies and procedures that go into the manual should be easy to use and consistent. The following list is a sample process that your medical practice could modify to fit your needs.

1. The designated HR professional drafts a new policy based on a newly identified need, a change in laws and regulations, or a shift in practice management strategies.
2. Annually, the designated HR professional reviews all policies and procedures. When a policy needs to be revised, the designated HR professional drafts a revised policy.
3. Supervisors and managers review draft policies and related procedures, and recommend any revisions and add comments.
4. The designated HR professional reviews all supervisor/manager comments and incorporates feedback into the policy as needed.
5. Your practice administrator reviews second drafts of policies and recommends revisions and adds comments.
6. The designated HR professional incorporates feedback from the administrator.
7. Your practice's legal counsel reviews the policy and makes needed changes.
8. Your practice administrator approves final policies and procedures.
9. The new or revised policies and procedures are placed into the policies and procedures manual and the employee handbook, and made available online.
10. The designated HR professional notifies all employees that a new policy has been implemented or an existing policy has been revised, including the location where employees can review it.

## Hot Trends to Watch

The healthcare environment never stops evolving, and many of these shifts and changes directly impact your medical practice and, thereby, your HRM policies. These trends may come from new legislation, cultural and demographic shifts, new technology, and employee fitness and wellness programs, which are summarized below.

**Trends to Watch**

- New legislation and regulations
- Multigenerational workforce
- New technological advances
- Employee wellness programs

### New Legislation and Regulations

A series of recent legislation since 2009 has reformed the American healthcare system. Although many requirements from healthcare reform have been enacted, HR professionals are still unclear of the exact impact the new legislation and regulations will have on medical practices. Healthcare reform has been enacted via two congressional bills: the Patient Protection and Affordable Care Act (PPACA) of 2010 and the Health Care and Education Reconciliation Act of 2010 that amended the PPACA. In addition, the American Recovery and Reinvestment Act (ARRA) of 2009 (the stimulus bill) and the Health Information Technology for Economic and Clinical Health (HITECH) Act, enacted as part of the stimulus bill, add many regulations to patient privacy and the use of electronic medical records. These regulations force designated HR professionals and the medical practice's legal counsel to stay abreast of the changing legislative environment to ensure compliance. New policies and procedures have to be developed or existing policies updated as legislation and regulations change.

### Multigenerational Workforce

Possibly for the first time, there are four distinct generations of employees in the workforce today: the so-called "Traditionalists" (born before 1946), the "Baby Boomers" (born 1946–1964), the "Generation Xers" (born 1965–1979), and the "Millennials" (born 1980–2000). People are tending to work more years since life expectancy is lengthening and retirement benefits and entitlements are being cut or may not enable the desired standard of living.

Traditionalists and Baby Boomers are reaching retirement. This trend is particularly affecting physicians and nursing vacancies where there may be a shortage of the younger generations entering into these professions. With such a high percentage of the workforce (Baby Boomers) reaching retirement age, there will be a worker and skills shortage that HR departments will encounter. Planning how to deal with retiring employees is crucial to ensure a smooth transition. Developing a succession plan, including leadership development opportunities for employees, can help lessen the impact of retiring workers.

A multigenerational workforce will require a variety of employee benefits offered by the medical group. Older workers need different benefit options than those of the younger generations. For example, a Baby Boomer may want long-term or elder-care benefits; a Generation Xer may be more interested in child-care programs; while a Millennial worker may be looking for more comprehensive health and dental coverage. In addition, domestic partner benefits are sometimes offered as a standard benefit offering.

Offering and administering a variety of benefits to employees will help medical practices acquire top talent and retain star employees.

### New Technological Advances

Over the past few years, medical practices and other employers have seen an explosion of new technologies affecting the work environment. The use of social networks has changed the way many medical practices recruit and screen candidates, mobile devices have changed traditional communication, and cloud computing will continue to advance the way HR departments manage your practice's human resources.

As more employees bring their iPhones, iPads, and Android devices to work, designated HR professionals must develop and/or update policies regarding the use of mobile devices, applications (apps), and social media. Mobile health, the transfer or ability to access healthcare information using mobile devices, is rapidly gaining popularity, particularly with the younger generations. Mobile health apps, which help providers care for patients, are quickly evolving into new, innovative ways to treat patients.

### Employee Wellness Programs

As healthcare costs and insurance premiums continue to escalate, countless employers emphasize employee fitness and wellness programs. Many employers use cash rewards and other incentives to encourage workers to improve their health by losing weight and quitting smoking. Successful employee wellness programs can pay off for employers because employees tend to be more productive and miss fewer days due to illness. Clinics and medical practices are in a unique position to promote healthy lifestyles for not only their employees but also for their patients.

## Summary

The *HR Policies and Procedures Manual for Medical Practices* includes HR policies designed in a template form throughout the manual so you can adapt them to your medical practice. Perhaps more importantly, it provides the background for each policy – why it is needed and its history, legal considerations, and other things that should be considered as you develop your medical practice's policies. In short, this manual provides that context for your policy-making.

This manual has been designed to help medical practices develop new and/or revise existing HR policies and procedures, possibly compiling them into a manual or handbook, that meet both your practice's and employees' needs. The chapters in this manual present information about the key HRM elements, from planning to recruitment to compensation to employee safety and health.

# CHAPTER 1

# Developing a Policies and Procedures Manual

Policy 1.01   Confidentiality and Annual Review Requirements

Policy 1.02   Human Resources Policy Revisions

As changes in American healthcare occur and technology evolves, so has human resource management (HRM) along with the methods medical practices and other healthcare organizations use to develop, communicate, and provide access to their human resources (HR) policies and procedures. Traditionally, most medical practices developed and printed an employee policies and procedures manual outlining policies that managers and supervisors use in their daily planning and decision making. Some medical practices also developed an employee handbook, which is a derivative of a policies and procedures manual, and distributed copies to staff members. The employee handbook explains the medical practice's policies, benefits, and rules, including employees' roles and responsibilities.

But today, most medical practices are foregoing the high cost of initially printing copies of policies and procedures manuals and employee handbooks and then reprinting updated versions. Instead, these documents are housed on the practice's intranet or server for easy access. Regardless of which method your medical practice uses, it is critical to establish a process to inform all management and staff when new policies are enacted or when existing policies are revised.

## Critical Elements of a Policies and Procedures Manual

Regardless of whether your medical practice's policies and procedures manual is printed or posted on the intranet, there are certain critical elements that need to be included. To set the tone of the manual, make sure it reflects:

- Your practice's basic employee-relations philosophies, ethical beliefs, and values about how management interacts with staff;
- The strategy of the organization;
- The vision for the future of your practice; and

- The information needed for making consistent, legally sound management decisions.

You may wish to preface the policies in the manual with a letter from the chief executive officer, senior administrator, or the board of directors to your managers and supervisors about leadership's commitment to ensure fair and consistent employment and performance policies. Such a letter or memorandum communicates leadership's support of the policies and explains the rationale and purpose of their policies and procedures. At the end of this chapter is a sample format (Form 1.1) to follow for elements in a policy as well as a sample memo (Form 1.2) to use as a guide.

In an introduction to the manual, identify:

- The purpose of the manual, the kind of policies it contains, and the practice's commitment to compliance;
- The users of both the manual and the employee handbook and how these items should be used; and
- The ways policies are made available to staff.

Every policies and procedures manual should have a table of contents so staff can quickly find the subject of interest. See Chapter 13, Employee Handbook, for more detailed information on how to develop an employee handbook.

The following list describes the typical elements that should be part of a policies and procedures manual:

- **Numbering system.** Use a numbering system to identify each section and each individual policy. You can use a standard system as utilized in this manual. For example, compensation may be Section 5.00, and policies concerning compensation are numbered 5.01, 5.02, and so on. Using a system like this, you can quickly find the subject matter and the specific policy you want.
- **Dating system.** Dating policies is important for tracking a policy's history and evolution. Record the date the policy was initially approved and the effective date for each revision. Doing both is absolutely necessary. Also note the person who approved the policy or change.
- **Packaging.** Packaging is important, whether your medical practice will use a printed manual, an electronic manual, or both. The goal is to make both versions as user friendly as possible. For printed versions, a standard three-ring binder with dividing tabs works well and expedites updating. For electronic versions, a detailed yet clear table of contents with hyperlinks works well for quick access to a specific section or policy.

Your medical practice's policies and procedures manual should be presented in a standard, easy-to-use format. Not only will this aid development, production, and updating, it will also help managers, supervisors, and staff by presenting policy information consistently.

## The Audience

Usually your managers and supervisors are the primary users of HR policies, whether in print or electronic forms. They are the individuals who have the responsibility to administer and put the policies into practice. When using a printed version, you may choose to give each manager and supervisor a copy of the policies and procedures manual, but it is more practical to limit the distribution to division managers. Otherwise, updating can become a logistical burden.

At the same time, all policies should be made available to each employee. It is inappropriate to keep them secret. Give employees access to the division's policies and procedures manual and also to the electronic version. It is particularly important to communicate any new policy or revised policy to all employees. Today, this communication is usually done via an e-mail to all employees. Explain the new or revised policy to managers so they can also communicate it to the workers. If your practice has an employee newsletter, this is a good place to outline the highlights of the new policy. Use the employee handbook as a quick, staff-oriented reference tool. The handbook distills policies in a brief, straightforward manner.

In the past, if policies and procedures were distributed broadly, it was customary for a controlled circulation form to be in each policies and procedures manual. The form was used to track to whom and when the manual was issued. If you limit distribution to a few locations, this tracking system is not necessary. The individual responsible for distributing and updating the policies and procedures manual can easily manage tracking a few manuals. Many practices require employees who have been terminated to return any printed copies of the policies and procedures manual to the HR manager.

## Producing the Manual

If your medical practice does not have a policies and procedures manual, it is recommended that you develop one. The following steps can be used when developing a policies and procedures manual for your medical practice.

1. **Establish a committee.** Establish a small committee to advise you when developing or revising the policies and procedures manual. You may also choose to use the senior management team. In any case, senior managers should be aware that development or revision of the policies and procedures manual is in process. The manual should be reviewed on a regular basis to ensure it is up to date. See Policies 1.01 and 1.02 at the end of the chapter.

2. **Establish a budget.** Assuming you will use internal resources for producing the manual and limit the number of printed manuals, this cost should be minimal and easy to monitor. The higher cost is staff time. The more people you involve in the development and review process, the more that staff productivity is reduced. Information technology (IT) costs should be included for programming the manual for your practice's intranet. Estimate the cost of designing your manual, which will be greater if you hire a graphic designer rather than utilizing internal resources such as Microsoft Word® or a desktop publishing application. If you will be printing copies of the manual, include printing costs in the budget. Also be sure to include any legal counsel and/or consultant costs.

3. **Set a timeline.** Decide on a publication deadline for the new or revised manual. From there, set a project schedule to meet that deadline. Assign an individual to be held accountable for reaching each milestone in the project schedule.

4. **Seek counsel.** Consult an outsider such as an employment attorney, your local employers' council, or your industry association, such as the Medical Group Management Association, about new laws and employment practice trends to ensure you are aware of any new policies or revisions needed.

5. **Decide the format and design.** Decide how the policies and procedures manual will look in both printed and electronic versions. Typically, the printed manuals are a standard 8½-×-11-inch size in a three-ring binder with dividing tabs, which is easy to update. As mentioned earlier, electronic versions should have hyperlinks embedded for quick access to the sections and individual policies. The design, including font type, should match the branding or other practice publications in use.

6. **Assign a primary policy developer.** This person is accountable for developing and/or updating the policies assigned by the committee.

7. **Review drafts with the committee.** The committee and a legal counsel, if necessary, should review the drafts of the new or revised policies. The committee will recommend revisions, and the primary policy developer will incorporate the feedback. The committee should seek supervisor input on specific polices and also test policy concepts on key employees. Many organizations now use online survey tools, such as SurveyMonkey®, to collect employee opinions and feedback on potential new policies or changes to existing policies. Often you will find that employees have insights and perspectives that help clarify policy direction.

8. **Compile the finalized policies.** Organize all final policies into sections in a logical order in the policies and procedures manual. Once the manual is formatted and approved by the committee, the physical copies should be printed and distributed and the electronic version should be made "live" on the intranet.

9. **Communicate to all employees.** Develop a communications plan to introduce new or revised policies not only to managers but to all staff members. Any related training for managers and supervisors should be developed and scheduled. Supervisors should be thoroughly trained so they can explain the policies to their staff and answer any questions. They are the best source of information regarding employees' reactions to policies, how policies are impacting employee morale and productivity, and how policies might be modified to achieve better results in the future. In a communication piece to all staff about the policies and procedures manual, explain the manual's contents and encourage questions. In addition, if printed copies are available, communicate where those copies are located (e.g., the administrator's office, HR department).

## Evaluating the Manual

Evaluating your policies and procedures manual is an important activity to ensure its effectiveness and relevancy. When evaluating your manual, determine if:

- The current policy-making and communication systems meet the needs of your organization, managers, and employees;
- Everyone understands the policies and believe they are appropriate; and
- The policies achieve the results needed by the organization in terms of employee relations and performance.

To evaluate your medical practice's policies and procedures manual, use both formal and informal approaches. An informal method is to encourage supervisors and managers to constantly provide feedback. For example, you may discover that several supervisors are getting requests for more flexible schedules. A division manager may believe that recruiting has become difficult because the pay structure is no longer competitive within the industry. Feedback like these examples will help you develop new or revise existing policies and procedures that are aligned with what employees are wanting. If supervisors aren't providing this feedback, ask them for it.

A more formal approach is to develop and administer a questionnaire to determine · managers' opinions about the policies and procedures manual. Use an online survey tool or send a questionnaire via e-mail to seek the information that will help you and senior management know whether certain policies are having a positive or negative impact on employee morale and productivity, and if new policies should be developed or revisions need to be made to existing policies. In the questionnaire, ask managers and supervisors to rate the following elements of the manual:

- Appearance/format/organization;
- Timeliness/relevance;
- Accuracy;
- Effectiveness;
- Comprehensiveness;
- Assistance for decision making; and
- Operational efficiency.

## Updating the Manual

Every medical practice should periodically review their policies and procedures manual and update it. A general rule is to review the policies and procedures manual annually, including having your legal counsel review it as well. Beyond the scheduled periodic review, there are various circumstances that could prompt an update. These situations could be:

**Tips for Staying on Top of New Policy Trends**

- Read, watch, and listen.
- Research new trends.
- Meet with the HR Policy Committee to determine plans of action.
- Keep senior management informed.
- Make any necessary updates to policies.

- A major new law or legislation is passed that may determine how you can recruit and manage employees;
- Your practice significantly increases in size;
- Internal trends occur, indicating your employees are leaving to pursue their careers with your competitors that have more attractive employment policies;
- Senior management or the board of directors has changed dramatically thereby changing management's philosophies in regard to managing human resources;
- New societal trends take place that may trigger changes in employment laws and general practices;
- Employment benefit development affecting your compensation packages and your competitiveness; or
- Some policies are so out of date that they are no longer relevant.

The life of a policies and procedures manual is short due to these previously mentioned circumstances. It should never be considered complete and final, but rather a work in progress. Realize that not only do employment laws change from time to time because of social trends, but they can also vary from state to state. Thus, it is critical that your legal counsel review your policies and procedures on a regular basis.

As stated previously, your medical practice should review the manual at least annually unless something triggers an immediate update, for example, a change in employment laws. The date of the annual review should be noted in the policies and procedures manual. Further, individual policies should be under review by the HR policy committee on a continuous basis. Your medical practice should have a policy regarding confidentiality and annual review requirements to ensure that all policies and procedures remain current. Policies 1.01 and 1.02 at the end of this chapter are sample policies that your medical practice can adapt to meet your specific needs.

There should be no surprises about any trend triggers. External factors such as societal trends and related government regulations, as well as benefit evolutions, are well publicized, not only in the HR publications and conferences but also by the consumer media. The local employer's council and the Society for Human Resource Management, among others, are great resources for keeping up to date on trends in the HR field.

## Summary

Your medical practice will benefit by developing and maintaining policies related to every aspect of its HRM, just as it benefits from operational and governing policies. Employees need to know not only what is expected from them, but also about employment laws and related management responsibilities. Packaging this information into a policies and procedures manual makes it convenient to reference them all in one place at one time.

Some medical practices include a code of ethics as a preface to the policies and procedures manual. However, it is usually better to include this in the section of the policies and procedures manual that features your practice's ethics policy.

After you have a system in place for policy-making, policy development, and policy updating, you will find that these policies ease communication and improve employee performance and satisfaction.

**Sample Policies**

**Policy 1.01**      <u>**Confidentiality and Annual Review Requirements**</u>

This is an example of a confidentiality statement and annual review requirements for a policies and procedures manual.

---

Policy 1.01             **CONFIDENTIALITY AND ANNUAL REVIEW REQUIREMENTS**

<u>Purpose:</u> To ensure that all *[Practice]* policies and procedures are reviewed periodically and held confidentially.

<u>Applies to:</u> Human Resources Department

<u>Policy:</u> It is the policy of *[Practice]* to review all policies in the *HR Policies and Procedures Manual* annually. The *HR Policies and Procedures Manual* is designed for the exclusive use of *[Practice]*. It is considered confidential information. Sharing this information with others is unacceptable unless the Administrator or designated HR professional has given permission to do so.

<u>Approved by:</u> Practice Administrator

<u>Effective date:</u> 1/1/20__

**Policy 1.02**     **Human Resources Policy Revisions**

This is an example of a policy regarding revisions of policies and procedures.

---

POLICY 1.02                    **HUMAN RESOURCES**
                               **POLICY REVISIONS**

Purpose: To ensure that all policies and procedures are up to date and meet changing requirements, needs, and legislation.

Applies to: Human Resources Department

Policy: *[Practice]* expects to revise human resources (HR) policies to meet changing needs. This shall be done consistently.

Procedures:

1. Any staff member of *[Practice]* may suggest policy revisions by doing so in writing to the designated HR professional.

2. The designated HR professional may be asked to research suggested revisions.

3. If appropriate, the designated HR professional drafts a revised policy for review by the Administrator, designee, or Policy Committee.

4. The Administrator or Policy Committee then accepts, rejects, or modifies the proposed revision and, if it is approved, sets an effective date for adopting the revised policy.

5. The revised policy is communicated to staff via all-employee messages in appropriate media. The printed *HR Policies and Procedures Manual*, the electronic manual, and the *Employee Handbook* are updated. Training is provided as needed to staff, supervisors, and managers.

Approved by: Practice Administrator

Effective date: 1/1/20__

**Sample Forms**

**Form 1.1**        <u>**Policy Format**</u>

This is an example of a policy format.

---

FORM 1.1                    **POLICY FORMAT**

Each policy should include the following information:
- Policy number;
- Policy name;
- Purpose;
- Applies to (which employees are covered by the policy);
- Policy (describe what the policy is);
- Procedures;
- Approved by (name and title of person who approved the policy for implementation); and
- Effective date.

**Form 1.2**                **Sample Policies and Procedures Manual Memo for Management**

This is an example of a memo from the medical practice's administrator to management and supervisory staff regarding the policies and procedures manual.

---

FORM 1.2                                      **MEMO**

January 1, 20__

To:        Management and Supervisory Staff
From:      Medical Practice Administrator
Re:        *HR Policies and Procedures Manual*

The management of *[Practice]* believes that each employee should be familiar with *[Practice's]* human resources (HR) policies and procedures that have been developed in accordance with employment laws and regulations, HR trends, compensation/benefit administration changes, and other employment matters. The *HR Policies and Procedures Manual* is designed to help each employee know what is expected of him or her and how the efforts of our staff can advance both *[Practice]* goals and individual interests.

The manual has been prepared to use as a reference to direct your management choices and employment decisions as well as be a guide for administering our policies in a fair and consistent manner. Our HR policies are regularly reviewed and updated. Copies of the manual are available in the designated HR professional's office.

Please thoroughly familiarize yourself with these polices. For further clarification of any of these policies, contact our designated HR professional.

# CHAPTER 2

# Employment Laws and Regulations

Policy 2.01    Americans with Disabilities Act

Policy 2.02    Equal Employment Opportunity

Policy 2.03    Immigration Reform and Control Act

Employment laws were originally geared toward protecting employees from employer exploitation; for example, child labor laws. As the employment laws became more sophisticated after World War II, they started to focus more on union-related issues, work-hour limitations, and wages. In the second half of the 20th century, the laws started to include more types of employers and many forms of civil rights, including equal employment opportunities, worker health and safety, disability accommodations, employee privacy, and personal leaves of absence. The justice system became involved particularly with cases focusing on affirmative action, wrongful discharge, and employment-at-will. In recent years, the focus has shifted more toward benefits for domestic partners, technology usage, and security issues.

## Key Federal Labor Laws

- Family and Medical Leave Act (FMLA)
- Occupational Safety and Health Act of 1970 (OSHA)
- Fair Labor Standards Act of 1938 (FLSA)
- Workers' Compensation Act

As society has endorsed government's regulation of employment, it has become imperative that those responsible for human resource management (HRM) put compliance with these laws at the top of their priority list.

## Regulating Government Departments and Agencies

The US Department of Labor (DOL) and the Equal Employment Opportunity Commission (EEOC) enforce federal employment laws. These mandates and the regulations that implement them cover many workplace activities for most employers and workers.

The DOL enforces laws and regulations covering:

- Wages and hours;
- Occupational safety and health;
- Workers' compensation (for federal employees);
- Employee benefit plans;
- Unions and their members;
- Employee protection;
- Uniformed service members' employment and reemployment rights;
- Employee polygraph protection;
- Whistleblower and retaliation protection;
- Garnishment of wages;
- Family and medical leave; and
- Immigrant workers.

Some state and local labor laws differ from the federal laws. Be sure to keep up to date not only with federal labor laws but also with your state and local laws.

The other government agency with significant impact on employment law is the EEOC. It regulates and enforces federal Equal Employment Opportunity (EEO) laws and discriminatory practices. The EEOC pinpoints many types of discrimination, including the following:

- Age;
- Disability;
- Equal pay and compensation;
- Genetic information;
- National origin;
- Pregnancy;
- Race/color;
- Religion;
- Retaliation;
- Sex; and
- Sexual harassment.

These laws underscore the importance of avoiding any form of discrimination within your medical practice. They impact nearly every HRM policy that you develop and implement. "Discriminatory practice" means that it is illegal to discriminate in any aspect of employment, including the following:

- Hiring and firing;
- Compensation, assignment, or classification of employees;
- Transfer, promotion, layoff, or recall;
- Job advertisements;

- Recruitment;
- Testing;
- Use of company facilities;
- Training and apprenticeship programs;
- Fringe benefits;
- Retirement plans;
- Disability leave; and
- Other terms and conditions of employment.

### Key Laws Prohibiting Discrimination

- Titles I and V of the Americans with Disabilities Act of 1990 (ADA)
- Title VII of the Civil Rights Act of 1964
- Equal Pay Act of 1963 (EPA)
- Age Discrimination in Employment Act of 1967 (ADEA)
- Genetic Information Nondiscrimination Act of 2008 (GINA)

## Major Employment Laws and Regulations

This section provides a brief discussion about the major employment laws and regulations. All managers and supervisors should become familiar with these laws and review their legal responsibilities. All managers and supervisors should also attend trainings on a general overview of employment laws as well as topic-specific training such as the FMLA. Your local employers' council or chamber of commerce typically offers training programs that may be helpful to your medical practice. As this is an abridged discussion of the key employment laws and regulations, and because legislation can change quite often, refer to the DOL (www.dol.gov) and EEOC (www.eeoc.gov) Websites for full and complete information about all employment laws.

### Americans with Disabilities Act of 1990 (ADA)

The ADA prohibits private employers, state and local governments, employment agencies, and labor unions from discriminating against qualified individuals with disabilities in job application procedures, hiring, firing, advancement, compensation, job training, and other employment aspects. The ADA covers employers with 15 or more employees. An individual with a disability, defined as a protected individual, is a person who has a physical or mental impairment that substantially limits one or more major life activities, has a record of such impairment, or is regarded as having such impairment.

Not every disabled individual is protected under the ADA; the person must also be qualified. A qualified employee or applicant with a disability is an individual who, with or without reasonable accommodation, can perform the essential functions of the job in question. "Essential functions," as presented in well-written job descriptions, are those functions that are essential to performance of the position in question. To determine whether a function is essential, examine whether:

- **The position exists to perform the function.** For example, positions involving phone responses can reasonably require that the employee be able to hear and speak if he or she will be assessing whether incoming calls are emergent, urgent, or nonemergent.
- **Only a limited number of other employees are available to perform the function.** For example, an essential function for a file clerk may be to answer the phone if only two employees are in a very busy office and they all handle a variety of tasks.

- **The function is highly specialized and the person is hired for his or her special expertise or ability to perform the function.** For example, fluency in Spanish is an essential expertise or ability to perform the function to communicate with Spanish-speaking patients.

Qualified individuals do not include job applicants or employees engaging in illegal use of drugs when the individual's usage is the basis for an employer's actions. For example, an employer terminates an employee for coming to work high on drugs and not being able to complete their essential functions. The terminated employee would not be considered a qualified individual under the ADA.

Under the ADA, discrimination may include limiting or classifying a job applicant or employee in an adverse way, denying employment opportunities or promotions to people who qualify, or not making reasonable accommodations to the known physical or mental limitations of disabled employees. Reasonable accommodations may include but are not limited to:

- Making existing facilities readily accessible to and usable by a person with disabilities. This accessibility is particularly important to healthcare providers because they are considered public accommodations under Title III.

- Job restructuring; modifying work schedules; reassigning the employee to a vacant position; acquiring or modifying equipment or devices; adjusting or modifying exams, training materials, or policies; and providing qualified readers or interpreters.

Reasonable accommodations by the employer are limited only if they are an "undue hardship" on its operations. *Undue hardship* is defined as an action that requires "significant difficulty or expense" in relation to the size of the employing organization, the resources available, and the nature of the operation.

Title V of the ADA protects individuals from coercion, intimidation, threat, harassment, interference, and retaliation in the exercise of their own rights or their encouragement of someone else's exercise of rights granted by the ADA. The EEOC enforces ADA complaints and claims.

The ADA Amendments Act of 2008 (ADAAA) effectively amended the ADA to broaden and clarify the definition of "disability." It was also designed to strike a balance between employer and employee interests that had been upset through various US Supreme Court rulings and EEOC regulations. A major change was that the ADAAA prohibits the consideration of a mitigating measure such as medication, assistive technology, accommodations, or modifications when determining whether an impairment substantially limits a major life activity. This includes if the impairment is episodic or in remission. The ADAAA also more fully defines what a major life activity is. According to the amendment, a major life activity includes but is not limited to:

- Caring for oneself;
- Performing manual tasks;
- Seeing, hearing, speaking, and breathing;
- Eating and sleeping;
- Walking, standing, bending, and lifting; and
- Learning, reading, concentrating, thinking, communicating, and working.

Also included in this list are major bodily functions such as functions of the immune system; normal cell growth; and digestive, bowel, bladder, neurological, brain, respiratory, circulatory, endocrine, and reproductive functions. A sample policy (Policy 2.01) on ADA compliance is at the end of this chapter.

**Civil Rights Act of 1964**

Title VII of the Civil Rights Act protects individuals against employment discrimination on the basis of race, color, sex, national origin, and religion. Title VII also protects individuals because of an association with another individual of a particular race, color, sex, national origin, or religion. This means that an employer cannot discriminate against a person because of his or her interracial association with another person such as an interracial marriage. It applies to employers with 15 or more employees. In 2012, the EEOC ruled that employment discrimination on the basis of gender identity or transgender status is also prohibited under Title VII.

In terms of race and color discrimination, Title VII states that equal employment opportunity cannot be denied to any person because of his or her racial group or perceived racial group or his or her other race-linked characteristics (such as hair texture, color, and/or facial features). It prohibits employment decisions based on stereotypes and assumptions about abilities, traits, or the performance of individuals of certain ethnicities. These prohibitions apply to all races, colors, and ethnicities. All employees and job applicants, regardless of their nation of origin, are entitled to the same employment opportunities. National origin discrimination means treating someone less favorably because he or she comes from a particular place, because of his or her ethnicity or accent, or because it is believed that he or she has a particular ethnic background.

Under Title VII, it is unlawful to discriminate against any employee or job applicant for employment because of his or her gender in regard to hiring, termination, promotion, compensation, job training, or any other term, condition, or privilege of employment. Title VII also prohibits employment decisions based on stereotypes and assumptions about abilities, traits, or the performance of individuals on the basis of sex. It prohibits both intentional discrimination and neutral job policies that disproportionately exclude individuals on the basis of sex and those that are not job related. Title VII's prohibitions against sex-based discrimination also cover sexual harassment and pregnancy-based discrimination.

Sexual harassment is a form of sex discrimination that violates Title VII. Unwelcome sexual advances, requests for sexual favors, and other verbal or physical conduct of a sexual nature constitute sexual harassment when this conduct explicitly or implicitly affects an individual's employment, unreasonably interferes with an individual's work performance, or creates an intimidating, hostile, or offensive work environment. A *hostile workplace* is defined as an environment where any type of EEO-related harassment occurs.

The Pregnancy Discrimination Act of 1978 amended the Civil Rights Act stating that discrimination on the basis of pregnancy, childbirth, or related medical conditions constitutes unlawful sex discrimination under Title VII. Women who are pregnant or affected by related conditions must be treated in the same manner as other applicants or employees with similar abilities or limitations. In regard to hiring, an employer cannot refuse to hire a pregnant woman because of her pregnancy, a pregnancy related condition, or the prejudices of coworkers, clients, or customers. In terms of pregnancy and maternity leave, an employer may not single out pregnancy-related conditions for special procedures to determine an employee's ability to work.

Title VII also prohibits employers from discriminating against individuals because of their religion in hiring, firing, and other terms and conditions of employment. Employers may not treat employees or applicants more or less favorably because of their religious beliefs or practices, except to the extent a religious accommodation is warranted. Employees cannot be forced to participate, or not participate, in a religious activity as a condition of employment. Employers must reasonably accommodate employees' sincerely held practices unless doing so would impose an undue hardship on the employer.

An employer may not fire, demote, harass, or otherwise retaliate against an individual for filing a charge of discrimination, participating in a discrimination proceeding, or otherwise opposing discrimination. The same laws that prohibit discrimination also prohibit retaliation against individuals who oppose unlawful discrimination or participate in an employment discrimination proceeding.

Executive Order 10925 of 1961, signed by President John F. Kennedy, was the first time the term *affirmative action* was used regarding workplace discrimination against race, color, and national origin, ensuring that protected applicants were employed and treated equally. In 1967, Executive Order 11375 added sex discrimination to the definition of affirmative action. The purpose of these executive orders was to pressure employers into compliance with the Civil Rights Act of 1964. Keep in mind that some states, such as California, Michigan, and Washington, have constitutional amendments banning affirmative action within these states.

The EEOC, which was created by Title VII, enforces the Civil Rights Act. The Equal Employment Opportunity Act of 1972 strengthened the EEOC by giving it the authority to institute legal action if conciliation fails in disputes involving employment discrimination. It extended the anti-discrimination provisions of Title VII of the Civil Rights Act to educational institutions and state and local governments. Policy 2.02 at the end of the chapter is a sample policy that addresses equal employment opportunity.

### Equal Pay Act of 1963 (EPA)
The EPA covers all employers who are covered by the federal wage and hour law under the Fair Labor Standards Act. It requires that men and women be given equal pay for equal work in the same establishment. The jobs need not be identical, but they must be substantially equal in skill, effort, responsibility, and working conditions. The job content, rather than the job title, determines whether jobs are substantially equal.

### Age Discrimination in Employment Act of 1967 (ADEA)
The ADEA protects individuals who are 40 years of age or older from employment discrimination based on age, and it applies to both employees and job applicants. It was amended in 1986 to prohibit mandatory retirement. Under the ADEA, it is unlawful to discriminate against a person because of his or her age with respect to any term, condition, or privilege of employment, including hiring, firing, promotion, layoff, compensation, benefits, job assignments, and training. The ADEA applies to employers with 20 or more employees. Employers can still discharge an employee regardless of his or her age for legitimate, nondiscriminatory reasons. In addition, the ADEA has an

exception that allows employers to discriminate on the basis of age for safety reasons referred to as a bona fide occupational qualification. An employer can ask an employee to waive his or her rights or claims under the ADEA either in the settlement of an ADEA administrative or court claim or in connection with an exit incentive program or other employment termination program. There are specific minimum standards that must be met in order for a waiver to be considered by the courts as knowing and voluntary, and thereby valid. Finally, employers have the right to offer *voluntary* retirement incentives to employees.

The EEOC adopted a selection process, the Uniform Guidelines on Employee Selection Procedures, that ensures the selection process does not adversely impact protected individuals. The guidelines safeguard against recruitment tools, such as employment tests, that may disproportionately screen out protected individuals from the selection process. These types of recruitment tools are unlawful since they are considered discriminatory unless they abide by the guidelines.

### Older Workers Benefit Protection Act of 1990 (OWBPA)

The OWBPA prohibits age discrimination in employee benefits and established the minimum standards for determining the validity of waivers of claims under the ADEA. The OWBPA requires employers offering group exit programs to provide notice of individuals covered and any time limitations. It also prohibits employers from denying employee benefits to older workers based on age.

### Genetic Information Nondiscrimination Act of 2008 (GINA)

Title II of GINA prohibits employers from an individual's genetic information when making hiring, firing, job placement, or promotion decisions with respect to compensation, terms, conditions, or privileges of employment. Genetic information as defined by GINA is an individual's genetic tests, the genetic tests of the individual's family members, the predisposition of a disease or disorder in the individual or family members, and medical history. GINA also prohibits employers to request, require, or purchase genetic information from an employee, job applicant, or family members except when the employee volunteers the information for services such as part of a wellness program. In addition, employers can ask for medical history when required by family and medical leaves, for law enforcement purposes, or for reasons regarding workplace safety.

GINA also requires employers who have access to an employee's genetic information to ensure confidentiality of such information. The information should be kept on separate forms and in separate files than personnel records. The documentation should be treated as a confidential medical record under the Health Insurance Portability and Accountability Act of 1996 (HIPAA) regulations.

### Fair Labor Standards Act of 1938 (FLSA)

The FLSA, as amended, established minimum wages, outlawed child labor, and established overtime pay, equal pay, and record-keeping affecting more than 50 million full-time and part-time workers. Some employees are exempt from the FLSA, including professional "white collar" workers. *Exempt* means these employees, including professional, administrative, and executive employees, are not eligible for overtime. In order to be considered "exempt," employees must be paid at least $455 per week and perform duties:

- Involving the management and/or general business operations of the organization;
- Requiring specialized academic training;
- In a computer field; or
- Selling the organization's services outside the place of business.

Exemptions are determined on a case-by-case basis, and job titles alone do not determine exemptions. Nonexempt employees are eligible for overtime pay in the event that they work more than 12 hours in a workday or when they work more than 40 hours in a workweek.

For example, consider whether an employee with the job title of nurse is exempt or nonexempt. To qualify as exempt, all of the following statements must be true:

- The employee is compensated by salary that is $455 per week or more; and
- The employee's primary duty must be the performance of work requiring advanced knowledge; namely, work that is predominantly intellectual in character and requires consistent exercise of discretion and judgment.

Typically, registered nurses who are paid on an hourly basis receive overtime pay. However, registered nurses who are registered by the appropriate state examining board generally meet the requirements for the learned professional exemption. If they are paid a salary of at least $455 per week, they may be classified as exempt.

Licensed practical nurses and other similar healthcare employees, however, generally do not qualify as exempt learned professionals, regardless of work experience and training, because possession of a specialized advanced academic degree is not a standard prerequisite for entry into such occupations, and thus they are entitled to overtime pay. The FLSA particularly focuses on ensuring that employees do receive minimum wage and overtime back wages. The DOL Wage and Hour Division sternly enforces these provisions.

### Family and Medical Leave Act of 1993 (FMLA)

The FMLA requires employers with 50 or more employees to provide employees up to 12 weeks of unpaid, job-protected leave to take care of a new child, whether for a birth or an adoption; to take care of a seriously ill immediate family member (parent, spouse, or child); or because of an employee's own serious health conditions. Many states have enacted laws with additional mandates to the FMLA. These additional mandates include FMLA compliance for organizations with fewer employees and an expanded definition of the immediate family to include domestic partners and their children, grandparents, and in-laws. Ensure that your medical practice is in compliance with your state's mandates.

### Occupational Safety and Health Act of 1970

The Occupational Safety and Health Administration (OSHA) established regulations to provide for the safety and health of employees on the job. The act aims to ensure better working conditions by working with employers and employees on work environment conditions. OSHA focuses on three strategies:

1. Strong, fair, and effective enforcement, especially of the most hazardous industries (those with high injury and illness rates);

2. Outreach, education, and compliance assistance; and

3. Partnerships and cooperative programs.

Under the act, employers are required to identify, track, and report occupational injury and illness trends.

### Consolidated Omnibus Budget Reconciliation Act of 1985 (COBRA)

COBRA provides certain former employees, retirees, spouses, former spouses, and dependent children the right to temporary continuation of health coverage at group rates. This coverage is only available when coverage is lost due to certain specific events. Group health coverage for COBRA participants is typically more expensive than health coverage for current employees. Usually, the employer pays a part of the premium for current employees while COBRA participants generally pay the entire premium themselves, which is often less expensive than individual health coverage.

### Employee Polygraph Protection Act of 1988 (EPPA)

The EPPA generally prevents employers from using polygraph tests, either for pre-employment screening or during the course of employment, with certain exemptions. Employers usually may not require or request any employee or job applicant to take a polygraph test; or discharge, discipline, or discriminate against an employee or job applicant for refusing to take a test; or for tests to be administered to certain job applicants in certain industries (such as security services and pharmaceuticals) and those reasonably suspected of involvement in a workplace incident (such as theft and embezzlement) that results in specific economic loss or injury to the employer. When polygraph tests are allowed, they are subject to strict standards.

### Employee Retirement Income Security Act of 1974 (ERISA)

The ERISA regulates employers who offer pensions or welfare benefit plans to their employees. Title I of ERISA is administered by the DOL's Employee Benefits Security Administration and imposes a wide range of fiduciary, disclosure, and reporting requirements on fiduciaries of pension and welfare benefit plans and on others having dealings with these plans. The ERISA does not require employers to provide pensions or health or other welfare benefit plans; however, it regulates those plans once established by an organization. The ERISA has been amended several times, including by the Pension Protection Act of 2006; the Worker, Retiree, and Employer Recovery Act of 2008; COBRA as mentioned previously; Newborns' and Mothers' Health Protection Act; the Mental Health Parity Act; the Women's Health and Cancer Rights Act; and HIPAA.

### Consumer Credit Protection Act of 2012 (CCPA)

Title III of the CCPA is enforced by the DOL Wage and Hour Division and protects employees from discharge by their employers because their wages have been garnished for any debt. The CCPA also sets limits on the amount of an employee's earnings that may be garnished in any one week. This is informally known as the federal wage garnishment law.

### Immigration Reform and Control Act of 1986 (IRCA)

The IRCA requires employers to hire only persons who may legally work in the United States, that is, US citizens, noncitizen nationals, lawful permanent residents, and aliens authorized to work in the United States. The employer must verify the identity and employment eligibility of anyone to be hired, which includes completing the Employment Eligibility Verification Form (Form I-9). To avoid discrimination problems, an employer should not ask for documentation until after a job offer is extended. Employers must keep each I-9 on file for at least three years or one year after employment ends, whichever is longer.

The IRCA prohibits employers from knowingly hiring, recruiting, or referring for work aliens who are not authorized to accept employment in the United States. *Knowing* includes not only actual knowledge but also constructive knowledge, that is, information that may fairly be inferred through notice of certain facts and circumstances that would lead a person to know about a certain condition. Inference cannot be based on a person's appearance or accent. See Policy 2.03 for a sample policy on immigration law.

### Uniformed Services Employment and Reemployment Rights Act of 1994 (USERRA)

The USERRA ensures that certain persons who serve in the armed forces have a right to reemployment with the employer they were with when they entered the service for five years of active duty. These persons include those called up from the reserves or National Guard. It also prohibits discrimination based on military service or obligation, including returning disabled veterans. These rights are administered by the Veterans' Employment and Training Service. Employers are required to report annually the organization's employment of veterans.

### Health Insurance Portability and Accountability Act of 1996 (HIPAA)

HIPAA is regulated by the DOL's Employee Benefits Security Administration. Although much of the focus of this act, especially in healthcare organizations, has been on the accountability for ensuring patient privacy and confidentiality, the act's original emphasis was on the portability of insurance benefits. Title I protects health insurance coverage for workers and their families when they change or lose their jobs. In particular, the act gives the employee protection in terms of existing health conditions.

### Patient Protection and Affordable Care Act (PPACA) and Health Care and Education Reconciliation Act of 2010

The PPACA and the Health Care and Education Reconciliation Act amending the PPACA were signed into law on March 23 and 30, 2010, respectively. Although several requirements have already become effective, many of the mandates are continuing to go into effect through 2018. In addition, many lawsuits were filed questioning the legality of the act; however, the act was upheld by the US Supreme Court's June 2012 ruling. Healthcare human resources (HR) experts are still trying to figure out exactly what impact this act will continue to have on employment issues. This following explanation is accurate as of this manual's publishing date.

Beginning in 2015, employers with more than 50 employees will face tax penalties if they do not provide all full-time employees affordable health coverage. If an employer does not follow this mandate, tax penalties will be imposed on a per-employee basis. Provisions in the act will help some eligible small healthcare organizations (those with less than 25 employees) that provide health insurance to their employees through subsidies and various tax credits. These subsidies will expire several years after the establishment of health insurance exchanges in each state by 2014. The health insurance exchanges are a marketplace for individuals and small businesses to shop for health insurance plans at a competitive price. Health insurance exchanges were certified and operational by January 1, 2014.

The PPACA also enacted changes to reimbursable expenditures on an employee's health flexible spending account (FSA), health savings account (HSA), and health reimbursable arrangement (HRA). Over-the-counter drugs are no longer reimbursable unless they are prescribed by a physician, except for insulin. Also, the penalty for employees who make withdrawals from their HSAs for nonmedical purposes increased to 20 percent. Beginning in 2013, employee FSA contributions were set at a maximum of $2,500 per employee.

The PPACA will also affect payroll and taxable deductions. The acts raise the employee portion of the Medicare tax by an additional 0.9 percent for individuals with an annual income of more than $200,000 or a household annual income of more than $250,000. This additional tax is levied on the combined wages of the employee and the employee's spouse in the case of a joint tax filing. Employers are required to withhold this additional tax similar to the existing Medicare (the Hospital Insurance or HI) payroll tax. This provision applies to wages received after December 31, 2012.

The PPACA also codifies many of the wellness program provisions from HIPAA. According to the PPACA, employers may establish wellness programs providing a minimum discount, rebate, or other reward for participation without violating any anti-discrimination rules for group health plans based on health status–related factors. The wellness incentive was increased to 30 percent of the cost of coverage in the PPACA.

**National Labor Relations Act of 1935 (Wagner Act) and Taft–Hartley Act**

The Wagner Act guarantees the right of employees to organize and bargain collectively through representatives of their own choice. It requires employers to bargain in good faith with recognized unions, and it created the National Labor Relations Board to administer the act.

**Posters Typically Required to Be Visible to Employees**

- Equal Employment Opportunity Act
- Family and Medical Leave Act
- Fair Labor Standards Act
- Occupational Safety and Health Act
- Uniformed Services Employment and Reemployment Rights Act
- Employee Polygraph Protection Act

The Labor-Management Relations Act of 1947 (Taft–Hartley Act) effectively amended the Wagner Act. The Taft–Hartley Act sought to balance the power of labor unions and management by prohibiting certain unfair labor practices by unions, protecting the individual worker's position from union coercion, and regulating union officers.

**Labor-Management Reporting and Disclosure Act of 1959 (Landrum–Griffin Act)**

The LMRDA or Landrum–Griffin Act established a so-called bill of rights for labor union members and strengthened provisions of the Taft–Hartley Act regulating internal union practices. The act was designed to stop corrupt practices and protect law-abiding unions.

## Communicating Laws and Regulations to Employees

Clear and concise policies and procedures documented in an employee handbook, a policies and procedures manual, and/or on your medical practice's intranet will help you and your staff's ability to comply with employment laws and regulations. Many of the laws and regulations mentioned previously have provisions requiring posters to be visible by all employees. Some medical practices have a bulletin board in the HR departments for these posters. Others put them in the employee break area or in other areas where there is considerable employee traffic. Each state has slightly different requirements, so be sure to check with your state to determine which posters must be visible at your medical practice.

All posters are available for download on the respective Websites for the US DOL and your state's DOL.

## Employment-At-Will

The concept of employment-at-will, or the ability of employers to dismiss an at-will employee for any reason and at any time, continues to be difficult since many employment protections enacted into law, court rulings, and state statutes have limited employers' rights to terminate employees at will. Employees can claim wrongful discharge and sue for damages if the discharge results from a broken promise made by the employer (oral, written, or implied) or a violation of public policy. More than 30 states recognize some exceptions to the employment-at-will doctrine. If an employer terminates an employee for a reason determined to be an exception to the at-will doctrine, that termination constitutes an unjust dismissal, and consequently, that employee can receive damages or reinstatement.

Your medical practice should focus on HRM policies that provide effective guidelines to promote consistency of management rather than emphasizing the limitation on employment-at-will. Documentation of these policies is important, including an HR manual that presents clear policies, especially those related to progressive discipline and termination.

Your employee handbook, which is discussed in chapter 13, should include a statement related to employment-at-will. See Form 13.1 for a sample statement taking into account current legal trends and HR practices. Your medical practice may wish to use this statement with any necessary adaptations to reflect your practice's management philosophy, your legal counsel's advice, and your state's laws.

## Avoiding Wrongful Discharge Actions

Today in medical practices, immediate terminations due to gross misconduct tend to be rare. Many terminations are performance related and preventable if selection, orientation, training, supervision, coaching, and discipline practices are carried out effectively. Proactive performance management can help protect your medical practice from wrongful discharge actions and unwarranted unemployment insurance claims. Some measures that will reduce the risk of liability follow.

- Develop a written policy that covers the grounds for termination. Like all policies, this one should be communicated to all employees through an employee handbook, the HR policies and procedures manual, and on your practice's intranet. This step may help protect against charges of termination without proper warning.

See Form 2.1 for a sample Termination Statement to use in your policies and procedures manual.

- Use clear and precise language, including terminology, when developing policies and procedures. Solicit your legal counsel to review the language in all of your medical practice's policies.

- Include specific disclaimers on job application forms, in policy materials, and in the employee handbook explaining that these documents do not constitute an employee contract.

- Educate managers about the importance of logging and documenting every termination action. Managers should keep precise records of training and retraining, coaching, performance improvement action plans and results, probationary and warning notices, remedial efforts, and other actions taken that should precede any termination action. The HR department should help the managers keep these records.

- Ensure that your practice's performance review forms and job descriptions accurately reflect the performance expected in job-related specific terms (e.g., objectives and behaviors) and are used by all managers to document each employee's strong and weak performance points. Managers must understand that they must write examples of behaviors that justify their ratings on the performance review forms. A common mistake is giving employees favorable annual performance review assessments and then terminating them.

- Reinforce to managers the importance of warning employees in advance when their actions could possibly lead to termination unless significant changes occur in their performance. These warnings should be documented in writing or have witnesses in attendance during an oral conversation (over the phone or in person).

- Train managers to stay alert for signs of poor performance such as decreased productivity, baseless complaints, and increased absenteeism and tardiness. HR professionals should assist managers to help with their direct reports through a committed effort to coaching, retraining, and concentrating on the specifics of successful performance.

- Communicate to managers frequently and effectively that termination of an employee is not solely their decision. The decision to terminate an employee must involve others (e.g., the supervisor's manager and a designated HR professional) to ensure that an employee cannot allege malice or personality conflict on the part of the supervisor. Consult your legal counsel or employers' council if a termination case appears to be complex and problematic. In addition, establish a procedure that only designated supervisors and managers are authorized to express and make oral and written hiring decisions.

- Consider establishing a severance package that includes limited-time continuation of health and life insurance benefits. Such a courtesy may preclude any charges of vindictiveness and may help mollify any injured feelings. Terminated employees who consider severance payments generous are less likely to initiate litigation, and the costs are typically much less than legal expenses.

- Consider purchasing defense and judgment insurance that protects employees against lawsuits arising from cases other than personal injury or property-damages suits, which are covered under general liability policies.

- Keep in mind that federal law protects employees against retaliation for raising certain concerns about a healthcare provider's compliance with health information privacy laws and laws intended to prevent waste, fraud, and abuse in healthcare. Termination decisions must not violate applicable nonretaliation laws.

- Conduct training for managers and supervisors on their responsibilities and employee rights, particularly those related to discipline and termination.

- Terminate employees only as a last resort and with great care and compassion. The exit interview should be isolated from other employees to avoid embarrassment for the terminated person, as well as to avoid upsetting and distracting other employees. The reasons for termination should be clearly explained. If the supervisor, manager, and designated HR professional have followed the appropriate pretermination steps, the termination should be no surprise to the employee. Termination can create ripples in the medical practice that go far beyond legal consideration, so handle all terminations with sensitivity.

## Helpful Resources

The DOL has developed several tools to ensure that America's employers and workers have access to clear and accurate information and assistance. These include:

- eLaws® Advisors (www.dol.gov/elaws/advisors.html) are Web-based interactive tools that help small businesses and workers understand most federal employment laws enforced by the DOL.

- The Wage and Hour Division's Website (www.dol.gov/mhd/) provides access to a wide range of services, and employment and regulatory information. The Wage and Hour Division of the DOL is responsible for enforcing all federal labor laws.

- The Equal Employment Opportunity Commission's Website (www.eeoc.gov) has a wealth of information about workplace discrimination laws and regulations.

In addition, your medical practice's legal counsel, industry and small business associations, your local employer's council and chamber of commerce, and other practices offer forums for learning about employment laws.

## Summary

The bottom line is that your medical practice must comply with employment laws. Keeping your medical practice's policies and procedures up to date with employment laws and regulations can be time-consuming and tedious as legislators review and change federal, state, and local laws frequently. Some changes occur because of social and political pressure. For example, the minimum wage is often raised as a political tactic that directly impacts most employers. Because legislative changes happen slowly, you typically have enough time to learn what and when new laws are coming and how they might affect your medical practice.

Many value resources are available to track new laws and legislative changes. The Medical Group Management Association carefully follows legislative actions and has lobbyists to ensure that federal politicians are aware of the industry implications of any regulatory change. Business associations and chambers of commerce also track these updates and put them into context for the healthcare industry. Federal and state government Websites also post new developments and legislative updates.

The role of human resources is to continually educate all supervisors, managers, and staff about these laws and their impact on the medical practice. Such education and compliance will help your medical practice deal more effectively with the many other functions of HRM.

**Sample Policies**

**Policy 2.01**     <u>**Americans with Disabilities Act**</u>

This is an example of a policy regarding compliance with the Americans with Disabilities Act.

---

POLICY 2.01         **AMERICANS WITH DISABILITIES ACT**

<u>Purpose:</u> To ensure *[Practice]* is in compliance with the Americans with Disabilities Act (ADA).

<u>Applies to:</u> All *[Practice]* employees.

<u>Policy:</u> *[Practice]* complies with the ADA.

<u>Procedures:</u>

1. The designated human resources (HR) professional shall be responsible for compliance with the ADA.
2. The designated HR professional shall review current and new job descriptions to ensure that they clearly state the essential functions, applicable skills, education and experience requirements, and any special requirements of each job position.
3. The designated HR professional shall review application forms and other hiring procedures to eliminate non-job-related questions about disabilities and ensure that supervisors and others involved in the selection process ask only whether the applicant can perform the essential functions of the job and how he or she will perform the functions.
4. Those involved in hiring shall evaluate carefully, with HR assistance, whether a disabled person can or cannot perform a particular job.
5. Pre-employment physical procedures shall be reviewed, recognizing that employers can only ask an applicant to take a pre-employment physical exam or complete a health history if everyone who applies for a job in that classification is also asked to do the same. Only those applicants who receive conditional employment offers can be required to take a physical exam.
6. Human resources policies and employee handbooks shall be reviewed to ensure compliance with the ADA and to make any necessary revisions related to recruiting, interviewing, pre-employment physical exams, and health histories.
7. The designated HR professional shall ensure that *[Practice]* physicians and managers understand ADA regulations.
8. *[Practice]* shall require a drug test for applicants who receive conditional employment offers.
9. The designated HR professional shall hold ADA training sessions for supervisors and managers, especially those involved in hiring and other key employment decisions. These sessions shall emphasize that career path opportunities should be accessible to all employees, including those who are disabled.

10. The designated HR professional, in conjunctions with an employee's supervisor, shall make available longer training periods and more frequent performance reviews for protected individuals needing reasonable accommodations. All managers shall be educated about what "reasonable accommodations" means.

11. The designated HR professional shall ensure that all hiring managers can articulate and document legitimate, nondiscriminatory, and credible facts on which any employment decision is based, including available accommodations considered and the specific reasons for employment rejection.

Approved by: Practice Administrator

Effective date: 1/1/20__

**Policy 2.02**   **Equal Employment Opportunity**

This is an example of a policy regarding compliance with anti-discrimination laws and regulations ensuring equal employment opportunity.

---

POLICY 2.02             **EQUAL EMPLOYMENT OPPORTUNITY**

Purpose: To ensure *[Practice]* is an equal opportunity employer.

Applies to: All *[Practice]* employees.

Policy: *[Practice]* is an equal opportunity employer. It is the policy of *[Practice]* to prohibit discrimination and harassment of any type.

Procedures:

1. The designated human resources (HR) professional shall be responsible for compliance with equal employment opportunity (EEO) and maintain personnel records in compliance with applicable laws and regulations.
2. Managers and supervisors are responsible for implementing the EEO policy.
3. The designated HR professional will provide training to employees on a regular basis regarding EEO laws and regulations.
4. *[Practice]* affords equal employment opportunities to employees and applicants, without regard to race, color, religion, sex, national origin, disability, genetic information, gender identity or expression, or veteran status.
5. *[Practice]* prohibits any and all discrimination in all aspects of the relationship between *[Practice]* and its employees including but not limited to:
   • Recruitment;
   • Employment;
   • Promotion;
   • Transfer;
   • Training;
   • Working conditions;
   • Wages and salary; and
   • Employee benefits.
6. *[Practice]* will display posters regarding EEO in areas highly visible to employees in compliance with applicable laws and regulations.
7. *[Practice]* forbids retaliation against any individual who files a charge of discrimination, reports harassment, or who assists, testifies, or participates in an EEO proceeding.
8. Employees are required to report to their immediate supervisor, the Practice Administrator, or the designated HR professional, any apparent discrimination or harassment.

9. The designated HR professional will promptly notify the Practice Administrator and legal counsel of all incidents or reports of discrimination or harassment.

10. *[Practice]* will promptly investigate all claims of discrimination or harassment and, if discrimination or harassment exists, will take appropriate disciplinary action, up to and including termination.

<u>Approved by:</u> Practice Administrator

<u>Effective date:</u> 1/1/20__

## Policy 2.03          **Immigration Reform and Control Act**

This is an example of policy regarding compliance with immigration law.

---

**POLICY 2.03          IMMIGRATION REFORM
AND CONTROL ACT**

<u>Purpose:</u> To ensure that *[Practice]* is in compliance with the Immigration Reform and Control Act (IRCA).

<u>Applies to:</u> All *[Practice]* employees.

<u>Policy:</u> *[Practice]* complies with the IRCA and other immigration laws and policies of the United States and the State of _____. It employs only US citizens and aliens legally authorized to work in the United States. It also complies with laws banning discrimination on the basis of citizenship or national origin.

<u>Procedures:</u>

1. The designated human resources (HR) professional is responsible for ensuring compliance with IRCA and state laws and regulations.

2. Each new employee shall complete Form I-9, Employment Eligibility Verification, and present appropriate documentation establishing identity and employment eligibility. An HR staff member must witness that documents were actually produced. Former employees who are rehired must also complete the form if they have not completed one with *[Practice]* within the past three years or if their previous Form I-9 is no longer on file or is invalid.

3. The designated HR professional shall implement and maintain the I-9 forms, ensuring that no potential for discrimination exists in the hiring procedures or job descriptions, and comply with regulations related to the hiring of foreign nationals.

4. I-9 forms shall be kept on file in a safe and accessible location for either three years after the person is hired or one year after the person is terminated, whichever is later.

<u>Approved by:</u> Practice Administrator

<u>Effective date:</u> 1/1/20__

### Sample Form

**Form 2.1**    <u>**Termination Statement**</u>

This is an example of a termination statement for a policies and procedures manual.

---

FORM 2.1                                **TERMINATION
                                           STATEMENT**

*[Practice]* reserves the right to terminate any employee with or without cause and with or
without notice at any time. Only the Administrator or designee has the authority to enter
into any agreement for employment for any specified period of time. In no event are these
human resources policies to be construed as, or determined to create, any contract by
implication. Only the Practice Administrator or designee has the authority to make this
commitment on behalf of the organization having the force and effect of a contract.

# CHAPTER 3

# Job Classification and Job Descriptions

Policy 3.01   Job Classification

## Job Classification

During the strategic planning process, one of the first steps is to look at the types of jobs and positions in your medical practice. Categorizing the various jobs into classes helps to improve efficiency and productivity. This process is called job classification. A sample Job Classification policy (Policy 3.01) is provided at the end of this chapter.

Job classification is a tool that groups similar jobs together to make them easier to manage. For example, a bookstore is categorized according to genre (e.g., travel, cooking, fiction, self-help) so shoppers can easily identify which types of books are where. Job classifications define which job descriptions fit into a specific category. For example, an administrative class of jobs might include all the positions whose duties are to perform, under supervision, difficult and responsible administrative work in an office, business, or finance setting.

### Job Classification Process

- Job analysis
- Job descriptions
- Job specifications and definitions

More specifically, job classification is the process of grouping job positions that have similar duties and responsibilities into classes. It involves slotting job descriptions into a series of classes that cover the range of jobs in your organization. Each class should be detailed enough to be descriptive, yet still general enough not to be limiting.

Job classification helps you make human resources (HR) decisions related to recruiting, selection, promotion, equal employment opportunities, performance evaluation, training and developing, and compensation. Job classification helps specifically with compensation decisions when, for example, you must:

- Determine the relative worth of the various jobs in your practice;
- Establish a pay plan that incorporates appropriate differentials among jobs; and
- Guard against and/or pay inequities.

**Job analysis reveals:**

- Work performed;
- Worker traits; and
- How the work relates to people, data, and things.

## Job Analysis

Job analysis helps everyone gain a better understanding of the content of an individual's work, the relationship of the work to your practice, and the qualifications the individual must have to fulfill all of the job tasks. Analyzing all of the jobs in your practice helps you manage HR responsibilities and helps managers and employees understand more fully the nature of your practice's work.

Job analysis is the systematic process of collecting and making certain judgments about all of the important information related to a specific job. The designated HR professional should execute a job analysis when your practice needs to create a new position, upgrade or downgrade a position, or redefine a position.

The analysis involves identifying exactly which skills an employee must have to fulfill the requirement of the job. When analyzing jobs, define the following parameters:

- Essential functions and related duties;
- Profession or occupation involved;
- Nonsupervisory responsibilities;
- Supervisory and administrative responsibilities;
- Physical demands;
- Accountabilities and desired outcomes;
- Working conditions;
- Technology requirements;
- Necessary knowledge (learned through education and experience), skills (demonstration of knowledge), and abilities (capacity for learning and doing);
- Appropriate behaviors; and
- Performance standards.

The Americans with Disabilities Act (ADA) brought to light the importance of a worker's qualification to do a job. Unless you can identify the essential functions of a position, you could inadvertently discriminate against someone who can do the job despite a disability.

### Job Analysis Steps

A job analysis requires the following three steps:

1. **Job identification.** Indicate the job title, job status, job code (if any), pay range, geographic location, and immediate supervisory reporting structure. In analyzing the skills needed, consider factors such as education, independent judgment, and initiative.

2. **Job description.** Describe the job tasks, reporting structure, physical requirements (including dexterity and motor skills, standing, twisting, sitting, reaching, bending, and lifting), and working conditions (i.e., the general work environment where the job will be performed, including job hazards). When describing the job duties and responsibilities, consider who assigns and supervises the work, as well as what the worker does. It is also important to know the level of difficulty for the job, the impact of error, and the interpersonal working relationships involved.

3. **Job qualifications.** Indicate the qualifications needed for successful job performance. It should be very clear that if a worker has the knowledge, skills, and abilities that match essential functions, he or she should be able to perform the job successfully. Typically, essential functions are listed on the performance evaluation form so there is a direct link between what is expected of the jobholder and how he or she performs the job.

Generally the designated HR professional coordinates the job analysis process with employees and their supervisors helping to collect detailed information about each position. A consultant who is a specialist in job analysis could also be hired. Methods for conducting a job analysis include questionnaires, interviews, checklists, diaries, observation, activity sampling, and critical incidents. Form 3.1 at the end of this chapter is a sample Job Analysis Questionnaire for employees and their supervisors to complete. The job analysis provides a great deal of specific information about the jobs in your practice. This information is used to create job descriptions.

Sometimes an organization will use personal interviews to collect information when conducting job analyses. Interviewing each employee can be time-consuming and expensive if using a consultant but can also provide more complete and accurate information. To obtain high-quality information, the interviewer must be highly skilled and experienced in conducting job analysis interviews. Form 3.2 at the end of the chapter is a list of sample Job Analysis Interview Questions that your practice can modify to fit your needs.

## Job Descriptions

Many terms can be used for job descriptions: *position descriptions* (a job description personalized for one specific individual), *job specifications* (all of the details of a job including knowledge, skills, and abilities needed), and *job descriptions* (a list of the job tasks, duties, and responsibilities). Typically, *job descriptions* encompass all of these other terms and is the term used in this manual.

Complete, current, and detailed job descriptions help new workers understand their jobs and remind existing employees what is expected of them. They guide employee selection and placement, help assess training and development needs, and serve as the foundation for performance standards. Formal job descriptions also protect organizations from charges of discrimination because they clearly detail what workers must be able to do as required by the ADA. In addition, a sample Job Description format is located at the end of this chapter (Form 3.3).

The Medical Group Management Association's *Job Description Manual for Medical Practices*[*] is a great and thorough resource for learning about, developing, and updating job descriptions that goes beyond this scope of this publication. To ensure that your medical practice follows through with job classifications, including job analyses and job descriptions, it is useful to have a job classification policy.

## Summary

The creation of job descriptions and classifications for your practice is a multifaceted process. First, based on the strategic planning of your practice, you identify the types of jobs needed currently and in the future. Next, you analyze each job in terms of its vital components – the what, why, and how of the job. Finally, you describe each job's responsibilities, qualifications, and relationships. This allows you to classify the jobs into categories and to move on to the next step of evaluating job worth: determining compensation rates.

When analyzing jobs, focus on the key job elements including duties, supervision received and exercised, interpersonal relationships involved, level of difficulty, impact of errors, physical demands, working conditions, and qualifications. After considering all these of factors, your task is to succinctly state the essential functions of the job. This information is critical in all human resource management functions: recruiting, training, supervision, and performance management.

---

[*]  *Job Description Manual for Medical Practices*, 3rd ed., by Courtney H. Price and Alys Novak (Englewood, CO: Medical Group Management Association, 2008).

### Sample Policy

**Policy 3.01**   ## Job Classification

This is an example of a job classification policy.

---

POLICY 3.01            **JOB CLASSIFICATION**

Purpose: To establish and maintain a job classification system.

Applies to: Human Resources Department

Policy: It is the policy of *[Practice]* to have a job classification system, including job analyses and job descriptions to aid in employee selection, promotion, compensation, and other personnel matters. The designated human resources professional maintains the job classification system.

Procedures:
1. A qualified individual will perform the job analysis.
2. The analysis will:
   - Identify the job accurately and completely; and
   - Describe the job tasks, including essential and nonessential functions, reporting structuring, physical requirements, working conditions, knowledge, skills, abilities, other requirements, and performance standards.
3. The job analyst will use the most appropriate method(s) to gather information about each job (i.e., questionnaire, interview, or observation).
4. The gathered information will be used to guide job evaluation, selection and placement, performance evaluation, training, wage and salary administration, and organizational analysis.

Approved by: Practice Administrator

Effective date: 1/1/20__

**Sample Forms**

**Form 3.1**  **Job Analysis Questionnaire**

This is a sample Job Analysis Questionnaire. Modify the template to fit your practice's needs.

---

FORM 3.1  **JOB ANALYSIS QUESTIONNAIRE**

The purpose of this questionnaire is to collect detailed information about a position and its duties, responsibilities, and educational and experience requirements as it currently exists. This information will be used to help develop or revise job descriptions, evaluate the job for appropriate classification, and ensure compliance through the Americans with Disabilities Act (ADA) and the Fair Labor Standards Act (FLSA).

Please provide information about the job itself and not about your performance in the job. Please complete the questionnaire as honestly, completely, and accurately as possible. Include duties related to special projects or temporary assignments *only if* these duties are required as a regular part of the job. This questionnaire is designed to collect information about most jobs in *[Practice]*; however, some job duties may not apply to your job. If two answers seem to fit the situation, select the one that works best. Your supervisor will also be asked about your job, but they are not allowed to change your responses. *[Practice]* recommends discussing your job duties and responsibilities with your supervisor to help you complete this questionnaire.

If you have any questions regarding this questionnaire or the job analysis process, please contact the designated human resources professional. Please submit the completed questionnaire to your immediate supervisor.

**Reason for Job Analysis:** Mark the reason for evaluating this position.

☐ Evaluate New Position | ☐ Evaluate Vacant Position | ☐ Evaluate Currently Held Position

| Name of Employee (Last, first, MI) | Date |
|---|---|
| **Job Title** | **Department** |
| **Name of Supervisor** | **Supervisor's Title** |

**Work Status:** Mark the work status of this position.

☐ Regular full-time  ☐ Temporary full-time
☐ Regular part-time  ☐ Temporary part-time

| **Employment Duration:** How long have you currently been in this position? | _____ Years | _____ Months |
|---|---|---|

**Primary Purpose of Position:** In one or two sentences, briefly describe the primary purpose or function of this position. Why does this position exist?

**Essential Duties and Responsibilities:** List the position's essential duties and responsibilities, listing the most important first, and estimate the average percentage of time spent on each. Only include duties and responsibilities that occupy at least 5% of the total job. Combine minor or occasional duties into *Other duties as assigned*. An example of duties and responsibilities with average percentage of time spent is provided below.

| | |
|---|---|
| 1. Coordinates with clinical staff to collect charge information for all patients | 25% |
| 2. Codes information about procedures performed and diagnosis on change | 20% |
| 3. Verifies and completes charge information in database and produces billing | 15% |
| 4. Processes and distributes copies of billings according to clinic policies | 15% |
| 5. Maintains required billing records, reports, files, etc. | 15% |
| 6. Other duties as assigned | 10% |
| Total | 100% |

| | |
|---|---|
| 1. | _____ % |
| 2. | _____ % |
| 3. | _____ % |
| 4. | _____ % |
| 5. | _____ % |
| 6. | _____ % |
| 7. | _____ % |
| 8. | _____ % |
| 9. | _____ % |
| 10. | _____ % |
| Total of all percentages should equal 100% | 100% |

**Minimum Requirements for Education:** Mark the box that best indicates the minimum training/education requirements of this job. This is not necessarily your level of education, but for the requirements of the job.

☐ High School Diploma or GED         ☐ Vocational/Technical School

☐ Some College/Associate's Degree      ☐ Bachelor's Degree

☐ Master's Degree                     ☐ Doctoral Degree

**Is continuing education required in the job's duties and responsibilities?**     ☐ No     ☐ Yes, please explain:

**Type of Experience Needed:** Describe the specific job experience that one should have to be successful in this position. For example, "billing experience in a healthcare organization" vs. "billing experience." Be sure that the experience stated is what is actually required by the job, not what is preferred.

**Amount of Experience Needed:** Mark the box that best indicates the minimum amount of time spent in performing similar work and acquiring the skills and knowledge to qualify for this position. This is not necessarily your amount of experience, but for job-related experience.

☐ Less than 6 months                              ☐ 3 to 5 years

☐ 6 months to 1 year                              ☐ 5 to 7 years

☐ 1 to 3 years                                    ☐ 7 years or more

**Type of Licensing/Certification Required:** Does this position require any licensing and/or certifications to do the job? For example, "current RN license in the State of Colorado."

☐ No  | ☐ Yes, please list the required (not preferred) licenses/certifications:

**Type of Skills Required:** Describe the specific skills required to do this job. For example, "proficiency in medical billing software" may be a requirement for a billing clerk.

**Supervisory/Leadership Responsibilities:** Mark the box that best indicates the nature of the direct supervisory and/or leadership responsibilities for this position.

☐ No supervisory responsibility                   ☐ Supervisor over one department

☐ Leader of a section of a department             ☐ Manager/Director/Administrator of multiple departments

**Amount of Direct Reports:** How many positions report directly to this position?

☐ None                                            ☐ 4–6 positions

☐ 1 position                                      ☐ 7 or more positions

☐ 2–3 positions

**Positions of Direct Reports:** List the title(s) of employee(s) whom this position directly supervises.

| Title | Number of Positions |
|---|---|
|  |  |
|  |  |
|  |  |
|  |  |
|  |  |

**External Contacts:** Does this position have contacts outside of *[Practice]* they must communicate with to complete routine functions of this job?

□ No   | □ Yes, please list the contacts, the purpose of the contact, and how often contact is made.

| Organization Name | Purpose | Frequency |
|---|---|---|
|  |  |  |
|  |  |  |
|  |  |  |
|  |  |  |
|  |  |  |
|  |  |  |

**Physical Demands and Working Conditions:** Indicate how much time is spent on each of the following to perform the essential job functions.

|  | None | Under ⅓ | To ⅔ | Over ⅔ |
|---|---|---|---|---|
| Standing | □ | □ | □ | □ |
| Walking | □ | □ | □ | □ |
| Sitting | □ | □ | □ | □ |
| Using hands to finger, handle, or feel | □ | □ | □ | □ |
| Reaching with hands and arms | □ | □ | □ | □ |
| Climbing (steps) or balancing | □ | □ | □ | □ |
| Squatting, stooping, kneeling, crouching, or crawling | □ | □ | □ | □ |
| Talking or hearing | □ | □ | □ | □ |
| Tasting or smelling | □ | □ | □ | □ |
| Lifting up to 10 pounds | □ | □ | □ | □ |
| Lifting up to 25 pounds | □ | □ | □ | □ |
| Lifting up to 50 pounds | □ | □ | □ | □ |
| Lifting up to 100 pounds | □ | □ | □ | □ |
| Time spent around blood and body fluids | □ | □ | □ | □ |
| Time spent around hazardous materials other than blood and body fluids | □ | □ | □ | □ |

**Equipment Used:** Please list all of the equipment that must be used to complete the duties and responsibilities of this job. For example, computers, X-ray machines, ultrasound, etc.

**Comments:** Please make any additional comments that would be helpful and important to understand this job.

| Employee Signature | Date |
|---|---|
|  |  |

**For Supervisor Use Only:** Do not edit, modify, or change the questionnaire!

**Employee Oversight:** Check the box that best describes the level of oversight under which this position operates.

☐ Receives clear and specific instructions and/or follows standardized practices, instructions, or procedures without ongoing supervision. Work is checked for accuracy, adequacy, and adherence to instructions. Employee consults with supervisor on matters not covered in the original instructions or by guidelines.

☐ Receives moderate to limited supervision working from objectives set by supervisor. Employee organizes and carries out most assignments in accordance with standard practices, instructions, procedures, or previous training. Employee handles some unusual situations independently of supervisor.

☐ Receives general direction working from established policies, procedures, and objectives. Employee plans and carries out assignments and resolves most conflicts that arise. Completed work is checked only to determine feasibility and compatibility with other work, or effectiveness in meeting objectives of the job.

☐ Receives only broad administrative guidance. Assignments are in terms of setting objectives within strategic planning goals. Employee has responsibility for planning, designing, and implementing programs, projects, and other initiatives and sets goals for a unit or department. Approval from higher supervision may be necessary only in terms of financial impact and availability of resources, but little reference to detail is discussed with the supervisor.

**Decision Making:** Briefly describe the typical and key decisions this position must make and what impact they may have on *[Practice]*.

**Comments:** Please review the questionnaire completed by the employee. Based on your understanding of the job as it currently exists, make any comments you have that would be helpful to understanding the position or any discrepancies that could not be resolved through discussion with the employee. This questionnaire is not meant to be a performance review, so please do not make any comments about the employee's performance.

| Supervisor Signature | Date |
|---|---|
|  |  |

**Form 3.2**      **Job Analysis Interview Questions**

This is a list of sample Job Analysis Interview Questions. Modify these questions to fit your medical practice's needs. Remember, the interviewer should be highly skilled and experienced in conducting job analysis interviews.

---

FORM 3.2           **JOB ANALYSIS
INTERVIEW QUESTIONS**

The following interviews can be used during a job analysis interview with employees.

Essential duties and responsibilities:
- What is the purpose of this job?
- What specific duties and responsibilities are performed?
- What percentage of time is spent on each of these duties?
- Do you use special tools or equipment to complete these duties?

Education and experience requirements:
- What is the minimum level of education required for this job?
- What type of continuing education, if any, must be completed for this job?
- What type of experience is required to do this job?
- What is the minimum level of related job experience for this job?
- What licenses or certifications are required for this job?

Skills and abilities:
- What special skills are needed to do this job?
- What specific knowledge is needed for this position?
- What specific abilities are needed for this job?

Working conditions:
- Describe the conditions involved in performing this job.
- Describe the physical demands of this position.
- What safety concerns or hazardous materials are related to this position?
- How frequently do you encounter these working or hazardous conditions?

Supervision and leadership:
- What are the leadership or supervisory responsibilities of this position?
- How many, if any, direct reports does this position have?

Contacts:

- Who within the practice must this position interact with to complete the job duties and functions?
- Who are the people/organizations you must communicate with outside of the practice to complete your job duties?
- How often must you communicate with them?

For supervisors only:

- Describe the level of oversight your direct reports require?
- Which direct reports have the authority to make decisions? What kinds of decisions do they make?
- What would be the result of a direct report's error?
- How is the quality of the direct report's work checked?
- What work is not reviewed?
- What guidelines govern the work of the direct reports?

## Form 3.3     Job Description Format

This is a sample format for a job description. Modify this format for your practice's use.

---

**FORM 3.3**

# "JOB TITLE"
# JOB DESCRIPTION

**Job Title:** Add the official job title.

**Reports To:** Add the job title of whom this position directly reports.

**Supervises:** List the job titles of whom this position directly supervises.

**Overtime Status:** ☐ Exempt    ☐ Nonexempt

**Job Summary:** Briefly summarize the purpose of this position, including key responsibilities and leadership duties.

**Primary Job Responsibilities:** List all primary job responsibilities.

**Other Job Responsibilities:** List any minor or additional job responsibilities.

**Education/Certification/Licenses:** List the minimum level of education required or preferred, all valid certifications required or preferred, and all valid licenses required or preferred for this position.

**Additional Requirements:** List any additional requirements such as Continuing Medical Education (CME) credits, any on-call requirements, or proficiency in electronic medical record systems.

**Experience:** List all required and preferred job-related experience needed to complete these responsibilities, including the minimum number of years of job-related experience.

**Knowledge, Skills, and Abilities:** List all knowledge, skills, and abilities required for this position, such as knowledge of pharmacological agents, excellent written and oral communication skills, and ability to interact with people of varied educational, socioeconomic, and ethnic backgrounds.

**Contacts:** List who this position has the most significant interaction, both within and outside the practice, such as clinical staff, patients, providers, vendors, regulatory agencies, community members, and so on.

**Physical Requirements:** Customize an ADA matrix, like the following one, to document the physical demands and working conditions of this position.

| Physical Activities | Amount of Time | | | |
|---|---|---|---|---|
| Place an **X** to indicate the amount of time spent on the following physical activities. | **None** | **Under ⅓** | **To ⅔** | **Over ⅔** |
| Stand | ____ | ____ | ____ | ____ |
| Walk | ____ | ____ | ____ | ____ |
| Sit | ____ | ____ | ____ | ____ |
| Drive | ____ | ____ | ____ | ____ |
| Use hands to finger, handle, or feel | ____ | ____ | ____ | ____ |
| Reach with hands and arms | ____ | ____ | ____ | ____ |
| Bend | ____ | ____ | ____ | ____ |
| Twist or Turn | ____ | ____ | ____ | ____ |
| Climb (steps) or balance | ____ | ____ | ____ | ____ |

| | | | | |
|---|---|---|---|---|
| Stoop, squat, kneel, crouch, or crawl | ___ | ___ | ___ | ___ |
| Talk or hear | ___ | ___ | ___ | ___ |
| Carry | ___ | ___ | ___ | ___ |
| Lift | ___ | ___ | ___ | ___ |
| Push or pull | ___ | ___ | ___ | ___ |
| Taste or smell | ___ | ___ | ___ | ___ |
| Other _____ | ___ | ___ | ___ | ___ |

**Vision**

Place an **X** to indicate whether these vision requirements apply.

| | Yes | No |
|---|---|---|
| Close vision (clear vision at 20 inches or less) | ___ | ___ |
| Distance vision (clear vision at 20 feet or more) | ___ | ___ |
| Color vision (ability to identify and distinguish colors) | ___ | ___ |
| Peripheral vision (ability to see an area up and down or left and right while eyes are fixed on a given point) | ___ | ___ |
| Adjust focus (ability to adjust the eye to bring an object into sharp focus) | ___ | ___ |
| Depth perception (three-dimensional vision, ability to judge distances and spatial relationships | ___ | ___ |
| Other _____ | ___ | ___ |

**Weight Lifted/Force Exerted**

Place an **X** to indicate the amount of time spent lifting weight or exerting force.

| | Amount of Time | | | |
|---|---|---|---|---|
| | None | Under $\frac{1}{3}$ | To $\frac{2}{3}$ | Over $\frac{2}{3}$ |
| Up to 10 pounds | ___ | ___ | ___ | ___ |
| Up to 25 pounds | ___ | ___ | ___ | ___ |
| Up to 50 pounds | ___ | ___ | ___ | ___ |
| Up to 100 pounds | ___ | ___ | ___ | ___ |
| More than 100 pounds | ___ | ___ | ___ | ___ |
| Other _____ | ___ | ___ | ___ | ___ |

**Environmental Conditions**

Place an **X** to indicate the amount of time spent exposed to these environmental conditions.

| | Amount of Time | | | |
|---|---|---|---|---|
| | None | Under $\frac{1}{3}$ | To $\frac{2}{3}$ | Over $\frac{2}{3}$ |
| Blood and bodily fluids | ___ | ___ | ___ | ___ |
| Hazardous materials other than blood and bodily fluids | ___ | ___ | ___ | ___ |
| Biohazards (bacteria, funguses, viruses) | ___ | ___ | ___ | ___ |
| Toxic, caustic, or poisonous substances | ___ | ___ | ___ | ___ |
| Communicable diseases | ___ | ___ | ___ | ___ |
| Radiation (ionizing, laser, microwave) | ___ | ___ | ___ | ___ |
| Chemicals | ___ | ___ | ___ | ___ |
| Wears protective clothing/equipment | ___ | ___ | ___ | ___ |
| Other _____ | ___ | ___ | ___ | ___ |

**Salary Range:** Add the salary range for this position.

**Approval Date:** Add the date on which this job description was initially approved or when an update was approved.

# CHAPTER 4

# Compensation

Compensation is something given or received for services rendered. This is a simple definition of a complex human resource management (HRM) function that not only involves many procedures, but also, and more importantly, results in policies that reflect the medical practice's commitment to an equitable, balanced compensation system that places value on the work of staff. Without such policies and the commitment to them, your practice will be severely handicapped in terms of performance, productivity, and retention of top talent.

*Compensation* is an all-encompassing term for not only wage and salary determination but also job evaluation (determining the relative worth of jobs), benefits (such as retirement plans and vacation), and incentives (rewards to encourage productivity and performance). Many factors controlling compensation are out of your control, including the cost of living in your area; the supply and demand of available, qualified staff; and your competitors, who compete not only for patients but workers as well. Managing compensation is a balancing act. Staff members must be satisfied through appropriate, yet competitive, compensation; and managers expect compensation not only to motivate

**Compensation impacts a worker's:**

- Ability to fulfill basic needs;
- Sense of achievement;
- Self-esteem;
- Self-fulfillment; and
- Self-worth.

employees and maximize productivity,
but also to be cost-effective.

Compensation means more to
employees than just the value of their
performance and the ability to complete assigned tasks. Compensation
also deeply involves psychological
factors including providing the basic
necessities of life: food, shelter, and
clothing. Even more important, compensation affects a person's self-worth and feelings
of achievement, self-esteem, and self-fulfillment. What's equitable in the eyes of the
employer is often seen as inadequate to the employee who feels more valuable than the
monetary and nonmonetary benefits received. A sense of inequity reduces motivation,
productivity, and loyalty.

**Components of a Compensation Package**

- Salary/Wage
- Benefits
- Incentives

Many publications are available, including those published by the Medical Group
Management Association (MGMA), that delve deeply into the compensation aspect
of HRM and go beyond the scope of this book. This publication only discusses the key
compensation topics important to understand when developing policies and procedures
for your medical practice.

## Developing a Compensation System

Creating the foundation for compensation administration begins by considering the following questions:

- Who is going to develop and oversee the compensation system?
- Who is going to provide expert advice?
- What is the budget for developing and maintaining the system?
- When will development occur and how will this ongoing task be carried out?
- Who can determine salary ranges and salary increases? How often and on what
  basis are these done?

It is often helpful to retain a consultant to set up a compensation system and to provide ongoing compensation consulting. Consider using a benefits consulting firm or
refer questions to an industry association, such as the MGMA, for information and
assistance. In any case, it is imperative that the senior management team is involved in
establishing the compensation philosophy and policy for your practice. Larger practices
often use a compensation committee representing different departments to ensure input
and consistency in compensation decisions.

The compensation committee or human resources (HR) professional should tackle the
hard questions about how to establish pay structures for various types of employees.
For example, should there be a difference between how clinical and nonclinical staff are
compensated? It should also decide how salaries/wages are complemented by benefits
and incentives. These three components compose the total compensation package that
job candidates consider when making a decision on whether to join your medical practice and that current employees consider when making a decision on whether to stay
with your practice.

As with the results of a job analysis that serves as input for evaluating a job and establishing a job structure as mentioned earlier, developing a compensation system begins with evaluating jobs based on the content of the work, the value of the work to the organization, the culture of the workplace, and external market forces. Compensation begins with job evaluation and moves on to establishing pay, benefits, and incentives.

## Job Evaluation

Job evaluation is the first and most important step in compensation administration. Utilizing the job descriptions helps determine the relative worth of a job in relation with other jobs in the medical practice. It involves formal comparison of the essential functions of various positions in order to rank each position in the organization. Although job content is a primary factor in evaluation, the market conditions, competition, worker supply and demand, and unemployment rates are also considered.

Job evaluation is a system procedure designed to aid in establishing pay differentials among jobs with a single employer. It helps you assess:

- A job's relative importance within the organization;
- The knowledge, skills, and abilities necessary to do the job;
- The difficulty level of one job compared to another; and
- The education, experience, and licensing requirements for the job.

**Popular Job Evaluation Methods**

- Ranking
- Job Classification
- Factor Comparison
- Point Factor

Using all of this information, you can develop an equitable and meaningful wage and salary system in line with federal and state laws. Several major laws are related to compensation practices (most described in Chapter 2, Employment Laws and Regulations), including:

- Age Discrimination in Employment Act;
- Civil Rights Act;
- Employee Retirement Income Security Act;
- Equal Pay Act;
- Fair Labor Standards Act;
- Family and Medical Leave Act;
- Health Maintenance Organization Act (requirement to offer a federally registered HMO option if other health plans are offered to employees);
- National Labor Relations Act (Wagner Act);
- Pregnancy Discrimination Act;
- Social Security Act;
- The federal Anti-Kickback Statute; and
- (for physicians) The Ethics in Patient Referrals Act (Stark law).

These are the primary federal laws that affect compensation. Also be aware of state laws, including minimum-wage requirements. Also be up to date on how Workers Compensation works.

There are many job evaluation methods. The four most popular methods are discussed in the following sections. There are advantages and disadvantages for each. In all cases, check your results with industry market data to make sure that your jobs match the market rate for similar jobs, which usually requires utilizing accurate market-pricing surveys. There is no perfect job evaluation method. You and your medical practice will need to decide which method works best for the type and size of your practice. In addition, Policy 4.01 at the end of this chapter is a sample policy related to job evaluation.

**Ranking Method**
The ranking method simply involves ranking the job descriptions in order from highest to lowest in each department based on a definition of value or contribution. It works best when there are just a few jobs (less than 30) to be evaluated. A matrix is then developed to show the compensation committee how the jobs rank across departments.

The designated HR professional or a committee can rank the jobs department by department. The ranker puts the job titles in order by value. A weighting system can also be used by giving jobs a subjective weight to reflect what the rankers believe they are worth. Jobs could also be evaluated in pairs by comparing two jobs side by side and then choosing one as more valuable to the organization than the other. The rankers then develop a chart showing all jobs within each department in order of most valuable to least valuable.

After all jobs are ranked, pay grades are established (entry level/beginner, junior, middle, senior, etc.) for every position in each department. Pay scales are then assigned for each pay grade after checking to see how similar jobs in the community are compensated. In this competitive compensation analysis process, establishing benchmarks is helpful. A benchmark job is a job common to the industry with easy-to-compare basic characteristics. Benchmark jobs have these characteristics:

• Well-known characteristics that are relatively stable over time;

• Commonalities across employers;

• Components representative of an entire range of jobs; and

• Acceptance in the external market for setting wages.

Benchmark jobs (or key jobs) are selected and then wages are compared with what other medical practices are paying their employees in the same job. For example, an X-ray technician position, which has similar functions across medical practices, can be used when validating the average pay in the community. By reviewing the market price of the benchmark jobs within the medical practice industry and your community, your medical practice can establish a pay scale. Advantages and disadvantages of the ranking method are shown in Exhibit 4.1.

**Exhibit 4.1 Ranking Method – Advantages and Disadvantages**

| Advantages | Disadvantages |
|---|---|
| • Simple<br>• Fast<br>• Easy to understand and explain to employees<br>• Least-expensive method | • Based on nonquantitative decisions rather than essential functions, knowledge, skills, and abilities needed for a job<br>• No standards for comparison<br>• Cumbersome when there are many jobs to evaluate |

## Job Classification Method

Classification is similar to the ranking method except that it involves organizing jobs into broad classes or categories based on job analysis findings and building a hierarchy. It uses some comparison standards, such as the complexity of the work and the amount of supervisory responsibility.

The designated HR professional or a committee groups each job into different classes (typically there are 7 to 14 classes). Many classes allow variability and diversity. Too many classes, however, inhibits their use as common denominators. Each class should be defined, and like job descriptions, class descriptions are only useful when they represent meaningful similarities and differences among jobs. After the classes are identified and defined, benchmark jobs are selected as reference points, similar to the job ranking method. Classification methods typically are occupation or industry specific. The government, for example, has a Defense Civilian Intelligence Personnel system based on job classifications. Advantages and disadvantages of the job classification method are shown in Exhibit 4.2.

**Exhibit 4.2   Job Classification Method – Advantages and Disadvantages**

| Advantages | Disadvantages |
|---|---|
| • Simple | • Standards used are not exact |
| • Fairly fast | • Jobs may be forced into a class that does not quite fit |
| • Easy to understand and explain to employees | • Relies on subjective judgments |
| | • May build biases based on gender, race, etc. |

## Factor Comparison Method

This approach is used to evaluate jobs using two criteria:

1. A set of compensable factors; and
2. Wages for benchmark jobs.

These criteria form a job comparison scale that can be used to set wages for nonbenchmark jobs. This method is one of the most complex and the least popular.

The designated HR professional or a committee usually determines the factor comparisons. Typically four or five compensable factors are used such as skills, responsibilities, effort (physical and mental), working conditions, and so on. For each benchmark job, the hourly wage is then divided up among the identified compensable factors. This produces a rate of pay for each factor for each benchmark job. After benchmark jobs have been factored, all other jobs are compared to the benchmarks and the rates of pay for each factor. For example, consider an administrative assistant position. The hourly wage might be $15 per hour, and the committee may value the factors in the following way:

- Hourly wage: $15
  - Skills: $4
  - Responsibilities $3
  
    Effort: $7.50
  - Working conditions: $0.50

Advantages and disadvantages of the factor comparison method are shown in Exhibit 4.3.

**Exhibit 4.3   Factor Comparison Method – Advantages and Disadvantages**

| Advantages | Disadvantages |
|---|---|
| • Value expressed in dollar amounts<br>• Can be easily applied to a variety of jobs<br>• Can be easily applied to newly created positions<br>• Adds flexibility | • Relies on subjective judgments<br>• May build biases based on gender, race, etc.<br>• Difficult to explain to employees<br>• Time-consuming |

### Point Factor Method

This system looks at a job's specific duties and responsibilities (essential functions) and awards points to each. It is an extension of the factor comparison method. The points are arbitrary, but they reflect the value your medical practice attaches to each function. Your practice would assign the highest point value to the essential function it most values, such as customer service, for example.

As with the factor comparison method, the point factor method uses a set of key factors (e.g., skills, responsibilities, effort, and working conditions). Each of the key factors is then sub-factored into levels and then divided further into prioritized degrees. Points are assigned for each degree and added up for each degree, level, and key factor to calculate a total point score for each job. Jobs are then grouped together by total score ranges and assigned to a wage or salary grade. Thereby, similar jobs are placed in the same wage or salary grade.

Typical key factors and levels may include those shown in Exhibit 4.4. Advantages and disadvantages of the point factor method are shown in Exhibit 4.5.

**Exhibit 4.4   Typical Key Factors**

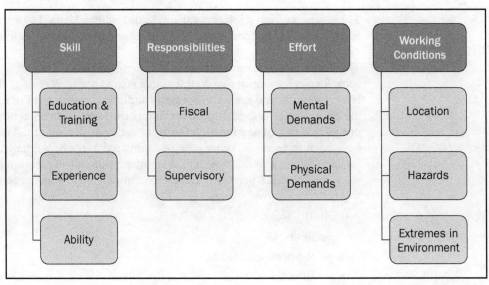

**Exhibit 4.5   Point Factor Method – Advantages and Disadvantages**

| Advantages | Disadvantages |
| --- | --- |
| • Value expressed in dollar amounts<br>• Can be easily applied to a variety of jobs<br>• Can be easily applied to newly created positions<br>• Helps eliminate bias | • Complex<br>• Time-consuming<br>• Pay judgments are subjective<br>• Difficult to explain to employees |

## Computing Pay

After each job has been evaluated, the next step is to determine the dollar value that each position is worth. Pay computation involves determining the:

- Number of pay structures needed;
- Number of pay grades within each structure;
- Minimum, midpoint, and maximum pay for each grade;
- Ways individuals can advance in pay grades;
- Record-keeping and reporting requirements; and
- Methods for communicating to employees about compensation.

Your medical practice's compensation committee has to determine where your practice wants to fit in the market in terms of compensation. For each job, the compensation committee determines where it is on the pay scale:

- Premium (6 to 10 percent above market rates);
- Fully competitive (5 percent above market rates);
- Competitive (equal to market rates); or
- Marginal (1 to 5 percent below market rates).

These decisions are critical when recruiting and retaining staff. By taking a premium or fully competitive position for a specific job, your practice may overcome the competition when qualified candidates are in short supply. However, if this philosophy is used for all jobs and at all times, your practice may quickly reach the salary budget. Usually, paying a premium is justified only for certain positions at certain times.

On the other hand, if your practice chooses to utilize a marginal scale, fewer qualified candidates may be willing to join your practice unless your total compensation package offers something of value to certain candidates. For example, you might offer medical assistants an extremely flexible schedule that appeals to mothers. Typically, using a competitive strategy works best as long as the option of using the other strategies for some positions is available.

### Setting the Pay Grades

Your medical practice may decide to have one or more pay structures for different categories of workers, that is, a different one for higher-level administrators. If your practice is a small group, however, a single pay structure is usually adequate.

For a small group, four to five pay grades within their single pay structure work well. For a larger group, there may be as many as 40 within a single pay structure. Regardless of the number of pay grades, keep in mind these tips:

- Cluster positions so that those of the same general value are assigned to the same pay grade;
- Place positions that are different in value in different pay grades; and
- Ensure that the pay grades reasonably conform to pay patterns in your labor market area.

The compensation committee or HR professional typically sets the minimum pay grade at a level that would be acceptable as a starting salary by 80 to 90 percent of the candidates. The midpoint should be high enough to retain employees when they have reached a high level of proficiency. The maximum would be used to retain the most competent employees.

For entry-level jobs, the range between each of the pay levels is small (e.g., 20 to 25 percent); at the higher-level positions, the range is usually broader (e.g., 35 to 40 percent) to ensure the flexibility needed to retain managers and administrators. Your medical practice should use a standard percentage difference (usually 5 to 10 percent) between midpoints for adjoining pay grades to ensure consistency in your pay structure. In healthcare organizations, there is often a small difference for lower-skilled employees, perhaps as low as 3 to 5 percent. At higher skill levels, usually there are higher midpoint differences between pay grades.

The pay range within each pay grade should provide opportunities for employee growth. Spreads typically vary from 10 to 25 percent on either side of the midpoint. Again, higher-level positions generally will have a wider pay grade range. The range spread is typically expressed in a percentage change from the midpoint. For example, the range spread for a pay grade might be ±10 percent from the midpoint.

After you have established the midpoint and the percentage range of each pay grade, the minimum and maximum pay rates for each pay grade can be computed as follows:

$$\text{maximum rate} = \text{midpoint} + (\text{range} \times \text{midpoint})$$

$$\text{minimum rate} = \text{midpoint} - (\text{range} \times \text{midpoint})$$

For example, your medical practice sets the midpoint for a job at $54,000 and the range at ±15%. To calculate the maximum and minimum rate, you would use the following formulas:

$$\text{maximum rate is } \$54,000 + (0.15 \times \$54,000) = \$62,100$$

$$\text{minimum rate is } \$54,000 - (0.15 \times \$54,000) = \$45,900$$

Therefore, the range for this pay grade is:

- Minimum: $45,900
- Midpoint: $54,000
- Maximum: $62,100

After the boundaries of the pay grade are set, the number of pay steps in the pay grade range can be determined. Typically, the number of steps varies from 5 to 12 within each pay grade. The percentage increase within the steps varies from about 2.5 to 5 percent. The compensation committee may decide to pay for performance or longevity, and set a wider range to reflect these objectives.

Ideally, an employee will start at the lower end of a pay grade and move toward the midpoint (usually the competitive market rate) fairly quickly, assuming the employee's performance is satisfactory. Thereafter, the rate of advancement tends to slow, with increases given more for exceptional performance. If a supervisor does not manage pay increases carefully, employees may be in jeopardy of becoming ineligible for a raise because they have reached the maximum end of their pay grade. This can happen if raises are given automatically. If some employees do not have the qualifications or desire to move up, their salaries should remain capped.

To ensure that your medical practice's pay grades and salary ranges are competitive, gather data on current salary and wage levels for comparable jobs in your industry and in your geographic area. Keep in mind that competitive wages in New York City are much different than competitive wages in Boise, Idaho. Many HR and compensation organizations publish salary and wage surveys, which can help you not only confirm that your pay structure is competitive, but also assure your employees they are earning a proper wage.

Excellent resources for these types of surveys are the American Management Association, the Society for Human Resource Management, the MGMA, the US Department of Labor (DOL), local chambers of commerce, and many private research and consulting firms. See Policy 4.02 for a sample policy on computing pay.

## Pay Raises and Adjustments

Salary increases are typically based on a variety of factors, including employee performance, available budget for increases, current economic conditions and future forecasts, increasing competition, and local industry trends. For example, in 2012 healthcare employees saw about a 2.7 percent base salary increase over 2011 salaries.[*] This number was the largest increase in salaries since the financial meltdown in 2008 to 2009. Criteria for increasing pay are:

- Merit;
- Length of service;
- Experience;
- Productivity; and
- Performance.

Occasionally, the medical practice's pay structure will need to be adjusted when internal changes or environmental variations occur. These changes include inflationary rates, changes in the relative value of a job to your practice, adjustments to job tasks and responsibilities, reorganizations, and developments of new technology.

---

[*]   2011–2012 Culpepper Salary Budget Survey, Culpepper & Associates, Inc. 2012.

**Pay Raises**

Three types of pay raises can be considered by medical practices:

1. Merit pay;
2. Longevity-Seniority pay; and
3. Pay-for-performance.

*Merit Pay*

A performance-based system, merit pay is a traditional method to financially reward employees who work hard and perform the best. Salary increases are scheduled at specific times, such as the anniversary date of employment, and the salary progresses through the pay grade range.

For a salary in the minimum to midpoint range, increases tend to happen more rapidly and are larger than those salaries around the midpoint, which are relatively stable and set to the local competitive market in that pay grade. Merit pay was originally designed to reward extraordinary performance; however, these annual small percentage increases have been customary for many years, and employees now expect them. This trend was partially fueled by many organizations giving high-performing employees the highest percentage increase (e.g., 3 to 5 percent), average performing employees a smaller percentage (e.g., 1 to 2 percent), and poorly performing employees no increase. Merit pay is now often seen as an entitlement, not a reward.

*Longevity-Seniority Pay*

This traditional system rewards length of service to an organization. Employees are eligible for a pay increase at set intervals. Increases tend to be the same for every employee with a satisfactory performance report. This system can reduce conflicts among the employee, the supervisor, and the union. It does not reward employees, however, for excellent performance, which can be demotivating to other hard-working staff. This system is rarely used today.

*Pay-for-Performance*

If your medical practice is committed to rewarding exceptional performance, you should design a system that gives salary increases to employees for taking on more responsibilities and achieving performance goals. With such a system, salary increases are neither automatic nor based on seniority or longevity.

Most practices use some type of a pay-for-performance method. To effectively utilize this type of system, your medical practice must have a performance evaluation system based on sound principles as the only way to avoid any potential discrimination claims or Equal Employment Opportunity challenges. (See Chapter 11, Managing Performance, for more information). Such a system typically sets standards to effectively measure performance, encourages managers to give continual feedback about performance, corrects poor performance, reinforces goals, and rewards results.

**Pay Adjustments**

Adjustments to the pay structure ensure that the medical practice achieves the three classic compensation goals:

1. Equal pay for equal work;
2. Competitive salaries; and

3. Rewards for performance.

Your practice can continually accomplish these goals by adjusting salary structure, pay grades, and individual salaries in these ways:

- Remaining competitive by annually reviewing your labor market's prevailing pay rates for comparable jobs and adjusting the medical practice's salary structure in unbiased ways;
- Retaining employees by rewarding outstanding performance through a competitive salary structure; and
- Making adjustments to employee salaries equitably when promotions or demotions occur.

There are three types of pay adjustments.

1. **Cost of Living Adjustment (COLA).** Cost of living adjustments are across-the-board increases/decreases to all employees because of inflation or labor market factors. These adjustments are typically an equal percentage to all employees. This changes the dollar amount for each pay grade and step within the salary structure but does not move any employee or job within the structure. A COLA increase used to be popular but is less common today. With the struggling economy, some organizations have frozen salaries or implemented a universal decrease to avoid laying off employees.

2. **Performance or longevity increase.** As previously discussed, merit pay is designed to reward performance but is often given automatically. Longevity and seniority increases are given when an employee reaches a particular anniversary of employment but are rarely used today. Performance increases are given when an employee achieves set goals as agreed on by their manager or supervisor. Adjustments are typically given when an employee is promoted and accepts higher-level job duties and responsibilities. Conversely, if an employee is demoted to a lower-level position, a salary decrease should occur. An employee may seek a less demanding position for personal reasons as well.

3. **Job classification increase.** This type of increase occurs when the supply of available qualified candidates for a job is so tight that the job becomes more valuable in the labor market. For example, the current national shortage of nurses has caused the worth of this job category to increase.

*Work Premiums and Overtime*
Healthcare organizations often ask employees to work outside the standard 8 a.m. to 5 p.m. routine. To compensate for these "off-hours," work premiums may be used to pay for overtime, and weekend and holiday work. Work premium policies must comply with federal overtime wage and hour laws.

Under the Fair Labor Standards Act (FLSA), an organization must pay a time-and-one-half premium for the time beyond 40 hours that a nonexempt employee works in one workweek. The hours worked beyond the 40 in one workweek is called overtime. This type of pay can be an effective way for managing costs when used prudently by having an employee occasionally work a few more hours so you don't need to hire another employee. On the other hand, overtime pay costs mount up quickly. It may be less costly to hire temporary staff to fill in extra hours needed. Also, if not managed properly, overtime authorization can inadvertently become automatic and result in higher staff costs. Monitor overtime costs to determine whether employees are stretching out their work in order to get overtime hours, or supervisors are slow to recognize that additional work hours are needed, or no one is paying attention to these extra costs.

Employees can quickly burn out if asked or expected to work extra hours on a regular basis. This has become a problem, for example, for nurses working in short-staffed hospitals. It is best to assign overtime work only to those qualified employees who voluntarily request extra work hours. The FLSA does involve various compensation compliance issues of which you should be aware. For specifics, refer to the FLSA regulations on the DOL's Website. The FLSA does allow inpatient healthcare providers to use an 8/80 pay period system; however, few medical practices have such facilities and qualify for this exemption.

*Call-In or Standby Premiums*

Occasionally, medical practices need employees to stand by to perform work assignments outside the normal working hours. Since such "on-call" assignments are an inconvenience to employees, premium compensation can be provided, usually at 1½ times their regular hourly rate. A minimum reporting premium policy may also be established that guarantees a certain amount of pay for being on call. A standard reporting premium is two to four hours of pay for reporting to work outside of normal working hours, regardless of how long the employee works.

Such policies may also apply to other types of jobs in the medical practice, particularly if your practice has an information technology (IT) department. Like most companies, healthcare organizations are dangerously vulnerable to computer downtimes as well as hacking and cyber-theft of patient, personal, and/or private information. For that reason, some larger medical practices have IT staff members on call 24 hours a day and provide premium pay for their availability. See Policy 4.03 for a sample policy on work premiums.

*Shift, Weekend, and Holiday Work*

Many healthcare organizations have irregular shifts like 4 p.m. to midnight or midnight to 8 a.m., for example. This scenario occurs more in a hospital setting, but there are some medical practices, such as those that perform cosmetic surgery, that have patients stay overnight. In these cases, it is common to add a shift differential rate of pay to the normal rate paid to nonexempt employees; this could be either a flat amount or a percentage. Salaried employees doing shift work sometimes receive an additional monthly increment to their base pay.

Some employees who work Monday through Friday receive premium pay for working on weekends or holidays even though the hours worked during the week do not exceed 40. Such "after-hours work" is often compensated at time and one-half. It is rare that an employee receives both overtime and weekend/holiday pay.

## Incentives

An incentive is something that incites action or greater effort from an employee. Incentives were first used as motivators for executives by giving them a share in profits. This concept has expanded since then to include offerings for all employees as a way to improve performance and productivity. Healthcare organizations and group practices have begun to utilize incentives, including reward programs designed for meeting cost-efficiencies, quality, and other performance goals. Profit-sharing programs are discussed further in the Chapter 5, Benefits.

Employee recognition and reward programs reinforce outstanding performance and provide acknowledgment, appreciation, and praise for going above and beyond expectations. Some medical practices give supervisors a small discretionary fund for awards, which could include gift cards, tickets to sporting events, or other rewards. Recognition and rewards can also be given for outstanding teamwork, an innovative new idea that saves your practice valuable time, or for attendance. Employee recognition and reward programs are beyond the scope of this publication; however, much has been written about this topic, especially in MGMA's *Acknowledge! Appreciate! Applaud! 172 Easy Ways to Reward Staff for Little or No Cost*[\*]. Policy 4.04 is a sample policy about incentive programs for medical practices.

## Retaining Compensation Information and Records

Keeping records of compensation data is important for governmental regulation compliance, budgeting, and informing employees about salaries and wages. The compensation information needed for budget purposes includes:

- Gross and net pay for each employee;
- Ratio of gross pay to net pay for the entire medical practice;
- Comparison of budgeted pay to actual pay;
- Breakdowns of compensation by team, department, classification, and pay grade; and
- Other pay statistics used for monitoring performance.

Payroll information needed to comply with governmental laws and regulations and to inform employees about their compensation includes:

- Employee identification number (if used by your practice);
- Social Security number;
- Base pay;
- Time worked;
- Premium pay, incentive pay, and bonuses;
- Tax deductions; and
- Benefits.

Payroll processing can be quite complex for medical practices because of the array of options such as flexible benefits, various retirement savings plans, leaves of absence, shift differentials, and other offerings. Your medical practice may find it beneficial to use a payroll vendor for processing. In any case, internal staff will need to collect, input, and report compensation data and be available to answer employee questions.

Payroll also brings up two decisions that your medical practice will have to make. First is to determine when paychecks will be issued. Commonly used options are on every Friday or every other Friday. Probably the more frequently used method is on the 15th and last day of each month. Your practice's finance department or your accountant can help determine the best schedule for your practice. The yearly pay calendar should be posted for all employees and supervisors at the beginning of each year.

---

[\*]   By Alys Novak and Courtney H. Price (Englewood, CO: Medical Group Management Association, 2011).

Secondly, you should determine whether your practice will offer direct deposit. This has become the most common method of paying employees. In fact, the National Federation of Independent Business estimates that about 60 percent of all workers in the United States have their paychecks directly deposited into their bank accounts. Many organizations, including the federal government, mandate direct deposit. Your practice's payroll department or payroll service provider can help determine whether offering direct deposit is advantageous for your medical practice.

**Compensation Information Employees Want**

Employees want the basic information about when and how they are paid, as well as how to read pay-stub details related to deductions and other items listed. Some organizations provide an annual compensation report for employees that details not only pay elements, but also benefits and incentives.

The amount of information provided to employees about compensation depends on your practice's philosophy. Before sharing payroll information, make sure you have a solid compensation program based on well-developed pay structures, pay grades, and salary rates and ranges. Make sure it will stand up to employee scrutiny as they compare what your practice offers with other organizations in the community.

Employees also want to know about payroll mechanics. Create clear communication with all employees about the pay schedule, how they will be paid (via check or direct deposit), whether time sheets are required, which employees are required to submit them, and what the deadline is for time-sheet submission. Typically, the HR manager will hold periodic meetings explaining your practice's compensation practices where employees can ask any salary questions.

## Helping Employees Understand Compensation

As previously mentioned, it is not only important to communicate to employees how and when they will be paid but also to help them understand their compensation to prevent employee backlash. Most compensation administration minefields and dilemmas can be avoided by educating employees about the compensation plan and being open about the steps taken to ensure it is equitable. Simply and briefly outline the following processes for your employees so there are no surprises. Not all may apply to your medical practice.

- Job analysis;
- Job evaluation;
- Salary grades;
- Salary ranges;
- Salary structure;
- Salary policy;
- Manager support;
- Employee communication; and
- Monitoring, evaluation, and updating.

Although these processes seem mechanical, there is always a psychological element. Emotions are triggered in the process. Employees need and want to understand the key factors that influence their compensation. For this reason, use real examples to explain how factors such as experience and education factor into the salary equation. For example, a person may seek a high level of compensation because he or she has certain experience or education. However, that experience or education may not be a job requirement. Consider, for example, someone who has a PhD in economics and six years of experience as a professor. Although their job does not require the type of education or experience the person has, the person probably feels underpaid. This example shows how important it is to match the job to the person's qualifications.

Consider another example. A newly graduated nurse is typically paid at the entry level of the nurse job classification. If he or she is graduating as a nurse practitioner, the job classification has a higher level, and may be even higher if the person has special qualifications highly demanded by the medical practice, such as pediatric nurse practitioner with several years of related experience.

In summation, it is critical that the HR department simplifies the complexities of compensation so that staff members not only understand them, but also believe that your practice's compensation administration is appropriate. Also keep in mind that compensation impacts other HR matters, including promotion, performance management, discipline, and grievance procedures.

## Summary

Administering compensation involves a detailed, complex set of tasks. However, when you have a well-conceived pay system in place and well-documented policies and procedures, the management of compensation is straightforward.

Remember to consistently:

- Match job positions and related job evaluation and compensation policies with the medical practice's current strategic plan.
- Review job position descriptions to keep them up to date with changes in duties or technology.
- Participate and analyze market salary surveys to ensure that your compensation packages are competitive.
- Consult with compensation and benefits specialists and service providers about trends and services.
- Explain your practice's compensation system to the new hire and through communication and documentation in the employee handbook, benefits statements, and other media.
- Educate supervisors about their part in the system, such as authorizing leaves of absence and recommending pay raises. Assist them with completing the necessary paperwork by sending them polite reminders and the proper forms.
- Ensure that compensation arrangements comply with applicable laws.

Ensure that your payroll system works effectively and that any glitches are handled quickly and smoothly. Nothing will affect morale more adversely than a payroll error. The bottom line on compensation is: Employees want to work for a medical practice they believe recognizes their worth and compensates them equitably and efficiently. In addition, current and potential employees want to work with an organization that balances its formal system with informal methods of recognition and reward.

**Sample Policies**

**Policy 4.01**        **Job Evaluation**

This is an example of a job evaluation policy.

---

POLICY 4.01                        **JOB EVALUATION**

Purpose: To establish and maintain a process to measure the worth of jobs and to establish pay grades.

Applies to: Human Resources Department

Policy: The policy of *[Practice]* is to have a job evaluation plan to measure the worth of jobs and to establish pay grades. Rates of pay are set for each position on the basis of internal and external salary surveys. The goal of *[Practice's]* job evaluation plan is to develop an equitable compensation system for employees based on job position values.

Procedures:

1. Written job descriptions are prepared for each job title based on information gained through job analysis.
2. Pay grades, based on job evaluation results, are established by *[Practice]*, and a salary range is assigned to each pay grade. The salary range provides a minimum, midpoint, and maximum range of rates and permits employees within one pay grade to be compensated at different rates of pay based on merit, length of service, experience, and individual productivity.
3. Management is responsible for assigning pay rates to employees with the established pay grade of the position occupied by the employee, based on the job evaluation results.
4. The individual who has been assigned compensation responsibility administers the job evaluation plan. Responsibilities of the job evaluation planner include:
   • Periodically reviewing job descriptions to ensure they adequately describe the job;
   • Reevaluating positions regularly to ensure currency as well as reviewing new job positions; and
   • Making adjustments to pay grades when justified.
5. A compensation salary review committee reviews wages and salaries on an as-needed basis and at least annually.

Approved by: Practice Administrator

Effective date: 1/1/20__

## Policy 4.02 **Pay Computation**

This is an example of a computing pay policy.

---

**POLICY 4.02** **PAY COMPUTATION**

Purpose: To ensure equitable compensation for each position.

Applies to: Human Resources Department

Policy: The policy of *[Practice]* is to provide equitable compensation for each employee based on the job position, individual performance, and *[Practice's]* pay computation plan.

Procedures:
1. The pay computation policy provides the basis for determining individual salary levels.
2. A pay computation plan ensures pay equity for employees.
3. Pay grades and salary ranges that are affordable, comparable to, or better than similar jobs within the local healthcare region and the industry are established for each position.
4. Within each pay grade, minimum, midpoint, maximum, and intermediate steps are established.
5. An employee's salary rate is always set within the pay grade assigned to a position.
6. The department manager determines the initial hiring rate and step, with approval of the division manager, the human resources (HR) department, and the finance director.
7. A performance- and/or longevity-related spread is established for an employee's pay rate throughout the pay grade.
8. A promoted employee is assigned a rate of pay within the pay grade for the new job position commensurate with his or her performance level.
9. A demoted employee is assigned a rate of pay within the pay grade of the new job position commensurate with his or her performance level.
10. *[Practice]* maintains open communication with employees regarding its compensation policy and emphasizes how its compensation plan compares to industry-wide norms.
11. The designated HR professional is responsible for developing and maintaining compensation guidelines and pay computation in conjunction with *[Practice's]* administration. It is responsible for communicating the compensation policy to employees through appropriate channels and explaining the pay computation plan.
12. Wage and salary surveys are used when considering salary adjustments. The compensation salary review committee reviews *[Practice's]* salary structure at least annually.
13. Employees are paid on the 15th day and the last day of each month. If the regular payday occurs on a Saturday, Sunday, or holiday, employees are paid on the last working day immediately preceding the regular payday. Employees are offered the option of having their pay deposited directly into their designated bank accounts.

14. On each payday, employees receive a statement showing gross pay, deductions, and net pay after deductions. City, state, federal, and Social Security (FICA) taxes, and employee contributions to the group's benefits plans, as well as any employee-incurred expenses such as parking or cafeteria charges, or donations to a charitable organization such as the United Way, are automatically deducted and show on the pay statement. Also shown is any additional compensation for expenses such as mileage. The statement also shows the amount of leave time taken and remaining.

15. Employees may request salary advances for vacations and emergencies. The department manager and HR director must approve such requests. When a payday falls within an employee's vacation period, the employee may receive, before beginning the vacation, the salary that normally would be paid on the next regularly scheduled payday. In the case of an emergency, an employee may be permitted to draw in advance of the scheduled payday the pay due to the day of the advance payment.

Approved by: Practice Administrator

Effective date: 1/1/20__

## Policy 4.03    **Work Premiums**

This is an example policy about work premiums.

---

**POLICY 4.03                    WORK PREMIUMS**

Purpose: To establish and maintain compensation guidelines for overtime, shift, call-in, and standby work.

Applies to: All *[Practice]* employees.

Policy: The policy of *[Practice]* is to pay work premiums for these types of work: overtime, shift, call-in, and standby.

Procedures:

1. Overtime compensation is paid to nonexempt employees who work more than 40 hours per week, or 8 hours per day, during an 80-hour work period for certain positions (as allowed by the Fair Labor Standards Act), during the normal workweek at 1½ times their regular hourly rate.

2. To the extent feasible, overtime assignments are distributed equally among full-time employees, giving preference to employees with greater seniority who are willing to work overtime.

3. To compensate nonexempt employees for inconveniences experienced when regularly assigned to late shifts, a shift differential is paid.

4. Shifts starting after noon and ending at midnight or earlier are paid a specified per-hour differential; shifts starting after 11 p.m. are paid a specified per-hour differential.

5. Shift differentials are not paid during any period of paid leave, such as vacation, compensatory time off, or holidays unless the employee is required to work on a holiday.

6. Employees who are called from home to perform work during off-duty hours are paid 1½ times the employee's regular hourly rate. A minimum of two hours of work is guaranteed in such cases. No employee is called in to perform work during off-duty hours without the prior authorization of the employee's department manager.

7. Employees are paid for a minimum of four work hours if they report to work as scheduled and their supervisor sends them home due to an insufficient workload.

Approved by: Practice Administrator

Effective date: 1/1/20__

**Policy 4.04**        **Incentives**

This is an example of an incentive policy.

---

POLICY 4.04                              **INCENTIVES**

Purpose: To establish and maintain an incentive program.

Applies to: All *[Practice]* employees.

Policy: The policy of *[Practice]* is to offer a variety of incentive programs to staff members to increase productivity and performance. *[Practice]* believes employees should be encouraged to make constructive efforts to improve the group's operations. Incentive programs primarily include profit sharing, suggestion systems, and special bonuses.

Procedures:

1. The designated human resources (HR) professional, in conjunction with senior management, is responsible for developing, maintaining, and revising *[Practice's]* incentive program and setting eligibility requirements.

2. Incentive programs are designed for nonexempt and exempt employees.

3. The designated HR professional establishes and administers a profit-sharing plan based on group earnings and employee compensation.

4. The designated HR professional administers the incentive program, including any form of employee stock option plan (ESOP) if made available, in conjunction with the finance department.

5. *[Practice]* gives cash awards or appropriate gifts to employees whose suggestions are implemented and contribute to cost reduction or improvements in operational procedures.

6. Managers give special bonuses to reward an employee's exceptional, long-term effort that results in improved productivity or meets specific group goals. Supervisors are encouraged to give special recognition and rewards to employees for above-standard performance and have access to discretionary funds to make on-the-spot rewards.

Approved by: Practice Administrator

Effective date: 1/1/20__

# CHAPTER 5

# Benefits

Companies began adding benefits in the late 1800s as a way to increase employee motivation and productivity. Benefits became an even greater part of the compensation packages during World War II and the Korean War, when the government imposed wage and price controls. Companies and unions pushed to increase benefits to satisfy worker demands. The benefit patterns set in the 1800s continue today, whether good or bad. Employer-paid pensions and healthcare packages, for example, have forced some industries, such as the automobile manufacturers and airlines, to the brink of bankruptcy and beyond under the soaring costs of these benefits.

On the other hand, benefits are often cost-effective for the employer and employee. For example, most employee benefits are not taxable. In addition, an employer can purchase group benefits at a far better price than an employee can as an individual. Benefits can also meet employee needs in ways that far outweigh their cost.

As a medical practice considers which benefits to offer each year, it is often useful to hire a benefits consultant who can keep you abreast of new trends and many of the options available, as well as the legal and financial implications.

Benefits have a significant financial and administrative impact on a business workforce, which has come to expect a comprehensive benefits program. An inadequate program can seriously hinder an organization's ability to attract and retain personnel. Designing the right benefits plans for your employees is a complex task in terms of legal aspects, funding, and selection of vendor or administrators. A comprehensive benefits plan includes health insurance, disability insurance, life insurance, retirement planning, flexible compensation (cafeteria) plans, and leave from work. It can also include other components such as bonuses, service awards, reimbursement for educational expenses, and other benefits appropriate to employee responsibility. The reasons to offer benefits are:

- To attract and keep capable employees;
- To be competitive with other companies;
- To foster good morale; and
- To provide opportunities for advancement and promotion.

A program with a combination of benefits is the most effective and efficient means of meeting economic security needs. For many employers, a benefits plan is an integral bargaining tool to attract employees. In some cases, employers pay the entire costs of a certain benefit, such as life insurance, and in other cases the employee contributes a portion of the cost, such as health insurance.

## Employee Benefits Legislation

Four major laws impact employee benefits. Firstly, the Social Security Act of 1935 established a system to provide old-age, survivors' disability, and retirement benefits to employees who work a certain number of years, with coverage for most jobs. Both employers and employees share in funding this program. Medicare amendments to the act in 1965 added hospital and medical insurance protection to people ages 65 and older and the disabled. Social Security and Medicare have been greatly scrutinized recently, as the Social Security funds are paying out more money than they are bringing in and because of rapidly increasing costs of Medicare. This problem has been exacerbated in the past several years and will continue as the baby boomers reach the age of 65 and people live longer. Many argue that Social Security will not be available for the younger generations, and Medicare will continue to add to the deficit. Thus, like any governmental program, you should stay on top of proposed and enacted changes.

The Social Security Act also requires that unemployment compensation be provided through state-sponsored programs. The laws of each state determine minimum and maximum coverage, using a formula to determine the amount of weekly base pay and length of time employed. This is completely funded by employers through a tax based on a percentage of the employer's payroll. Watch unemployment claims closely since such claims can be quite expensive. The best approach is to prevent unwarranted claims to unemployment benefits.

Another claim that can be expensive and must be managed carefully is Workers' Compensation. This program was designed to provide cash benefits and medical care when a worker is injured on the job, or to his or her survivors if a worker is fatally injured on the job. Each state has its own Workers' Compensation program, and it is usually compulsory for employers with a certain number of employees to carry Workers' Compensation insurance with a state-approved insurance company. Even if insurance is elective, most employers carry some kind of insurance to cover claims. As discussed later, the best way to deal with Workers' Compensation claims is to prevent them by having an outstanding employee safety program.

## Major Laws Impacting Benefits

- Social Security Act of 1935
- Employee Retirement Income Security Act of 1974
- Health Maintenance Organization Act of 1973
- Patient Protection and Affordable Care Act of 2010

Secondly, the Employee Retirement Income Security Act of 1974 (ERISA) closely regulates aspects of employee benefits, including disclosure of benefits to employees. ERISA assigns the administrator of an organization's benefit plan the responsibility for complying with the disclosure requirements of the act. Also, employee benefit plans covered by the act must contain a reasonable procedure for administering employee claims and reviewing claim denials.

The third key law is the Health Maintenance Organization Act of 1973. As amended, it requires that membership in a qualified health maintenance organization (HMO) be offered as an option to employees covered under the act and to their dependents residing within the service area of the HMO.

Finally, the Patient Protection and Affordable Care Act of 2010 (PPACA) and the Health Care and Education Reconciliation Act of 2010 have and will continue to have sweeping changes to employee benefits, particularly in healthcare coverage for employees. According to the laws, organizations with 50 or more employees will be required to offer their full-time employees healthcare insurance beginning in 2015. In addition, employee contributions to health savings plans were capped starting in 2013. To help better fund Medicare, these two acts also increase the employee portion of the payroll tax for Medicare for the highest earners on wages earned after December 31, 2012. Because the exact impact of these laws is far from certain, stay up to date and consult with your legal counsel and benefits consultant to ensure that your medical practice stays in compliance and can plan and prepare for the upcoming changes.

## Types of Benefits

Employee benefits fall into three categories:
1. Mandatory (as required by law);
2. Protection and income (types of insurance); and
3. Service (types of lifestyle benefits).

This section lists the different benefits that your medical practice can consider under each of the types.

### Mandatory Benefits

Employers are required by law to provide some benefits to their employees. Some of these laws do not affect smaller medical practices. Your legal counsel or benefits consultant can help determine from which of these benefits your practice may be exempt. In addition, some states have adopted variances to these required benefits that you should verify with your state. The mandatory benefits are:

- Social Security;
- Family and Medical Leave Act (FMLA);
- Overtime;
- Workers' Compensation;
- Unemployment insurance;
- Time off for jury duty; and
- Military leave.

### Protection and Income Benefits

Protection and income benefits provide employees with ways to continue their income if they cannot work, plan for retirement, and pay for healthcare. Not all of these benefits may be offered to employees, but certain components can be offered in different combinations to maximize employee protection while controlling costs for the employer. This type of benefit includes those discussed in the following paragraphs.

> **Protection and Income Benefits**
>
> - Income continuation plans
> - Retirement plans
> - Health protection plans

*Income Continuation Plans*

These plans protect an employee's income in case the employee is not able to work due to a disability, injury, death, or termination. Plans include:

- Short-term disability;
- Long-term disability;
- Nonoccupational disability;
- Supplemental disability insurance;
- Accidental death and dismemberment insurance;
- Life insurance;
- Group universal life insurance;
- Severance pay; and
- Employment contracts.

*Retirements Plans*

Retirement plans provide instruments for workers to save money for their retirement. These plans are designed to help employees accumulate capital and meet financial goals. The defined contribution plans are discussed in detail later in this chapter. These include:

- Defined benefit plans (i.e., pensions); and
- Defined contribution plans:
    - Individual retirement accounts (SIMPLE IRAs);
    - 401(k) plans;
    - 403(b) plans for nonprofit organizations only;
    - Profit-sharing plans; and
    - Equity-based compensation plans.

*Health Protection Plans*

Health protection plans are the most costly kind of benefit, with frequent increases in cost. Many employers ask the employee to contribute to a portion of the costs of some of these benefits such as medical insurance. These types of plans include:

- Major medical insurance or basic medical, hospital, and surgical insurance;
- Health maintenance organizations (HMOs);
- Retiree medical insurance;
- Health savings accounts (HSAs);
- Flexible spending accounts (FSAs);
- Comprehensive physical exams;
- Critical illness plans;
- Dental plans;
- Vision care plans; and
- Hearing aid insurance.

**Service Benefits**

These benefits are paid by the organization and come in two categories: time off work and income equivalent payments and incurred expense reimbursements.

*Time Off Work*

Offering at least some of these benefits is a standard employee benefit. The paid time off benefits are discussed in detail later in this chapter. These benefits may include:

- Holiday;
- Vacation;
- Personal time;
- Sick time;
- Sabbaticals;
- Paid bereavement leave;
- Paid military leave;

**Service Benefits**

- Time off work
- Income equivalent payments and incurred expense reimbursements

- Court leave; and
- Inclement weather leaves.

*Income Equivalent Payments and Incurred Expense Reimbursements*
Income equivalent payments and incurred expense reimbursements focus on services that improve the quality of life. These include:

- Employee assistance and counseling;
- Financial planning;
- Preretirement planning;
- Long-term care;
- Tuition reimbursement assistance;
- Education subsidies;
- Adoption assistance;
- Wellness programs;
- Child care; and
- Elder care.

See Policy 5.01 at the end of this chapter for a sample employee benefits policy.

## Defined Contribution Plans

Defined contribution plans are individual retirement plans in which employers can contribute a set amount or percentage of money each year for an employee. Depending on the type of defined contribution plan, the employee can also contribute a dollar amount or percentage of his or her pay, deducted pretax, each paycheck. The employee also earns a return (or loss) on his or her investments into these types of accounts. Most of these plans have restrictions on them of not only how much employers can contribute each year but also when and how the employee can access the funds without penalty.

Defined contribution plans are regulated by the ERISA and by various Internal Revenue Service (IRS) tax codes. The ERISA protects these retirement plans from mismanagement and misuse of assets. The act also sets requirements and restrictions on defined contribution plans such as a minimum standard of participation, vesting, benefit accrual, and funding. The ERISA also ensures that the plan fiduciary acts solely in the best interests of the participants and beneficiaries. The IRS publishes each year the contribution limits for retirement plans. If you are considering such programs, use a benefits consultant, as well as your financial and legal advisors, to stay in compliance.

### Individual Retirement Accounts (IRAs)

Employers with fewer than 100 employees can offer a Savings Incentive Match Plan for Employees Individual Retirement Account, or SIMPLE IRA, helping employees to save for retirement. Employee contributions to SIMPLE IRAs are a pretax salary reduction; however, the deductions are subject to Social Security, Medicare, and unemployment taxes. SIMPLE IRAs do not require the employee to make regular contributions, but the employer must contribute a minimum amount each year based on a percentage of an employee's annual compensation. Work with your practice's benefits consultant and financial advisor for compliance issues.

### 401(k) and 403(b) Plans

401(k) and 403(b) plans are another retirement savings vehicle employers can offer their employees. Both of these retirement plans are considered tax-deferred, meaning employee contributions are deducted pretax from their paychecks but are then taxed when a withdrawal is made. Earnings (or losses) from investment activities are also tax-deferred. Organizations can offer both 401(k) and 403(b) plans as long as they qualify for the 403(b). Most organizations hire an administrator to oversee and manage their plans. Your medical practices benefits consultant and financial advisor can help find plan administrators and ensure compliance with the regulations and tax code.

401(k) plans allow employers to choose to contribute to an employee's account to up a certain amount. Many organizations require employees to have a predetermined number of years of service before the organization's matching is at the employees' disposal. This is called vesting. 401(k) plans also have strict rules about when an employee can begin to withdraw their money and have stiff penalties for early withdrawals. However, 401(k) plans do allow employees to take out a loan on their individual plan. In addition, the IRS sets limits on the amount of money an employee can contribute pre-tax each year and how much an employer can match yearly.

403(b) plans are only for the employees of tax-exempt nonprofit organizations. As with the 401(k), it was named after Section 403(b) of the Internal Revenue Code. Sometimes these plans are also referred to a tax-sheltered annuity; however, they are no longer restricted to only annuities as they once were. These plans operate very similarly to the 401(k) plans with limits to the amount of annual contributions, early withdrawal penalties, and loans taken on the account.

### Profit-Sharing Plans

Profit-sharing plans give employees a share in an organization's profits and build an invaluable sense of ownership. Employees typically receive a percentage of profit. Employees are not usually allowed to contribute to this type of benefit. This includes any procedures by which employers pay, or make available to employees, special current or deferred sums based on the organization's profits. Profits can be distributed to employees by:

1. Cash or current payment plans that distribute a predetermined amount through cash, stock, or both quickly after earning the profit;
2. Deferred retirement plans that place the funds in a retirement account for future distributions; or
3. A combination of both.

### Equity-Based Plans

Many physician-owned practices do not utilize equity-based plans since the issuing of equity brings about potentially uncomfortable situations. The medical practice's owners must be willing to give away some of their control and ownership to employees, including sharing sensitive information such as detailed financial matters. However, offering equity can be a good way to attract and retain top talent. This benefit gives employees a greater financial and psychological stake in the success of your practice as well as linking employees' long-term interests to your practice's financial future. Before offering such a benefit, consider how you will share information so employee owners are knowledgeable about the company, its performance, their working environment, and how they will participate in stock ownership.

## Time Off Work and Leave of Absence Benefits

According to the Employee Benefit Research Institute, time off work or leave is one the most common benefits offered by employers and is available to the vast majority of full-time employees. Time off from work improves the employee's physical and mental well-being and benefits employers with increased productivity and morale. Many employees expect time off and/or leave benefits. Paid time off (PTO) includes holidays, sick leave, and earned vacation and personal days. A leave of absence is any authorized absence from regularly scheduled work hours. Organizations typically use either a traditional PTO system or a PTO plan to manage and track employees' time off.

### PTO Bank System

PTO bank systems or plans are very popular for organizations in the healthcare industry. A PTO plan allows employees to accrue paid time off in a "bank" and use the days as they want. PTO plans do not differentiate among vacation, personal, and sick days as traditional PTO systems do; rather, employees are given a set amount of time (e.g., 20+ days) they can use throughout the year. Most organizations that utilize PTO plans also have additional programs for jury duty and bereavement. PTO plans give employees a great deal of flexibility, and they can use their time off as they see fit. A potential downside of a PTO plan is that an employee may begin to view all of his or her allotted days off as vacation and, therefore, tend not to take a day off if he or she is sick.

Some organizations allow their employees to trade unused days for cash at the end of the year or roll them over to the next year. In addition, many organizations also give cash for unused days off at termination or retirement, based on the employee's years of service. Limits can be set for the number of hours or days that can be cashed-in or rolled-over by employees. The reason for this limit is that this time becomes an accrued expense for the medical practice, which can be a heavy burden on its financial statements. See Policy 5.02 for a sample PTO policy.

### Traditional Time Off Work System

Some medical practices prefer to offer separate time off designated as vacation, holiday, and sick days, described in the following paragraphs.

*Vacation*

Vacation days are usually earned and accrued from the date of hire, but occasionally require a waiting period of three to six months before an employee can use this benefit. Vacations are considered a physical and mental health benefit to help rejuvenate energy and enthusiasm, resulting in improved productivity and morale. Vacation days are a standard part of a compensation package and can be used effectively as a competitive factor. Most employees today will demand at least some vacation days. Sometimes organizations offer more vacation days based on seniority and longevity. Typically, employees are given 10 vacation days (two weeks) per year to start. However, this benefit may increase to three or four weeks as the length of service increases.

When developing a vacation policy, consider the following:
- Which system (PTO bank or traditional) will be the most cost-effective for your practice;
- How much vacation time will be given to employees;

- How to give these benefits in the most equitable way;
- Which employees will be eligible for the benefit (e.g., after a grace period, part-time employees on a pro-rated basis);
- Times of the year when vacation cannot be taken;
- The number of employees who can vacation at the same time with undue absenteeism; and
- When and how employees can request and receive approval for taking vacation (e.g., at least two weeks prior).

Policy 5.03 at the end of the chapter is a sample vacation leave policy.

*Holidays*

Holiday time off is perhaps the most expected benefit by employees unless they are involved in an industry having a 24/7 schedule. Although hospitals, nursing homes, and some other healthcare organizations operate in such an environment, few medical practices do unless they offer urgent-care or emergency services. Patients and employees expect medical practices to be closed on at least six holidays: New Year's Day, Memorial Day, Independence Day, Labor Day, Thanksgiving, and Christmas. Should the holiday fall on a Saturday or Sunday, organizations usually observe it on the preceding Friday or the following Monday, respectively.

Most medical practices offer the aforementioned six holidays and, depending on your practice, may offer others such as the day after Thanksgiving or Christmas Eve. For example, a pediatric practice is less likely to offer additional holidays because of the nature of pediatric illness, whereas a dermatology practice may have more flexibility in scheduling patients.

Many organizations offer floating holidays or an additional one to three days per year for employees to use at their own discretion. Those organizations that do offer floating holidays as a benefit must have clear policies outlining that unused floating holidays do not roll over to the following year, must be approved by the supervisor, and are accrued throughout the year. Floating holidays are considered additional vacation days, and employees should be compensated in cash for unused days at the end of the year, at termination, or at retirement.

Medical practices that require employees to work on holidays usually give employees alternative time off with pay at the discretion of the employee and with approval of management. On the other hand, employees may receive premium pay for working a holiday. Some organizations offer more personalized forms of holiday time off, such as giving employees time off on their birthdays.

Under the Civil Rights Act, employers are required to make reasonable accommodation to an employee's religious observance or practice as long as that accommodation does not cause undue hardship on the business. You can deny requests for time off for a religious reason and suggest the employee take a vacation or personal day for these purposes. Or you can ask the employee to use a floating holiday if your medical practice offers such a benefit to employees. Your medical practice's policy on holidays should address these requests for observance of religious holidays.

When developing a holiday policy, consider the following:
- Which holidays your practice will observe;
- Which day a holiday will be observed if it falls over a weekend;
- How your practice will handle absences before or after a holiday;
- Which employees will be eligible for holiday pay for full-time and part-time employees; and
- What the rate of pay will be for working on a holiday.

Policy 5.04 at the end of the chapter is a sample holiday policy.

*Sick Leave*

Sick days provide income for employees during time of illness or injury. Typically, organizations provide 6 to 12 sick days per year, and it is usually accrued at a specific rate. Sometimes the number of sick days is tied to the length of service. There is usually a limit to the number of sick days that can be accumulated. For an extended illness, short-term disability and accident disability insurance apply. For a longer-term illness, long-term insurance and Social Security apply. Family and medical leave under the Family and Medical Leave Act (FMLA) may also come into play for employees needing extensive time off, as discussed later.

If your medical practice established a set number of sick days, some employees may feel entitled to use all of them, regardless of whether they are sick, resulting in sick leave abuse and absenteeism. Oftentimes, employees can take up to three sick days with no questions asked; however, many organizations require medical evidence such as a letter from a physician. Some organizations allow employees to roll over unused sick days to the next year.

When a person is ill, taking a sick day and staying home benefits the entire practice as well as the individual. Too often, individuals come to work when they are ill and spread germs to others. They should be encouraged to stay home and use their sick days when they are ill.

When developing a sick leave policy, consider the following:
- Which employees will be eligible for sick days;
- How many sick days will be allocated to employees;
- The procedure for reporting in sick and investigating sick leave abuse;
- Whether your practice will allow using sick days to care for family members; and
- How unused sick days will be handled at the end of the year, upon termination, and at retirement.

Policy 5.05 at the end of the chapter is a sample sick leave policy.

*Personal Leave*

Personal leave allows employees to be absent for personal business, educational pursuits, civic functions, extended vacations, emergencies, and other personal reasons. Usually, all full-time employees are eligible for such a personal leave, which is designated as such only when an extended leave does not qualify for an FMLA leave of absence or a military leave.

Some practices may grant employees a set number of personal days employees can use each year. In addition, some practices may permit long absences. Others may require employees to resign and reapply for any open position after an extended period off with no guarantee that the employee can return to the same job. In the past, such leaves were often granted at the discretion of the supervisors, which caused inconsistency and could generate charges of favoritism or discrimination.

A standard policy based on your practice's staffing needs, work load, and the employee's performance protects against such claims. Some organizations make the leave available to anyone who has completed the initial orientation period; others deny such leaves until the person has served at least one year. The person may be required to use earned leave before being allowed to take unpaid time off.

When developing a personal leave policy, consider the following:
- Your practice's staffing situation and work load;
- The employee's performance record;
- The process for requesting a leave, including an explanation of the reason for the leave;
- The minimum amount of service time that will be required to be eligible for personal leave;
- How many days will be given or allowed;
- The review process;
- Who will be in charge of approving an extended leave (e.g., immediate supervisor, department manager, designated human resources (HR) professional, or other senior manager); and
- Whether any part of the leave will be paid.

Policy 5.06 at the end of the chapter is a sample personal leave policy.

*Inclement Weather Leave*
Inclement weather conditions time off occurs when severe weather or natural disasters prevent employees from coming to work. Depending on the type of medical practice, such conditions may merely disrupt staff and patient care for a brief time or may trigger the emergency management triaging plans.

Natural disasters, such as hurricanes, tornadoes, earthquakes, blizzards, and floods, do happen, and the designated HR professional should be very knowledgeable of how to handle practice operations in a disaster. In addition, the designated HR professional should serve on your practice's emergency management team, which is discussed further in chapter 9.

Planning for the occasional heavy snow or rain can guide your weather policy. Typically, some departments (e.g., nonessential staff) would not be required to report to work in such situations, whereas essential staff to the operations of your practice would have to report. To ensure that critical operations are being performed, a solid backup plan should be in place in case certain staff members cannot make it to your practice. In some states, for example, it is not unusual to have an occasional blizzard that blocks streets, making driving impossible.

Essential staff members who are required to report in such instances are usually paid extra to ensure they arrive at work during weather emergencies. If, however, they are unable to make it, be careful how they are disciplined. Always remember that staff and patient safety is paramount. In nonemergency situations, some employees will choose to use their vacation or PTO days, or they may be allowed to make up missing time.

When developing an inclement weather policy, consider the following:

- Select who will make the decision when to put the inclement weather policy into effect;
- Determine how your practice closing will be announced to employees (e.g., e-mail blasts to all employees, Website announcement, a recorded message on a designated phone line, through news stations). Usually the message will state that only essential personnel must report;
- Decide whether administrative employees can work from home if a storm is predicted;
- Determine how the building or offices will be unlocked to allow essential personnel in and develop a plan for when they cannot get into the office;
- Determine who will be in charge if only essential personnel report; and
- Decide whether to allow employees to make up time if they miss work in a non-emergency situation.

See Policy 5.07 for a sample inclement weather policy.

*Sabbaticals*

Some organizations use a traditional academic method of offering sabbaticals. This type of leave may be unpaid, but other benefits do continue. Sabbaticals are typically when employees want to take a career break.

## Leaves of Absence

*Leave of absence* is defined as time away from work while maintaining the status of employee. Leaves of absence are usually of a predetermined length of time or end after a certain event occurs. They can also be either paid or unpaid leaves. In addition, medical practices with a certain number of employees are required by law to allow employees to take particular types of leave.

*Family and Medical Leave Act*

The FMLA states the covered employers must grant an eligible employee as many as 12 workweeks of unpaid leave during any 12-month period for one or more of the following reasons:

- Birth and care of a newborn child of the employee;
- Placement of a child with the employee for adoption or foster care;
- Care of an immediate family member (spouse, child, or parent) with a serious health condition;
- Serious health condition of the employee preventing them from working as defined as an illness, injury, impairment, or a physical or mental condition that involves an inpatient medical care facility or continuing treatment by a healthcare provider.

A covered employer is one with at least 50 employees who work within 75 miles of each other. Eligible employees must have been employed for at least one year and have completed at least 1,250 hours of service in the 12 months preceding the requested leave.

An FMLA leave is not paid; however, an employer may require an employee to use accrued sick days, vacation days, personal days, or family leave for some or all of a leave for birth, adoption, or foster care placement. For anticipated leaves, such as the addition of a child, the employee may be required to request advanced notice in writing. For emergency situations, such as the sudden illness of a family member, verbal notice should be made within two days. For leaves of serious health conditions, the employee may choose or the employer may require the employee to use accrued paid sick or medical leave.

Family leave, as recognized by the act, is when the employee's health is not involved. Family leave is identified as time off for parenting and for healthcare of a minor or disabled child, spouse, or parent. For a serious health condition leave, an employee may have an intermittent leave or a reduced work schedule leave when determined medically necessary by a healthcare provider. The employer may, in this case, transfer the employee to an alternate position, but the pay and benefits must be equivalent.

Employees do not use FMLA leaves all that frequently. When such leaves do occur, your medical practice should request the employee on leave to report monthly regarding their intention to return or to begin a full schedule. Upon return, the employee must be restored to the same or equivalent position. In any case, failure to return to work at the end of the leave results in termination unless additional leave would be a reasonable accommodation under the Americans with Disabilities Act. Supervisors will probably need help from the HR department to deal with the details of an FMLA leave. For example, supervisors are often confused by intermittent leave, which takes considerable management. Policy 5.08 at the end of the chapter is a sample policy on FMLA leave.

*Military Leave*
Federal laws prohibit employers from forcing employees to use personal vacation leave for mandatory military duties, including training in the National Guard or reserves and call for active duty. A military leave policy helps employees fulfill their military obligations and gives employers an opportunity to demonstrate their patriotism.

If an employee enlists, is drafted, or is called to active duty, the statute states that employees may spend as many as five years in active duty, and if, after discharge, they apply for their previous position within 90 days, the employer is required to reinstate the employee at a comparable job level with some exceptions. When developing a policy on military leave, consider the following:
- How the employee will be paid during military training leave;
- How many days will be allowed (typically 15 per year) for training and for travel time (typically 4 days); and
- How vacation and sick leave benefits will be handled during military leave.

Policy 5.09 is a sample military leave policy.

*Disability Leave*

Disability leave, either short-term or long-term, occurs when employees cannot work because of an accident or health-related problems. Short-term disability insurance plans typically provide payment (50 to 80 percent of base pay) for as many as 25 weeks while the insured employee is absent from work. During the waiting period for the payment to begin, the employee will usually use sick days. Disability situations can trigger FMLA consideration, as noted previously. Long-term disability insurance provides incapacitated employees with long-term security when they have extra medical expenses and are unable to produce income. Most of the plans are funded in conjunction with an organization's pension plan or through self-insurance funding. Some medical practices offer this as a paid benefit. Others offer it as a voluntary benefit where the employee funds 100 percent of the cost as a deduction from their paychecks. Policy 5.10 is a sample policy on disability leave.

*Bereavement Leave*

Bereavement leave is not required by law but is typically granted to full- and part-time employees in the event of an immediate family member's death. *Immediate family member* is typically defined as the employee's spouse, parents, children, siblings, grandparents, grandchildren, stepchildren, father-in-law, mother-in-law, sister-in-law, brother-in-law, son-in-law, or daughter-in-law. However, some organizations have begun to include domestic partners in the definition. The leave is usually for a maximum of three consecutive working days. Additional leave may be arranged by using available PTO. Bereavement leave for other than immediate family typically must be taken by using PTO and must be approved by the immediate supervisor. Some organizations may allow an employee to take a one-day bereavement leave for a close nonfamily member's death. Proof of death may be requested. See Policy 5.11 for a sample bereavement leave policy.

*Court Leave*

Court leaves are granted when employees are summoned to act as jurors or court witnesses. Similar to military leave, such service is considered a civic duty and should not be a financial hardship for employees. Most employers pay for such time off, either for jury duty or for court testimony related to their professional job responsibilities. For other matters, employees are required to take vacation or personal leave. If court duty lasts an extended period, usually an unpaid leave is arranged.

Three basic methods for providing compensation for authorized court leave are:

1. Employees are required to submit documentation of any pay received;
2. Employees are reimbursed the difference between court compensation and their regular pay; and
3. Employees are paid their regular pay and are allowed to keep the small amount paid by the court.

Method #3 is the most popular method used by most employers. See Policy 5.12 for a sample court leave policy.

*Requesting Leave*

Establishing a policy on leaves of absence ensures uniform treatment and gives managers a consistent way to evaluate such requests. In terms of decision making, your practice may choose to allow a supervisor to make this decision in conjunction with the department manager, or the HR director may decide. It is always important to have HR's input to ensure a company-wide perspective.

Employees should complete a leave request form in advance of vacation or personal leave, whether it is from the PTO bank, their vacation or personal days, or floating holidays. Because sick days cannot usually be predicted, sick leave should be reported when the employee returns to work. Military leave, court leave, and disability leave are usually granted to the employee when properly documented, following the same procedure.

When developing a policy on requesting leave, consider the following:
- Who will establish the written policies and procedures;
- How the policies and procedures will be communicated to employees; and
- How supervisors will be trained on implementing the guidelines so the decisions on granting leave are handled consistently and equitably.

Policy 5.13 at the end of the chapter is a sample leave request policy. In addition, if your medical practice does not use a PTO plan, your practice should have a form for employees to use when requesting leave. The form can either be downloadable from the intranet and e-mailed to the decision maker or some large practices may have an online form for employees to complete and submit via the intranet. A sample Employee Leave Request Form (Form 5.1) is provided at the end of this chapter.

## The Cost of Benefits

Benefits usually represent a fairly high percentage of total payroll costs. Benefit costs, as a percentage of total compensation, have increased slightly since 2004 as employers look for ways to reduce costs. As of March 2013, benefits accounted for 30.9 percent of total compensation as compared to about 28 percent in 2004.* In addition, retirement benefits and health insurance accounted for 3.6 percent and 7.8 percent of total compensation in 2013, respectively. Because of the increasing cost of providing health insurance to employees, the cost of benefits is expected to continue to increase over the next several years. However, as previously discussed, employers are shifting a larger portion of the cost of benefits to the employees, thereby controlling the employers' cost burden.

When your medical practice considers which benefits to offer, keep these costs firmly in mind. Determine how much your practice is willing to and able to spend. Using a benefits consultant can help you determine the optimal annual cost of benefits for your practice. Also, compare your practice's benefits to total compensation ratio and which benefits are offered to other medical practices in your area to determine whether your practice is competitive. Employers with less competitive benefits tend to lose employees to employers with more competitive benefits offerings.

## Communicating Benefits

Keep your practice's employees updated on the most current information regarding benefits. Use regular communication channels such as employee newsletters, meetings, and internal communications to review and discuss benefits. Communications should

---

\*  Employer Costs for Employee Compensation Historical Listing, March 2013, Bureau of Labor Statistics National Compensation Survey, July 17, 2013.

cover what benefits are offered by your practice, how they compare with similar group practices, what each benefit would cost the employee, and how they will benefit the employee and their family. You can also provide a year-end statement of the value of benefits.

Using a benefits consultant and benefits service providers can be extremely helpful to both the medical practice and its employees. They can assist in developing communications to help employees stay better informed, including secure Websites to help employees track and monitor their benefits, insurance claims, FSA and HSA balances, and retirement accounts.

It is also useful to share information about industry, national, and local benefit trends related to costs and offerings. Keep your employees up to date on healthcare costs and how your practice works carefully each year to get the best possible arrangements with insurance providers. Most importantly, impart to your employees a sense of shared responsibility for the cost of benefits. Specifically explain cost-sharing and deductibles at the time of benefits enrollment and provide a general statement in your employee handbook on how your practice constantly evaluates their benefits package and its costs to ensure they do not jeopardize the financial health of the organization.

## The Changing Employee Benefits Landscape

As the United States struggles to emerge from the economic downturn, many new trends in employee benefits are also surfacing. Many executive teams and especially the designated HR professional have been challenged to understand the changing landscape since the 2010 healthcare reform (the PPACA and the Health Care and Education Reconciliation Act). Many are unsure of exactly how the reform will affect health insurance premiums, what types of health insurance will be offered, and what health insurance will cost as different pieces of the legislation are instituted. Your legal counsel and benefits consultant will be valuable resources to help you understand the potential changes to requirements, coverage, and costs.

As previously mentioned, many organizations are passing on increasing benefits costs to their employees, which has helped employers keep benefits costs somewhat stable as the costs continue to rise. Increasing health insurance premiums, in particular, are causing employers to select plans with higher deductibles and/or reduced health benefits (such as coverage levels and family care), to offer HSAs or FSAs, and/or to have employees contribute more for coverage. Since 2010, employees are contributing 17 percent more for singles and 27 percent more for families on health insurance. This cost-shifting trend is partially due to the healthcare reform acts authorizing dependents up to the age of 26 to be covered under their parents' plan.

Employers are beginning to offer more voluntary benefits to their employees as a way to control costs. Voluntary benefits are those that the employee pays 100 percent of the cost. This approach offers employees a wide variety of benefits from which to choose while keeping costs down. Many employers are migrating previously employer-paid benefits to voluntary benefits. In addition, many employers look at wellness programs as a way to reduce the costs of healthcare programs. However, wellness programs are a long-term strategy to decreasing healthcare costs and oftentimes do not have a proven return on investment.

## Summary

Employee benefits consultants and/or services are vital in helping put together a balanced benefits package to fit the needs of your employees. They can help determine the types of benefits to offer your employees while keeping costs in consideration. Many employee benefits services are full service where they offer consulting advice, have insurance plans and voluntary benefits from which you can select, and help ensure compliance with employee benefits laws and regulations.

Benefits are a critical decision factor when an employee is considering a job offer. A competitive benefits package helps drive performance and attracts and retains top talent. A poorly organized or weak benefits program can inhibit the success of the medical practice.

## Sample Policies

**Policy 5.01**     ### Employee Benefits

This policy is an example of an employee benefits policy. *The particular laws of each state may differ, and this suggested policy should not be implemented without considering applicable state law.*

---

**POLICY 5.01**        **EMPLOYEE BENEFITS**

Purpose: To establish and maintain an employee benefits program.

Applies to: All *[Practice]* employees.

Policy: The policy of *[Practice]* is to provide its employees with adequate economic and personal security as part of their employment. *[Practice]* benefits have been designed to meet this goal in an equitable manner consistent with *[Practice]* objectives. *[Practice]* protects the interests of benefits plan participants and beneficiaries by making full disclosure of the employee benefits plan and its administration.

The designated human resources (HR) professional or associated administrator, in conjunction with senior management and the director of finance, is responsible for establishing the benefits package, monitoring it, and periodically reviewing and updating benefits. Employee preferences are usually surveyed biannually to ensure that current interests are considered. As appropriate, a benefits fair, sponsored by benefits vendors or service providers prior to the annual sign-up date, may be held as a way to inform employees about the various components of the package.

Procedures:
1. The designated HR professional is responsible for providing employees with summary descriptions of their benefits plan, including eligibility, on a regular basis and always prior to the annual sign-up period.

2. In the event a benefit is added or withdrawn from the plan, employees are adequately notified.

3. Employees have the privilege of not participating in any part of the benefits plans. This decision is communicated to the HR department and documented.

4. Employees are allowed to change their benefit selections annually, at a time specified by *[Practice]*, unless there is a life status change event such as marriage, divorce, and birth or adoption of a child.

5. Management, upon written request of any participant or beneficiary, furnishes complete copies of the latest updated summary of the group's benefits plan.

6. Participants or beneficiaries whose claim for benefits under the employee benefits plan has been denied shall be furnished with a written notice containing the reason for denial and appropriate information as to the steps to be taken if he or she wishes to submit a claim for review. If such a review is requested, the designated HR professional reviews the denial and furnishes his or her decision on the claim.

7. Employees eligible for coverage under *[Practice's]* health benefits plan have the option of membership in a qualified health maintenance organization.

Approved by: Practice Administrator

Effective date: 1/1/20__

## Policy 5.02        **Paid Time Off**

This policy is an example of a paid time off policy.

---

**POLICY 5.02                    PAID TIME OFF**

Purpose: To establish and maintain paid time off for employees.

Applies to: All *[Practice]* employees.

Policy: *[Practice]* provides paid time off (PTO) to compensate for vacations, short-term illnesses, and personal time off.

Procedures:

1. Paid time off may be used for vacations, short-term illnesses, or personal needs. Employees cannot borrow or lend PTO, but they can donate PTO using an approved process.

2. Employees must request PTO at least two weeks in advance by requesting such leave in writing. Before approving PTO requests, supervisors consider *[Practice]* workload needs and staffing.

3. PTO is accumulated by full- and part-time employees from the day they are hired. Employees may not use PTO until they complete the 90-day provisionary period.

4. Full-time employees may accrue 12 hours of PTO every month during their first year; then 16 hours monthly through the fifth year; 20 hours monthly through the tenth year; and 24 hours monthly every year starting with the 11th year of service.

5. Earned, unused PTO is paid when an employee leaves the company. Employees may accumulate a maximum of 240 hours.

Approved by: Practice Administrator

Effective date: 1/1/20__

**Policy 5.03**     <u>Vacation Leave</u>

This policy is an example of a vacation leave policy. The amount of vacation leave can be based on job classification, providing a different schedule for exempt and nonexempt employees. *This is a suggested policy for educational and illustrative purposes only. The particular laws of each state may differ, and this suggested policy should not be implemented without considering applicable state law.*

---

POLICY 5.03                **VACATION LEAVE**

<u>Purpose:</u> To establish and maintain a vacation leave program for employees.

<u>Applies to:</u> All *[Practice]* employees.

<u>Policy:</u> The policy of *[Practice]* is to grant annual vacation leave with pay to eligible employees in accordance with established guidelines.

<u>Procedures:</u>

1.  Full- and regular part-time employees are eligible for vacation leave during the calendar year after the first six months of employment. Regular part-time employees are entitled to vacation on a prorated basis. Temporary and provisional employees are not eligible to earn vacation leave benefits.

2.  The designated human resources (HR) professional, in conjunction with the Administrator or designee, determine how many vacation days employees receive, based on length of service. Vacation leave benefits are reviewed and modified periodically.

3.  Management makes every effort to grant vacation leave to employees based on their requests. However, the department manager must provide for adequate staffing levels, and employees should cooperate with their department manager when scheduling vacation leave. The department manager is responsible for approving vacation leave requests.

4.  If a conflict occurs among employees when scheduling vacation leave within a department, priority is established on the basis of seniority, with the most senior employee getting first choice in scheduling vacation leave.

5.  The following vacation leave guidelines, based on the number of years of continuous, full-time employment, are used in granting vacation leave.

| Years of Service | Vacation Days |
|---|---|
| 1–5 years | 10 |
| 6–10 years | 15 |
| 11–15 years | 18 |
| 16–20 years | 20 |
| 21 years or more | 22 |

6.  Vacation is earned annually at the end of the employee's first year of employment. Therefore, no vacation is paid until the employee has completed one year of service.

7. Vacation pay for full- and regular part-time employees consists of the employee's regular rate of pay for the vacation period.

8. Employees may take and be paid for their vacation as it accrues, with prior approval from the department manager.

9. Vacation days are not cumulative and normally must be taken in the year earned. Any exception to this provision must have written approval of the Practice Administrator.

10. Employees are not paid for unused vacation remaining at the end of each vacation year. However, if the employee is required by *[Practice]* to cancel vacation plans and the vacation cannot be rescheduled before the end of the year, the employee is permitted to reschedule the vacation within the next 90 days.

11. If a holiday falls during the vacation period, an additional day is granted that may be taken during the scheduled vacation period or at another time during the anniversary year.

12. The anniversary date of an employee is used in determining the eligibility date for vacations. Anniversary dates of employment are adjusted for any leaves without pay totaling more than 30 consecutive days.

13. Vacations should not be scheduled during peak work periods.

14. Pay for vacation is issued at the regular pay period. If an employee has an urgent reason for requesting his or her regular paycheck before leaving on vacation, the department manager must make such a request in writing to the designated HR professional, who determines whether an exception can be made.

15. Upon separation from employment with *[Practice]*, an employee receives vacation pay for any unused vacation accrued during the year in which termination occurs.

16. Sick leave is usually not paid during vacation leave. However, if a major illness occurs during vacation, the employee may present a physician's certificate for any illness more than three days in duration. The department manager and the HR director consider each request and make a final decision on whether to grant sick leave.

17. Vacation leave requests must be made in writing, using the leave request form, as far in advance as possible, with at least one month's advance notice desired. Department managers make final approvals of regular vacation requests.

18. An employee who retires is entitled to take full vacation during the vacation year in which retirement occurs.

19. Vacation leave is not granted to extend an employee's period of employment beyond the last day worked.

20. When a change in the employee's status occurs, the following policies apply:

    - The employee retains vacation leave accrued in full- or part-time status. For example, a full-time employee transferring to part-time status does not lose any vacation benefits already acquired as a full-time employee. A part-time employee transferring to full-time status retains any benefits accrued as a part-time employee.

    - A full- or part-time employee transferring to temporary status has accrued vacation leave benefits frozen for the period of temporary status. A temporary-status employee may not use any vacation leave benefits previously accrued while on temporary status but, upon return to permanent status, is entitled to previously accrued vacation leave benefits.

Approved by: Practice Administrator

Effective date: 1/1/20___

**Policy 5.04**      **Holidays**

This is an example of a holiday policy. *This is a suggested policy for educational and illustrative purposes only. The particular laws of each state may differ, and this suggested policy should not be implemented without considering applicable state law.*

---

POLICY 5.04                              HOLIDAYS

Purpose: To establish and maintain the holiday schedule observed by *[Practice]*.

Applies to: All *[Practice]* employees.

Policy: It is the policy of *[Practice]* to observe certain holidays each year as established by the group's management. Each holiday observed by *[Practice]* is a day off with pay for most employees. The following holidays are observed by *[Practice]* annually:

- New Year's Day;
- Memorial Day;
- Independence Day;
- Labor Day;
- Thanksgiving;
- Christmas; and
- Two to four floating holidays.

Procedures:

1. In December, the designated human resources (HR) professional posts any changes in the holiday policy for the following year.
2. Full-time employees receive their regular rate of pay for each holiday. Part-time employees receive holiday pay only for holidays on which they normally would be scheduled to work, and only for their regularly scheduled number of hours.
3. Temporary employees are not eligible to receive holiday pay.
4. To receive holiday pay, an eligible employee must be at work or on an authorized absence for the workdays immediately preceding and following the day on which the holiday is observed. If an employee submits a request for sick leave on these days, the employee must render a physician's statement supporting this request. Management reserves the right to approve or disapprove the sick leave request.
5. A holiday that occurs on a Saturday is observed on the preceding Friday. A holiday that occurs on a Sunday is observed on the following Monday.
6. If the holiday occurs during an employee's vacation period, an additional day of vacation is granted at a time mutually convenient to the employee and management.
7. *[Practice]* recognizes that some employees may wish to observe certain days not included in the group's holiday schedule, such as religious holidays. In these instances, an employee should request a floating holiday. Management makes every effort to accommodate this request if such absence does not result in an undue hardship on *[Practice]*.

Approved by: Practice Administrator

Effective date: 1/1/20__

**Policy 5.05**   <u>Sick Leave</u>

This is an example of a sick leave policy.

**POLICY 5.05**          **SICK LEAVE**

<u>Purpose:</u> To establish and maintain a sick leave program.

<u>Applies to:</u> All *[Practice]* employees.

<u>Policy:</u> The policy of *[Practice]* is to compensate eligible employees during absences for illness or injury up to an established limit. In accordance with the Family and Medical Leave Act (FMLA), employees who have been employed for at least one year and have completed at least 1,250 hours of service in the prior 12 months are eligible for as many as 12 weeks of unpaid leave because of a serious health condition that makes it impossible to perform their job functions.

<u>Procedures:</u>

1. Full-time and regular part-time employees are entitled to sick leave. Regular part-time employees are entitled to sick leave on a prorated basis. Temporary employees are not eligible for sick leave.

2. During the first three months of employment, new employees are not eligible to earn sick leave benefits. However, time off without pay is allowed in the event of illness or injury.

3. Employees are eligible to use sick leave only when the employee is incapacitated by sickness or injury; for disabilities caused or contributed to by pregnancy, miscarriage, abortion, childbirth, and recovery therefrom; for medical, dental, or optical examination or treatment, including examinations for military service or disability payments; or for necessary care and attendance during sickness.

4. Employees earn eight hours of sick leave per month of continuous service. Regular part-time employees accrue a proportionate amount.

5. Part-time employees receive sick leave credit in accordance with the following schedule, based on one month of continuous service:

| Number of Hours | Sick Leave Credit | Sick Leave Days |
|:---:|:---:|:---:|
| Less than 40 | 0 | 0 |
| 40–59 | ½ | 4 |
| 60–70 | ¾ | 6 |

6. Sick leave may be accumulated to a limit of 90 working days. On each anniversary date, hours accrued in excess of 90 days can be converted to vacation leave on the basis of eight hours (one day) of vacation for each 16 hours (two days) of sick leave, to as many as six additional days of vacation leave within the calendar year following the eligibility date for conversion. Converted vacation time must be taken by the pay period before the employee's next anniversary date.

7. To encourage good attendance, the following bonus leave program has been developed:

   - Full-time employees are granted one additional day of vacation for each six-month period of perfect attendance. *Perfect attendance* is defined as having no absences from work due to illness or injury, or unauthorized absences. This means using no sick leave for any reason during a six-month period. The six continuous months can begin at any time. Part-time employees working more than 20 hours per week may receive additional vacation benefits on a prorated basis for each six continuous months of perfect attendance.

   - Full-time employees may trade unused sick leave in excess of 30 days for a bonus award according to a specific schedule.

8. To receive sick leave, employees must adhere to the regulations about notifying their department. Unless otherwise established by the department manager, employees who are ill or unable to report to work must call their supervisor before their scheduled starting time so that staff coverage can be arranged.

9. If requested by a supervisor, an employee may be required to furnish a physician's statement that supports the sick leave request.

10. Excessive use of sick leave may be cause for disciplinary action, which may include dismissal. *Excessive use of sick leave* is defined as using more than six days of sick leave during a 12-month period, except for extenuating circumstances or major illness.

11. For absences because of illness in excess of five consecutive working days, a request for sick leave must be supported by a physician's statement (including diagnosis and prognosis satisfactory to management) that states:

    - The employee was physically unable to perform his or her duties during this period; and

    - He or she is physically able to return to work.

12. Any physician's statement may be reviewed by the administration, which could include an evaluation by a *[Practice]* physician. Management makes the final decision whether to approve any sick leave request.

13. When a leave of absence for illness is requested and approved, sick leave and vacation leave must be approved before an employee may be placed on unpaid leave of absence under the Family and Medical Leave Act.

14. When a change in the employee's status occurs, the following policies apply:

    - A full-time employee who has accumulated sick leave and transfers to part-time status retains sick leave accumulated. The employee accrues future sick leave hours based on a prorated schedule.

    - A full-time employee who has accumulated sick leave hours and transfers to temporary status has the accrued sick leave frozen during the tenure of the temporary status. Upon return to full- or regular part-time status, the accrued benefits are reinstated. Frozen sick leave hours may not be used or converted to vacation leave or pay.

15. Sick leave is normally not paid during vacation.

16. Payment is not made at the termination of employment for unused sick leave.

17. Sick leave is not granted in advance of accrual.

18. After six continuous months of service, vacation leave may be used for sick leave when sick leave has been exhausted and department manager approval is obtained.

Approved by: Practice Administrator

Effective date: 1/1/20__

## Policy 5.06    **Personal Leave of Absence**

This is an example of a personal leave of absence policy.

---

POLICY 5.06              **PERSONAL LEAVE OF ABSENCE**

Purpose: To establish and maintain a personal leave of absence program.

Applies to: All *[Practice]* employees.

Policy: The policy of *[Practice]* is to grant eligible employees unpaid personal leaves of absence when it is in the best interests of the employee and *[Practice]*.

Procedures:

1.  Unpaid personal leaves of absence may be granted to full- and regular part-time employees who have completed at least one continuous year of service.

2.  Management makes every effort to grant a leave of absence request when it is properly justified and in the best interests of the employee and *[Practice]*.

3.  A formal leave request form must be completed by the employee, which includes an explanation for the leave of absence. The leave request form is submitted to the department manager.

4.  The department manager forwards the leave of absence request to the designated HR professional for approval. The designated HR professional makes the final decision concerning the request.

5.  Management considers the staffing needs of *[Practice]* first and then reviews the work and employment record of the employee in determining whether to grant a leave of absence request.

6.  As a standard rule, requests for absence are granted for family and medical leaves governed by the Family and Medical Leave Act for a period of up to 12 weeks, and for military leave.

7.  Extensions of a personal leave of absence beyond 30 days are granted only in extenuating circumstances.

8.  Requests for a leave of absence or an extension of leave must be submitted to the department manager at least 30 days prior to the start of the leave, unless an emergency occurs.

9.  An employee who returns to work at the conclusion of a family or medical leave of absence is restored to his or her former position or to a comparable position at the same rate of pay.

10. If the employee fails to return to work at the conclusion of an approved personal leave of absence, the leave is cancelled and employment is terminated, unless additional leave would be a reasonable accommodation under the Americans with Disabilities Act. The effective date of termination is the last day worked.

11. Any *[Practice]* benefits that the employee previously received before the leave of absence began do not continue during the period of absence. Employees may make arrangements to pay for their own medical insurance premiums during an approved leave of absence.

Approved by: Practice Administrator

Effective date: 1/1/20__

**Policy 5.07**    <u>**Inclement Weather Conditions**</u>

This is an example of an inclement weather conditions policy.

---

**POLICY 5.07**          **INCLEMENT WEATHER CONDITIONS**

<u>Purpose:</u> To establish and maintain procedures during inclement weather conditions.

<u>Applies to:</u> All *[Practice]* employees.

<u>Policy:</u> It is the policy of *[Practice]* that in the event of emergency weather conditions such as heavy snowfall or a tornado, the Practice Administrator or designee can declare an official weather emergency. When on official weather emergency is declared, the following procedures are put into effect.

<u>Procedures:</u>
1. If the Practice Administrator or designee declares an early closing, covered employees are paid for their entire shift. Those employees required to remain are paid at the rate of time and one-half for hours worked after the early closing.

2. Regular employees who arrive within one hour of their regular time or at the beginning of a delayed starting time on an official weather emergency are paid from their regular starting time. Those covered employees arriving later than indicated are paid from the time of their arrival.

3. If the administrator or designee declares a full closing, regular employees do not report to work. In addition, they receive their regular pay for the day if they arrange to make up the time or to use leave time. Those designated as covered employees who must report to work are paid at the rate of time and one-half for hours worked during the emergency.

4. Should an employee not report to work, arrive late, or leave early during severe weather, he or she has the option of charging such time as vacation or personal time or not being paid for those hours.

5. If inclement weather or some other unforeseen circumstance causes *[Practice]* to close for a day, an announcement shall broadcast over local news stations.

<u>Approved by:</u> Practice Administrator

<u>Effective date:</u> 1/1/20__

## Policy 5.08    Family and Medical Leave Act

This is an example of a Family and Medical Leave Act policy.

---

POLICY 5.08          **FAMILY AND MEDICAL
LEAVE ACT**

Purpose: To ensure compliance with the Family and Medical Leave Act (FMLA).

Applies to: All *[Practice]* employees.

Policy: The policy of *[Practice]* is to comply with the FMLA and to follow its requirements related to leaves of absence, eligibility, scheduling and notice, mandatory leave, supplemental leave, benefits during leave, and return rights.

Procedures:

1.  An employee may request leave from work for the purposes of:
    *   A birth, adoption, or foster care placement of a child;
    *   Care for a spouse, child, or parent with a serious health condition; or
    *   A serious health condition that renders the employee unable to perform his or her employment duties.

2.  To be eligible for leave under the FMLA, an employee must have been employed by *[Practice]* for more than 12 consecutive months and must have worked at least 1,250 hours in the preceding 12 months.

3.  A leave of absence request must be completed for leaves, whether paid or unpaid. An employee intending to take leave is required to give advance notice in a reasonable and practical manner. In situations involving leave for a serious health condition, every reasonable effort to schedule medical treatment so that it does not unduly disrupt *[Practice]* operations should be made before a leave is considered.

4.  An employee requesting medical leave must provide medical certification that indicates a serious health condition exists and that provides other information as requested. A serious health condition means an illness, injury, impairment, or condition involving:
    *   Inpatient care in a hospital, nursing home, or hospice; or
    *   Outpatient care that requires continuing treatment and supervision by a healthcare provider.

5.  Eligible employees are entitled to the following mandatory leaves of absence under the law:
    *   An employee may take as many as 12 weeks of leave in a 12-month period for the birth of the employee's natural child or the placement of a child with the employee for adoption or foster care. Birth leave may be a combination of parental leave and pregnancy leave. Parental leave is time off work for employees who are physically able to return to work but choose to stay home and care for newborn children. Pregnancy leave is characterized by a physical disability because of childbirth or a related medical condition.
    *   An employee may take as many as 12 weeks of family leave in a 12-month period to care for his or her child, spouse, or parent with a serious health condition.

- An employee who has a serious health condition that renders the employee unable to perform his or her duties may take medical leave for as many as 12 weeks in a 12-month period.

6. An employee may choose or may be required to use sick leave or time accrued to them during a medical leave. None of the leaves under the FMLA are paid.

7. During the period of leave, participants in the group health insurance plan continue to receive coverage on the same basis as applied immediately before the leave began for a period of time determined by the nature of the leave situation. Any employment benefit that accrued before a family or medical leave began is held in reserve. Employees are informed if benefits cease and if and when anniversary day adjustments apply.

8. Employees who return to work in 12 weeks or less are returned to their same position or an equivalent one.

Approved by: Practice Administrator

Effective date: 1/1/20__

**Policy 5.09**        <u>**Military Leave**</u>

This is an example of a military leave policy.

---

POLICY **5.09**                    **MILITARY LEAVE**

<u>Purpose:</u> To establish and maintain guidelines for military leave.

<u>Applies to:</u> All *[Practice]* employees.

<u>Policy:</u> The policy of *[Practice]* is to grant military leave to eligible employees who are called to active military duty or are required to attend annual military training encampment with the United States government or any political subdivision thereof.

<u>Procedures:</u>

1.  Employees, except temporary employees, are eligible for military leave.
2.  One 15-calendar-day period of military training leave is granted annually.
3.  In the event the military training is optional, the employee is allowed vacation time for this purpose.
4.  If the amount of pay, subject to income tax provisions, received for military training is greater than the pay that would be earned by the employee, such leave is without pay. If the military pay, subject to income tax provisions, received by the employee is less than he or she would earn from *[Practice]*, *[Practice]* pays the employee the difference between the military pay and his or her regular pay.
5.  If an employee is inducted into active military service or the Armed Forces of the United States or is called from a Reserve or National Guard unit into active duty, or if emergency duty is declared by the proper authority of the state, then the employee is placed on military leave without pay.
6.  Military leave without pay is granted for the duration of active military service, not to exceed five years, plus 90 days from the date of discharge. Extensions are granted if an employee is required to serve a longer period of time involuntarily because of war or national emergency.
7.  Vacation and sick leave credits are not earned during military leave without pay.
8.  Employees must make application for return from military leave without pay within 90 days from the date of discharge from military service.
9.  A return from military leave without pay is conditional upon submitting a certificate of satisfactory completion of military service.
10. Failure to apply for a return to employment from military leave without pay within the time limit previously stated is considered a resignation.
11. A written request must be submitted to the employee's supervisor at least two weeks in advance, indicating the starting and ending date of the military training leave. To receive this benefit, the employee must furnish a copy of his or her military orders signed by an authorized military officer.
12. The length of military training leave granted to an employee depends on his or her military orders, not to exceed 15 calendar days annually.

13. If an employee is disabled while on military training leave or military leave without pay, and rendered incapable of performing the duties of the position previously occupied at *[Practice]*, the employee is offered the best available position for which he or she qualifies, providing the employee reapplies within the previously stated time limit.

<u>Approved by:</u> Practice Administrator

<u>Effective date:</u> 1/1/20__

## Policy 5.10    Disability Leave

This is an example of a disability leave policy.

---

Policy 5.10                    **DISABILITY LEAVE**

Purpose: To establish and maintain guidelines for disability leave.

Applies to: All *[Practice]* employees.

Policy: The policy of *[Practice]* is to provide short- and long-term disability insurance plans, in conjunction with benefits available through government sources.

Procedures:

1. The designated human resources professional, in conjunction with the Practice Administrator, determines the amount and duration of disability payments. Short- and long-term disability plans equal at least the minimum required by state law.

2. Full- and part-time employees are eligible for disability leave. Temporary employees are not eligible.

3. Employees are eligible for disability leave when they are physically unable to perform the duties of their position or another position within *[Practice]* due to injury or occupational disease incurred in the course of their employment.

4. Disability benefits are not awarded when the disability is an aggravation of a known medical condition that existed prior to employment with *[Practice]*. Such benefits are not awarded when the disability is the result of aggravation of a pre-existing disability arising from other employment for which the employee has received a permanent partial award, nor when the employee receives a civil judgment or settlement for permanent disability arising from a nonindustrial injury.

5. Every employee who sustains an injury in the course of his or her employment must notify the immediate supervisor within the time period specified by local law.

6. If the employee fails to report an injury, he or she loses one day's disability leave for each day's failure to report.

7. Employees on disability leave may be required to be examined periodically by a *[Practice]* physician. Compliance with this requirement is a condition for continuing disability leave with pay.

8. Disability leaves are not granted beyond an employee's date of retirement.

Approved by: Practice Administrator

Effective date: 1/1/20__

## Policy 5.11          **Bereavement Leave**

This is an example of a bereavement leave policy. *This is a suggested policy for educational and illustrative purposes only. The particular laws of each state may differ, and this suggested policy should not be implemented without considering applicable state law.*

---

**POLICY 5.11                    BEREAVEMENT LEAVE**

<u>Purpose:</u> To establish and maintain guidelines for bereavement leave.

<u>Applies to:</u> All *[Practice]* employees.

<u>Policy:</u> It is the policy of *[Practice]* to grant bereavement leave with pay to eligible employees in accordance with established guidelines.

<u>Procedures:</u>

1. Full- and regular part-time employees are eligible for paid bereavement leave during the calendar year after the first six months of employment. Temporary and provisionary employees are not eligible for paid bereavement leave.

2. During the first six months of employment, new employees are not eligible for paid bereavement leave benefits. However, time off without pay is allowed in the event of the death of an immediate family member or other relative.

3. Eligible employees are allowed up to three consecutive days of leave with pay in the event of the death of the employee's spouse, child, parent, parent-in-law, sibling, stepparent, stepbrother, stepsister, stepson, or stepdaughter.

4. Eligible employees are allowed one day of leave with pay in the event of the death of the employee's brother-in-law, sister-in-law, son-in-law, daughter-in-law, aunt, uncle, grandparent, or grandchild.

5. Employees may use accumulated sick leave to attend the funeral of a friend or any other individual upon the approval to the employee's department managers.

6. Full-time employees receive their regular rate of pay during the bereavement leave. Part-time employees receive their regular rate of pay only for days on which they normally would be scheduled to work, and only for their regularly scheduled number of hours.

7. Bereavement leave is not normally paid during vacation or any other type of leave.

8. The department manager should be notified immediately when the employee needs to request bereavement leave. The department manager makes every effort to grant bereavement leave to employees based on their requests.

9. Request for an extension to a bereavement leave must be approved by the department manager. If approved, employees must use accumulated sick leave after the allotted bereavement leave is exhausted.

10. If requested by the supervisor, an employee may be required to furnish some proof of death that supports the bereavement leave request.

<u>Approved by:</u> Practice Administrator

<u>Effective date:</u> 1/1/20__

## Policy 5.12          Court Leave

This is an example of a court leave policy.

---

**POLICY 5.12**                          **COURT LEAVE**

Purpose: To establish and maintain guidelines for court leave.

Applies to: All *[Practice]* employees.

Policy: The policy of *[Practice]* is to grant court leave to eligible employees when they are summoned to report for jury duty to any federal, state, or municipal court, or when they are subpoenaed to testify as witnesses concerning matters arising out of their professional job responsibilities.

Procedures:

1.  Full-time employees who submit a jury summons from a federal, state, or municipal court, or who submit a subpoena to testify as a witness concerning *[Practice]* business, shall be granted court leave with full pay to serve in that capacity.

2.  An employee who is called, summoned as a juror, or subpoenaed as a witness presents his or her supervisor the original summons or subpoena from the court to qualify for paid court leave.

3.  At the conclusion of such duty, a signed statement from the clerk of the court or other evidence showing the actual time of attendance must be turned in to the immediate supervisor.

4.  Court leave is intended to apply only to those times when the employee is needed for court service. It shall not be considered as paid leave during the time period when the employee has been excused from court service and does not return to work.

Approved by: Practice Administrator

Effective date: 1/1/20__

**Policy 5.13**          <u>**Leave Request**</u>

This is an example of a leave request policy.

---

POLICY **5.13**                    **LEAVE REQUEST**

<u>Purpose:</u> To establish and maintain guidelines for requesting a leave of absence.

<u>Applies to:</u> All *[Practice]* employees.

<u>Policy:</u> It is the policy of *[Practice]* to grant various types of leave to employees. Management makes every effort to accommodate an employee's request for leave.

<u>Procedures:</u>
1. All employee requests for a leave of absence must be submitted in writing using *[Practice]*'s leave request forms.
2. For all leaves of absence except for brief sickness, a written request on the leave request form indicating the type of leave, its duration, and the dates of departure and return must be approved by the appropriate supervisor prior to taking the leave.
3. The employee's leave request form should be submitted to the appropriate supervisor as soon as possible, but not less than two weeks before the leave starts unless it is an unexpected emergency.
4. Exceptions to the two-week minimum for requesting nonemergency leave are made on a case-by-case basis, based on staffing requirements and management's discretion. Only authorized exceptions are made.
5. Sick leave information should be provided on the leave request and submitted for approval immediately upon the employee's return to work.
6. Supporting documents or copies of these documents should be attached to the leave request form. These might include physician statements, subpoenas, summonses, or military orders.
7. Record-keeping of employee requests for leave is the responsibility of the appropriate supervisor. A copy of the leave request form is provided for the Human Resources Department.
8. Employees must report back to work the next scheduled workday following the last day of leave.
9. Supervisors may grant an extension of a leave request if circumstances warrant such a request.
10. Unless an absence is substantiated by a leave request form and approved by the supervisor in accordance with these procedures, an employee is not paid for any absence from scheduled work.
11. Failure to follow this procedure may be cause for disciplinary action.
12. In the event that an employee does not report for work at the expiration of an approved leave of absence, employment is terminated and seniority rights with *[Practice]* forfeited, unless additional leave would be a reasonable accommodation under the Americans with Disabilities Act.

<u>Approved by:</u> Practice Administrator

<u>Effective date:</u> 1/1/20__

## Sample Form

### Form 5.1    Employee Leave Request Form

This is a sample Employee Leave Request Form template. Modify this template to fit your practice's needs.

---

FORM 5.1              **EMPLOYEE LEAVE REQUEST FORM**

| **Name** (Last, first, MI) | | | | | | **Date of Request** |
|---|---|---|---|---|---|---|

| Department | | | | | | |
|---|---|---|---|---|---|---|

| **Type of Leave/Absence Requested** (Check appropriate box(es) below) | **Date** | | **Time** | | **Total** | |
|---|---|---|---|---|---|---|
| | From | To | From | To | **Hours** | |
| □ **Vacation** | | | | | | |
| □ **Sick Leave** | | | | | | |
| □ **Personal Leave** | | | | | | |
| □ **Floating Holiday** | | | | | | |
| □ **Court Leave** | | | | | | |
| □ **Bereavement Leave** | | | | | | **Relationship to Deceased** |
| □ **Military Leave** | | | | | | □ **Training** <br> □ **Active Duty** |
| □ **Disability Leave** | | | | | | |
| □ **Other** | | | | | | **Explain** |
| □ **Family and Medical Leave** <br> Contact your supervisor for additional information about your entitlements and responsibilities under the FMLA. | | | | | | □ **Birth/Adoption/Foster Care** <br> □ **Serious health condition of family member** <br> □ **Serious health condition of self** |

**Required Documentation:** A doctor's statement is required if sick leave is more than three days; proof of service is required if court leave is requested; a medical certification of a serious health condition may be required for disability leave under the FMLA.

| □ **Documentation Attached** | □ **Documentation Not Attached:** Explain. |
|---|---|

**Certification:** I hereby request leave/approved absence as indicated above and certify that such leave/absence is requested for the purpose indicated. I understand that I must comply with *[Practice's]* policies and procedures for requesting leave/approved absence (and provide additional documentation, including medical certification, if required) and that falsification on this form may be grounds for disciplinary action including termination.

| Employee Signature | Date |
| --- | --- |
| | |

| Official Action on Request:   □ Approved          □ Disapproved |
| --- |
| **Reason for Disapproval** |

CHAPTER 6

# Recruitment and Selection

Effective recruiting involves identifying the future employment needs of your practice (based on its strategic plan), reviewing job descriptions, and determining the best type of recruiting method to attract top talent. To recruit applicants with the appropriate qualifications, the designated human resources (HR) professional must communicate with supervisors who will be managing the new hires. The designated HR professional should also ensure that all federal and state laws are followed, including your practice's equal employment opportunity and Americans with Disabilities Act (ADA) policies.

## Common Recruiting Methods

Recruitment programs should be an active, ongoing process of identifying applicants and encouraging them to apply for vacant and/or upcoming positions at your medical practice. Recruitment methods utilized depend on the size of your group, its location, goals for the program, funding, and the type of positions being filled. It is important for your practice to continually look for qualified candidates. Even when positions aren't available, keeping an up-to-date and accessible employee recruitment database of highly qualified candidates can

### Common Recruiting Methods

- Promotions
- Employee referrals
- Internet
- Headhunters/Executive search firms
- Agencies
- Walk-ins/Write-ins
- Colleges and universities
- Advertising
- Other healthcare organizations

strengthen your practice's recruitment process. It is important to keep track of only the highest qualified candidates so they can quickly be contacted when a position becomes available.

### Promotions

When appropriate, your group's first source of recruitment should be promotion from within. Such a policy encourages staff members to improve their skills and fosters increased productivity and employee morale. Employees are more likely to make a long-term commitment to their jobs and your practice if they realize that good performance is recognized and rewarded. Although this is not always possible because of specialized clinical skills necessary for medical service positions, whenever job vacancies occur above entry level, they should be offered first, if feasible, to current employees. When promoting from within your group, the candidate should always be interviewed as if he or she was not already an employee. Not every current employee is the right fit for an open position. An employee who has excellent performance reviews may not necessarily be the most highly qualified for the new position. For example, many people do not like or are not comfortable in management roles.

### Employee Referrals

Employee referrals are an excellent source for recruiting candidates. Employee morale will be improved when employees find that their recruitment recommendations are considered and accepted. Giving cash or other types of recognition bonuses to employees who refer candidates who are then hired is relatively inexpensive and can produce highly qualified and motivated applicants.

### Internet

Online sources are extremely popular recruitment methods and continue to evolve as new technologies are introduced. Recruiters are using three main Internet sources: organizational Websites, job boards, and social media.

#### Organizational Websites

Many group practices use their own Website as a recruiting tool. An employment opportunities page can easily be added to an existing Website, informing potential applicants of open positions, listing the job description, and providing instructions for how to apply. Be cautious of relying too heavily on your medical practice's Website for drawing the targeted potential applicants. Your current and future patients may visit your Website more often than qualified potential applicants searching for job postings. Most group practices that utilize their organization's Website for recruiting and branding combine this method with employee referrals, attending job fairs, advertising, job boards, and so on.

No matter how elaborate your medical practice decides to make their recruitment pages, keep in mind that the page is an extension of the medical practice's brand and will leave an impression on potential applicants. Ensure that the page grabs the visitor's attention, is easy to navigate, and explains the hiring process. Most pages will

**Popular Job Boards for Healthcare Providers**

- www.healthecareers.com
- www.mgma.com/jobs
- www.careervitals.com
- www.healthcarejobsite.com
- www.practicelink.com
- www.craigslist.org

include the open position's job title, job description, and instructions for how to apply, including a way to submit a résumé or an application via an online form. Lastly, ensure that the Website auto-generates or the recruiter quickly sends an e-mail to the applicant notifying them that their résumé has been received. An unattractive, poorly designed Website may turn the most highly qualified potential candidates away from your group.

*Job Boards*

Many healthcare organizations rely heavily on job boards to find qualified applicants. Many job boards charge a fee for submitting a job posting while others are free. Although job boards may bring in many applicants, they also attract many underskilled and/or unqualified candidates, and therefore require a thorough applicant screening process to sift out unqualified candidates.

There are hundreds of available job boards including those that focus on a geographic area, a specificity such as healthcare, and even salary level such as entry-level positions and executive searches. Selecting the right job board is important to finding qualified candidates who could be a good fit with your practice.

*Social Networks*

Increasingly, healthcare organizations use social networks to find highly qualified candidates. Organizations are using a variety of social media to recruit candidates for open positions. This method can be costly in terms of time spent, and some charge a fee to list job openings. In addition, they may not be as targeted as your practice needs. Some recruiters routinely use social networks like Facebook and LinkedIn to identify candidates by searching for desired qualifications, geographic areas, and/or work experience. Recruiters also post information about job openings on their personal social media accounts like Twitter, hoping that others will pass along information about the job opening to their friends who may be qualified and interested in their open positions. Listing job openings on social media accounts is a quick and cost-free recruitment tool that may identify qualified candidates and is not time-consuming. However, the true success of recruiters finding qualified candidates using social media outlets has not yet been determined.

Recruiters and the hiring manager do routinely use different social networks to screen candidates. Besides contacting a candidate's references, they will also look at the candidate's Facebook page, Twitter feed, LinkedIn account, and other media sources to learn more about the candidate's personal and professional life. Sometimes seeing a candidate's activities on social media can help the medical practice determine whether he or she will be a good fit with your practice's culture and values.

**Headhunters and Executive Search Firms**

Headhunters are often a good resource to find qualified job candidates. There are many types of search firms that identify and screen qualified applicants for recruiters. Retained search firms usually focus on executive-level positions and charge for services rendered even if a candidate is not offered employment. Executive search firms also specialize in recruiting for senior-level management positions. Contingent-fee recruiting firms typically recruit for lower-level positions like administrative assistants, bookkeepers, and so forth, and charge for their services when a candidate is hired. The designated HR professional should interview, ask for references, and carefully select search firms before contracting with them.

Headhunters and executive search firms provide candidates based on the criteria you give them and will only provide you with candidates who fit your job description. The designated HR professional should check the candidate's references and interview candidates recruited by headhunters and executive search firms just as he or she would for all other applicants.

### Agencies

Public and private agencies can also be excellent sources of recruitment. State and federal employment agencies often provide free applicant screening services. Depending on the type of position to be filled, you may want to list job openings with these services. Many of these agencies are equipped to do testing, which could be invaluable to smaller groups that do not have the resources to test on their own.

Private employment agencies may charge a fee for using their services, and you should check their references before contracting with one. Nevertheless, your practice may want to develop a close relationship with private agencies that have a good success record of identifying highly qualified applicants. This may be particularly beneficial for smaller groups that may not have internal resources to do their own recruitment and screening.

### Walk-Ins/Write-Ins

A walk-in or write-in applicant is often attracted to the medical practice because of its reputation and may not be responding to a specific job opening. To generate goodwill within the community and to invest in future recruitment needs, arrange for a brief interview with each walk-in, even if positions are not available. Prompt and courteous responses to write-ins should be made and recorded, so an active recruitment database can be reviewed as positions become available. The best kind of recruiting occurs before a position needs to be filled when you work ahead of time to establish a highly qualified pool of candidates.

### Colleges and Universities

College campuses and technical schools can also produce excellent applicants. Most of these institutions develop programs in which employers periodically visit groups of students to supply them with general recruiting and job opportunity information. Online job databases through the institution's career services center allows employers to post open positions for students to browse. Career fairs are also held periodically to introduce students to potential employers. Working closely with school placement officers can produce well-educated, highly qualified applicants.

### Advertising

Advertising in newspapers, magazines, and trade publications is another recruitment tool. Most healthcare organizations have found that trade publication advertising is more successful, especially for administrative and/or managerial positions. The media selected depends on the cost, the success of each media in previous recruitment efforts, and skills required for the position.

## Complying with Recruitment Regulations

Employment procedures for recruitment, selection, and placements must meet the terms and conditions specified in Title VII of the Civil Rights Act of 1964 and the Age

Discrimination in Employment Act of 1967. Policies governing recruitment must be reviewed for compliance with federal anti-discrimination provisions to ensure that these policies do not discriminate against any potential employee because of race, color, religion, gender, gender identity, transgender, sexual orientation, national origin, disability, or age. Under most federal equal employment opportunity laws, it is illegal to indicate a preference based on age, race, color, religion, national origin, sexual orientation, or handicap in advertisements relating to employment, unless a bona fide occupational qualification for a particular job is identified.

The Equal Employment Opportunity Commission (EEOC) prohibits any kind of action that could have a negative effect on applicants, potential candidates, or employees of a particular age, race, color, religion, national origin, gender, gender identity, transgender, sexual orientation, or disability. The EEOC enforces these anti-discrimination laws and regulations from advertising for open positions, application forms, and the selection and hiring process. Consequently, all advertising or other recruitment literature should contain the following phrase: "*[Practice]* is an equal opportunity employer." To comply with these mandates, your practice should also use a variety of recruitment media sources to ensure you reach a wide variety of people.

Application forms, in particular, are an area of potential problems because many pieces of personal information are collected about the applicant. To prevent potential claims of discrimination on application forms, the form must focus on objective, job-related qualifications that presumably give each applicant an opportunity to obtain employment. A sample Application for Employment form (Form 6.1) is located at the end of this chapter and can be modified to fit your practice's needs. As a general rule, a pre-employment inquiry that disproportionately filters out protected individuals is illegal, unless the inquiry is justified for a legitimate business reason. Employers should periodically review their application form to ensure that the information sought is job related and in compliance with applicable federal and state laws. States have slightly varying employment discrimination laws that may go beyond federal regulations. Therefore, consult with your legal counsel and review your state's laws in addition to federal laws to ensure compliance. A sample affidavit that should appear on all application forms is at the end of this chapter (Form 6.2). Interviews, selection tests, and background checks are also areas of possible discrimination and should be scrutinized to ensure that a group of applicants is not being inadvertently discriminated against.

## Common Selection Methods

Your medical practice's selection process should identify the most highly qualified applicants. It is one of the most critical HR functions and has serious management and public relations impact. For example, hurried interviews and skipped reference checking can result in an unqualified applicant being hired. Yet unnecessary long waits and lengthy decision-making processes can result in an unfavorable impression of your practice in the community. The basic aim of selection is to provide consistency to hiring practices, based on job criteria that adhere to anti-discrimination requirements. The selection process should be objective, nondiscriminatory, and conducted in a manner that promotes positive impressions and long-term success for both your practice and the applicant.

As with recruitment, review all policies governing the hiring practices to ensure they do not discriminate against any employee or applicant because of race, color, gender, gender identity, transgender, religion, national origin, age, or disability. State laws may also prohibit discrimination on the basis of additional categories, such as marital status, sexual orientation, or public welfare status. The Uniform Guidelines on Employment Selection Procedures* were issued by the EEOC, Civil Service Commission, Department of Justice to provide guidance on how to comply with these laws. The guidelines apply to tests and other selection procedures used as a basis for any employment decision. Employment decisions include, but are not limited to, hiring, promotion, demotion, referral, retention, and selection for training or transfer. Policy 6.01 at the end of this chapter is a sample fitness for duty policy.

### Interviews

The most commonly used selection technique is an interview, usually conducted on a one-to-one basis. The interview must also meet that standards of job-relatedness and nondiscrimination. Thus, the same person should conduct interviews whenever possible, and the interviewer should ask a standard set of questions for each position. Many employers believe that the interview is the quickest, safest, and fairest selection method, as well as being less costly and easier to validate than written tests. Utilizing a variety of interviews is an excellent way to get a feel for the applicant's professional behavior. To maximize the probability of choosing the best possible employee, many HR professionals recommend that no applicant should be hired unless given two interviews.

**Common Selection Methods**

- Interviews
- Reference checks
- Criminal background checks

Phone interviews are an excellent start to the selection process. They are a cost-effective and fast way to prescreen and filter job candidates. Phone interviews are effective for gathering information about past work experience and education before a personal interview is offered. This is also a way the interviewer can evaluate the speaking skills and phone etiquette of the applicant.

Group interviews involve a panel of interviewers questioning several applicants scheduled closely together to determine who is the most qualified. These group interviews help interviewers evaluate applicants while the responses of previously interviewed candidates are still fresh in their minds. The interviewers should be carefully selected for each position. For example, the designated HR professional responsible for recruitment should conduct the phone interview, and the direct manager or supervisor should interview the most highly qualified candidates. In addition, employees who will work closely with the person ultimately hired can conduct an interview with the highest qualified candidates as well.

The medical practice should provide interviewers with interview instructions and a list of appropriate and nondiscriminatory questions to ask. A variety of open-ended and hypothetical problem-solving questions should be asked. Avoid asking questions that the candidate can simply answer with only a "yes" or "no" answer.

---

\*   29 CFR 1607.

**Reference Checks**

Reference checks involve verifying the information provided by an applicant as well as obtaining additional information about previous job performance. This information is used to evaluate a candidate's background and is a good indicator of future performance.

Thorough reference checks are strongly recommended in the healthcare industry. Many medical professionals have already demonstrated their proficiency through licensure, but the level and degree of competency and professionalism can only be determined by questioning former employers. Interviewers should always verify the status of the applicant's license. Furthermore, it is critical to verify the status of all credentials, including education and previous employment. It is not uncommon for applicants to lie on their résumés and employment applications about their credentials and other licenses. Detecting fraud at first glance can be difficult and emphasizes the importance of carefully reviewing résumés/applications before calling references. Follow these guidelines when reviewing résumés:

- Compare dates of graduation with dates of certification.

- Review all professional affiliations and identify those that do not quite fit or are misspelled.

- List all past employers the applicant reports are now out of business and supervisors who have left the organization. Many times this information is false and easy to verify.

- Be sensitive to gaps to employment; they can signal potential problems, including those previous jobs from which an applicant has been terminated or possibly when he or she spent time incarcerated.

Applicants who overstate their job qualifications may become unsatisfactory or harmful employees in your practice. As a warning, include a statement on your employment application form to the effect that résumé fraud results in immediate disqualification and/or termination. Proof of résumé fraud can be vital evidence in employer lawsuits.

Before checking references, the employer needs a signed consent from the applicant, authorizing the employer to contact prior employers or educational institutions attended. This consent statement can be included in the application form. An example of a Reference Check Consent and Authorization Form is located at the end of this chapter (Form 6.3). Your group practice may wish to consider using this type of language with necessary adaptations to make it reflect your practice's specific management philosophy, organizational needs, and staff size.

The other side of reference checks is providing information about current or former employees to other organizations. Many organizations have a policy to give only the essential information about a former employee, such as dates of employment, title of last job, and salary. The legal ramifications of reference checks have caused employers to be cautious; lawsuits have been filed because former employers did – or did not – provide reference information. Although employers generally enjoy a qualified privilege to references, unsubstantiated statements can destroy the privilege. The trend has been to share only information that was documented and can be easily defended.

Under certain circumstances, legal ramifications may also exist for an employer who does not exercise reasonable care in its selection of an employee if that employee later harms another in the course of his or her employment. Despite the reluctance of some employers to comment on former employees' performance, employers should still try to contact references and verify the information provided by the applicant. Employers who are hiring should ask former employers about the dates of employment, title, duties and functions, quality of work, attendance and punctuality, ability to get along with coworkers, job performance, stated reason for leaving employment, and whether the former employers would rehire the individual. A written record should be kept of all reference checks and the information obtained. Additionally, all information obtained through reference checking should be held confidentially and should not be given to an applicant or referred to during the course of the interview and screening process. Your group may need to emphasize interviews and using trial periods, instead of relying on former employers' comments about an applicant to verify a person's competence. Policy 6.02 at the end of this chapter is a sample reference checks policy.

**Criminal Background Checks**

Many states have laws requiring certain types of healthcare employers to perform criminal background or history checks. For example, employees who provide direct care to patients with physical or developmental disabilities or patients receiving inpatient, home, or hospice care are usually required to consent to a criminal background check. In some states, applicants who have been convicted of certain crimes, such as murder, assault, robbery, theft, sex crimes, and drug related cannot be employed in these positions. Most state laws apply to hospitals, nursing homes, home health agencies, hospices, community centers, and assisted living centers.

The EEOC and some federal courts have taken the position that an employer cannot automatically reject an applicant because of a criminal conviction. You must evaluate whether and how the crime is related to the job sought. For example, a conviction for sexual assault is highly relevant for an applicant seeking a position with unsupervised patient contact. However, a conviction for failing to file income tax returns may have little relevance to a candidate's suitability for a maintenance or clerical position.

Generally, employers have no obligation to tell applicants what they plan to look into as part of their consideration of an applicant; although under federal law, criminal background and credit checks require prior disclosure to the applicant. There are advantages to informing applicants that they may be subject to a criminal background check. First, applicants cannot claim that they did not know about the possibility of a criminal background check. Second, it may prevent applicants from lying on their application forms. Lastly, it may prevent some people from submitting their application because they do not want to undergo a criminal background check.

The depth of the investigation should be directly related to the vulnerability of the public if a dangerous person is put into the position. Minimal investigation is called for in the case of an outside grounds keeper; however, a staff position that involves unsupervised contact with patients should receive substantial scrutiny. If a person is transferred into a patient-contact job, it is wise to run a more detailed background check.

An example of a consent statement for a Criminal Background Check Authorization and Consent form is located at the end of this chapter (Form 6.4). Your practice may wish to adopt this statement with necessary adaptations to reflect your group's specific management philosophy, organizational needs, and staff size. Because state laws vary and may affect the legal requirements, your practice should also be familiar with these laws.

**Credit Report Checks**

Employers frequently check candidates' credit reports if the job duties involve handling money. If your medical practice orders a candidate's credit report, the Fair Credit Reporting Act requires you to disclose to candidates that you may use credit report findings in the selection process prior to pulling the report. The Federal Trade Commission, which enforces the law, requires a stand-alone disclosure and authorization form to be completed by each applicant. Form 6.5 at the end of this chapter is a sample Credit Report Authorization and Consent Form. In addition, the employer must provide candidates a copy of the report, inform them which consumer reporting company was used, and state their rights under the Fair Credit Reporting Act if the results eliminate them from the selection process.

**Anti-Discrimination Requirements for Selection**

As mentioned previously, policies and procedures governing your medical practice's selection process should be reviewed to ensure they do not discriminate against any employee or applicant because of race, color, gender, gender identity, transgender, religion, national origin, age, or disability. Some states have laws and regulations that protect other classes of people, including sexual orientation.

*The Equal Employment Opportunity Commission*

The purpose of the EEOC is to enforce the anti-discrimination in employment laws, including during the selection decision process. Thus, each employer must maintain records or other information that indicates the impact any selection tests or other selection procedures have upon employment opportunities identifiable by race, gender, or ethnic group. These records must be made available for inspection.

Employers are required to track the types of applicants they encounter. This is usually done through a software applicant tracking system as a service application. Oftentimes, applicant tracking systems are part of a larger human resources information system (HRIS). Many companies offer inexpensive software and Web-based applicant tracking systems for organizations of all sizes. Alternatively, some HR departments use an applicant tracking form that captures data such as name, date, race, gender, veteran, disabled, position applied for, whether interviewed, and whether hired. In the case of an EEOC audit, auditors will ask to see applicant-tracking statistics related to EEOC factors in terms of how many applicants applied, how many were interviewed, and how many were hired.

When any selection procedure adversely impacts the employment opportunities of any race, gender, ethnicity, age, or other protected class, the employer must validate that the procedure evaluates future job performance. The EEOC's Uniform Guidelines on Employee Selection Procedures contain technical standards and instructions for conducting validity studies and documenting validity evidence. Keep in mind, if an employer's selection process is challenged, the employer carries the burden of persuasion to prove that business necessity required the procedure.

*Americans with Disabilities Act*

The ADA prohibits discrimination in an employment decision on the basis of a known disability if the individual can perform the essential job functions with or without reasonable accommodation. The ADA's prohibition against discrimination in an employment decision means that a person's disability cannot factor into any decision concerning hiring, advancement, transfer, discharge, training, compensation, and other condition of employment. The ADA defines a disability as "a physical or mental impairment that substantially limits one or more of the major life activities of such individual." Disability also applies to an individual who has "a record of such impairment" or one who is perceived as having such impairment. The ADA protects only disabled individuals who are qualified; if a disabled individual is not qualified, he or she need not be considered for that position.

Although the ADA does not require employers to provide job descriptions of the essential functions of a job, if a job description exists at the time of the job notice or interview, it is considered evidence of the essential function if a discrimination charge is later raised. Thus, employers who use job descriptions are strongly advised to accurately reflect the essential functions.

An employer's obligation to provide reasonable accommodations extends to the application process as well. Thus, an employer must make the application process available to disabled individuals. To minimize discrimination charges against the application process, an employer may wish to express in its job notice that applicants who need accommodation in the application process should feel free to request it.

Inability to perform a single job does not constitute a disability; rather, the individual must be restricted from either a class of jobs or a broad range of jobs in various classes. For example, a surgeon with shaky hands is not disabled, because he can still teach or consult. However, a laborer who has a bad back, which prevents him or her from lifting, is considered disabled. The ADA encompasses people with HIV and AIDS and sometimes alcoholism and drug addiction. Individuals who employers perceive as high risk for incurring work-related injuries are protected. Obese people or individuals with cosmetic disfigurements cannot be discriminated against under the ADA's definition of disabled, which includes not only actual impairment but also perception of impairment.

Employers cannot ask job applicants whether they are disabled or require them to submit to a medical examination before extending an employment offer. However, an employer can ask whether the applicant is able to perform the position's job functions. Only in limited situations can an employer refuse to hire or take other adverse employment actions because of an employee's disability. An employer may defend against a discrimination charge if selection criteria are job related and based on business necessity and if no reasonable accommodation is available. If a disabled applicant poses a significant health or safety risk to others that cannot be eliminated by a reasonable accommodation, the employer may also exclude the individual from an employment consideration – only if one of the stated job qualifications is that the employee cannot pose a direct threat to the health or safety of his or her coworkers.

## Offers of Employment

Once your medical practice has selected the most qualified candidate for a position, the offer of employment is made. Offers can be made either verbally or in writing. Remind interviewers that verbal representations may result in unintended contractual commitments for your practice. Verbal offers should always be followed up with a written offer of employment. Written correspondence with applicants should be carefully reviewed by your legal counsel to ensure that representations do not result in unwanted contractual obligations.

Your practice is advised to develop a standard offer letter, reviewed by your legal counsel, to avoid making unintended promises regarding employment; the letter should include an employment-at-will clause. Avoid any definitive promises by your practice. The salary should be framed in the shortest possible time period, such as hourly wage or monthly salary. The letter should also state a time limit for acceptance of the offer and should include any pre-employment responsibilities of the applicant. Under the ADA, your practice may offer a job on the condition of satisfactory results of post-offer medical exams or drug tests.

**Health Examinations**

To decrease the possibility of discrimination in the hiring process, the ADA prohibits employers from making pre-employment inquiries about a candidate's disabilities. An employer may only ask whether an applicant can perform the job functions with or without reasonable accommodation. Even if the applicant volunteers information about a disability, the employer should only discuss the individual's ability to perform the essential functions of the job.

Requiring medical examinations of applicants is restricted by the ADA. Employers may require an applicant to submit to a medical examination only after conditionally offering the applicant a job. It is not sufficient for ADA compliance for the employer to simply narrow down the selection to the final applicants. Although the offer can be contingent upon a satisfactory health examination, a subsequent withdrawal of the offer based on the examination results must be related to an employee's ability to perform the job. Only results of such examination that indicate the person is unable to perform the essential functions of the position may be used to deny employment to the applicant. An employer may also withdraw an offer if the applicant's disability poses a direct threat to the applicant or others in the workplace, and the threat cannot be eliminated by reasonable accommodation.

Post-offer medical examinations must be required for all candidates in the same job category to whom an employer makes offers. Employers who use medical examinations must treat the results as confidential medical records. The results may only be released to certain individuals in limited circumstances, as indicated by law.

Health examinations of current employees may only be conducted if they are job related and necessary to the operation of the business. For example, safety concerns or a sudden unexplained decrease in job performance might warrant a medical examination of an employee. The examination may not include tests or inquiries that are not related to the employee's ability to perform the job. Employers may also conduct examinations pursuant to an employee health program, but only if participation is voluntary and the results are kept confidential.

The underlying purpose of requiring health examinations is to obtain information on health status. Along with determining whether the applicant is physically able to carry out the job functions, health examinations can protect the employer from invalid Workers' Compensation claims in cases where injuries or illness were present when an employee was hired.

Medical practices may choose to use health histories, physical exams, or both, depending on the health status of the applicant and the physical requirements of the position. In healthcare organizations, health screening is particularly relevant for employees directly involved with hands-on patient care. To ensure employees do not have a health condition that jeopardizes patients' health, require all such caregivers to complete a health screening questionnaire signed by their physician as soon as possible after hire. Your medical practice may also choose to use a simple immunization history form that does not need to be signed by a physician. Health histories help to evaluate the current medical, physical, and mental conditions of an employee or applicant to determine overall job suitability. If the person's health history reveals any serious medical, physical, or mental problems that might interfere with successful and safe job performance, the medical practice has the right to request a medical examination to determine the current medical status and extent of previous injuries, diseases including HIV and AIDS, or handicaps. For example, if the candidate has a history of back problems and applies for a licensed practice nurse position, which requires heavy lifting of as much as 100 pounds, the medical practice would want a further detailed medical evaluation of the applicant's ability to lift.

Health examinations also help employers determine, with the help of a physician, if a disabled applicant can perform the essential functions of a job with or without reasonable accommodations as well as determining the particular accommodations. The physician's advice on accommodations is the emphasis.

Policy 6.03, at the end of this chapter, is a sample of a policy for health examinations. Because state laws vary and may affect the legal requirements, your practice should consult your legal counsel and become familiar with these laws.

### Drug Testing

Under the ADA, a test to detect the illegal use of drugs is not considered a medical examination. Thus, employers may administer drug tests to applicants to discover illegal use of drugs. Employers may also prohibit employees from being under the influence of alcohol, illegal drugs such as cocaine and heroin, and illegal use of prescription drugs in the workplace. An employee or applicant found to be currently using drugs in an illegal manner is not protected as a qualified individual with a disability. An employer may make employment decisions on the basis of current illegal drug use. Employers should be careful, however, to ensure that the drug test results they rely on are accurate.

Although the ADA does not prohibit drug testing of applicants, employers should be aware that drug tests can indicate the existence of a disability. Use of a specific prescription drug, shown in the results, could indicate the presence of a particular disability. The disability could then be considered "known," and a duty to reasonably accommodate it might arise. Employers who choose to utilize drug tests should test all applicants as a condition of employment.

## Hiring People with Close Relationships

Nepotism implies favoritism toward relatives, including undeserved rewards and unfairly granting employment or other advantages. Traditionally, nepotism refers to hiring or advancing relatives solely because of their relationship with an employee, officer, or shareholder in an organization without regard for their qualifications. Today, organizations are faced with a wider range of related people including immediate family members, in-laws, step relatives, grandparents, and domestic partners.

The most stringent policies regarding close relationships in the workplace imposed by an organization prohibit hiring anyone with a close relation to an individual employed anywhere in the organization. Thus, employment of a person in one site prevents a relative from being hired to work in any location. A less-restrictive policy bars employment only of employees with close relationships in the same facility, whereas a more liberal policy permits employment in the same site, but not within the same department or area. Finally, many policies prohibit people with close relationships from holding positions in which one person directly supervises another or has some influence over the other's pay, promotion, or work situation.

In carrying out strict policies regarding close relationships in the workplace, employers must proceed cautiously when deciding who to retain. If these decisions disparately impact females or older workers, employers are left open to discrimination charges. Employers are generally advised to let the individuals involved make the choice, and then, if possible, transfer to another department, rather than terminate, that person who decides to leave. However, the decision should be on an objective and neutral basis.

Medical practices that have operated effectively without a policy regarding close relationships in the workplace may not need to implement one. Flexibility in closely related people may help recruit good candidates. Should a problem arise, a rule can be established addressing the situation providing the business necessity justification. Policy 6.04 is a sample policy regarding close relationships in the workplace.

## Negligent Hiring

Negligent hiring is a legal theory that says an employer who fails to take reasonable precautions to ensure that employees will not harm a coworker can be held liable. With disturbing and increasing frequency, disgruntled employees are taking out their anger and frustration on coworkers or customers (i.e., patients). Lawsuits can then claim that the employer did not do an adequate job of investigating the employee's background before hiring. The injured party argues that if the employer had done an adequate investigation, it would have learned of the employee's violent tendencies. Thus, the employer's negligence resulted in harm that was foreseeable.

There are steps you can take to substantially reduce your medical practice's exposure to claims of negligent hiring, while also preventing complaints of discrimination, breach of confidentiality, and defamation:

1. Use an application form that has been reviewed by legal counsel.
2. Conduct a telephone interview with qualified candidates to review their résumé, application form, and past work experiences. Ask about any lapses in employment history.
3. Interview qualified candidates face-to-face in private.
4. Discuss and have the applicant sign the reference check consent form and the criminal background check consent form.
5. If the applicant's duties require driving, obtain proof of a valid driver's license and, in some circumstances, discuss and have the applicant sign a driving record consent form.
6. Contact the applicant's references.

7. Conduct employment reference checks by contacting all previous employers to verify truthfulness on employment history.

8. Confirm educational and licensure credentials provided by the applicant.

9. Order a criminal background check and/or the applicant's driving record if necessary.

The more information your practice seeks and the more information you obtain about an applicant, the better prepared you are to make hiring decisions. In conducting interviews, criminal background checks, and other investigative efforts, it is imperative that you first understand what the applicable federal and state laws require, permit, and prohibit. Check with your legal counsel about these issues.

## Summary

Your medical practice must have solid recruiting and selection policies in order to recruit and hire top talent. You should use several recruiting methods that are appropriate for you medical practice's strategic plan, position type, and size. Throughout the recruiting process, your medical practice must abide by all government regulations regarding equal employment, including but not limited to the Civil Rights Act of 1964 and the Americans with Disabilities Act of 1990. The selection process also needs to follow these regulations. You should avoid asking applicants any questions that may put them at a disadvantage due to their nationality, race, gender, gender identity, transgender, age, or disability.

## Sample Policies

**Policy 6.01**            ## Fitness for Duty

This is an example of a fitness for duty policy. *This is a suggested policy for educational and illustrative purposes only. The particular laws of each state may differ, and this suggested general policy should not be implemented without considering applicable federal and state laws.*

---

POLICY **6.01**              **FITNESS FOR DUTY**

Purpose: To ensure that all employees are physically, mentally, and emotionally able to perform the essential job functions with or without reasonable accommodation.

Applies to: All *[Practice]* employees.

Policy: All *[Practice]* employees must be fit for duty. This includes physical, mental, and emotional fitness. In the event that an employee demonstrates any inability to function appropriately in his or her position, he or she is referred to the employee health nurse or the employee assistance coordinator. The employee may then be required to furnish a physician's note indicating ability to perform essential job duties with or without necessary accommodations.

If the employee demonstrates physical or mental manifestations reasonably leading to suspicion of drug or alcohol misuse or abuse, *[Practice]* reserves the right to require appropriate blood or urine testing to determine if misuse or abuse has occurred. A positive result from these tests results in the employee not being allowed to work until the situation has been resolved. Failure to cooperate in testing or resolution efforts may result in termination.

The employee health nurse must evaluate employees who have been ill or injured and wish to return to work.

Employees who are exposed to or contract a communicable disease must report this information to the employee health nurse immediately, in compliance with infection control policies. *[Practice]* provides services to assist employees in these situations.

See the employee health nurse or the designated human resources professional for more information.

Approved by: Practice Administrator

Effective date: 1/1/20__

**Policy 6.02**          <u>**Reference Checks**</u>

This is an example of a reference check policy. *This is a suggested policy for educational and illustrative purposes only. The particular laws of each state may differ, and this suggested general policy should not be implemented without considering applicable federal and state laws.*

---

POLICY 6.02                    **REFERENCE CHECKS**

<u>Purpose:</u> To establish and maintain guidelines for reference check requests.

<u>Applies to:</u> All *[Practice]* employees.

<u>Policy:</u> It is the policy of *[Practice]* to disclose only the date of hire, date of separation, and position held unless the former employee provides and signs an acceptable statement releasing *[Practice]* of any and all liability for the information provided. If such statement is signed, *[Practice]* may release the following documented information:

1. Positions held;
2. Date of hire;
3. Salary level;
4. Promotions;
5. Performance evaluations;
6. Attendance; and
7. Date of separation.

Any release of information will be in compliance with federal and state laws.

<u>Approved by:</u> Practice Administrator

<u>Effective date:</u> 1/1/20__

## Policy 6.03          Health Examinations

This is an example of a health examinations policy. *This is a suggested policy for educational and illustrative purposes only. The particular laws of each state may differ, and this suggested general policy should not be implemented without considering applicable federal and state laws.*

---

POLICY 6.03          **HEALTH EXAMINATIONS**

Purpose: To establish and maintain guidelines for health examinations.

Applies to: All *[Practice]* employees.

Policy: The policy of *[Practice]* is to require its employees to have a health examination under the circumstances outlined below.

Procedures:

1.  After a conditional job offer, all individuals are required to satisfactorily complete a health examination form and have it signed by their physician as soon as possible after hire. Some health examinations may be required to include a physician's report and medical records when there is a concern about the person's ability to perform the job.

2.  Management reserves the right to request that an employee have a physical examination at any time when the health and safety of the employee or patients is in question.

3.  Health and physical examinations administered at the request of management are paid for by the group.

4.  Any medical examinations paid for by *[Practice]* are the group's property and treated as confidential.

5.  When *[Practice]* requires a physician's report concerning an illness suffered by an employee, the examination is at *[Practice's]* expense and performed by a physician selected by the group. Employees who are not satisfied with the physician's report may submit one from a physician of their own choice and at their own expense. *[Practice's]* physician evaluates results of this examination and makes a final determination.

6.  Employees returning from sick leave may be required to have a physical examination, limited to the condition causing the absence, to determine their capability to satisfactorily perform their regular job duties.

7.  Employees who are exposed to any occupational health hazard, such as toxic materials, fumes, or nuclear radiation, are required to have a physical examination, limited to the substances to which employees are exposed. The physician determines whether exposed employees require medical treatment and/or whether they may be permitted to continue their jobs.

Approved by: Practice Administrator

Effective date: 1/1/20__

**Policy 6.04**     <u>**Close Relationships in the Workplace**</u>

This is an example of a policy about close relationships in the workplace. *This is a suggested policy for educational and illustrative purposes only. The particular laws of each state may differ, and this suggested general policy should not be implemented without considering applicable federal and state laws.*

---

POLICY 6.04          **CLOSE RELATIONSHIPS
IN THE WORKPLACE**

<u>Purpose:</u> To establish and maintain guidelines for close relationships in the workplace.

<u>Applies to:</u> All *[Practice]* employees.

<u>Policy:</u> The policy of *[Practice]* is to permit employment of people with close relationships to employees provided that it does not create a real, potential, or perceived conflict of interest. An employment decision of any kind including, but not limited to, placement, hiring, salary, or promotion is not based in whole or in part on whether an employee has a relative presently employed by *[Practice]*, except in accordance with these criteria:

- *[Practice]* will not place one such person under the direct supervision of the other person;
- *[Practice]* will not place one person in the same area or department employing the other person;
- If an applicant would be hired except for *[Practice's]* policy of not placing a "relative" under the supervision of the other or in the same area or department as the other, the affected individuals are informed and must decide which person will be employed.

*Relative* is defined as a spouse, domestic partner, parent, legal guardian, child, sibling, grandparent, grandchild, or in-law/step (father, mother, brother, sister, son, daughter) of the employee. This also includes employees who are in a dating relationship.

Should the marriage or dating relationship of current employees result in one person working under the direct supervision of the other person or in the same area or department as the other person, if feasible, one individual is given the opportunity to transfer outside the department. If the transfer is not feasible, the couple is given an opportunity to choose which person resigns. Should the couple choose not to make that determination, the less-senior person is terminated.

Employees with close relationships will be held accountable for any negative impact on the workplace due to such relationship. A negative impact on the workplace includes any perception of favoritism by other employees, or any perception of harassment without regard to whether actual favoritism or harassment exists.

<u>Approved by:</u> Practice Administrator

<u>Effective date:</u> 1/1/20__

## Sample Forms

**Form 6.1**       **Application for Employment**

This is a sample Application for Employment form you can modify to fit your medical practice's needs. Consult with your legal counsel to ensure compliance with federal and state laws.

---

FORM 6.1                **APPLICATION FOR EMPLOYMENT**

Please complete this form by typing or printing in ink.

**GENERAL INFORMATION**

| Last Name | First Name | Middle Initial | Date of Application |
|---|---|---|---|
| **Home Phone**<br>( ) – | **Cell Phone**<br>( ) – | **E-mail Address** | |

| **Current Address** (Street number and name) | **Apt. #** | **City, State, Zip Code** |
|---|---|---|

**Are you legally entitled to work in the United States?** □ Yes □ No | **Are you 18 or older?** □ Yes □ No

**Have you ever been convicted of a law violation (other than minor traffic violations)?** A "yes" response does not disqualify you from employment, since the nature of the offense, date, and the job for which you are applying will be considered.

□ No □ Yes, please explain:

**Are you currently employed or engaged in any other business?** □ No □ Yes, please explain:

**Have you ever applied here before?** □ No □ Yes, please explain:

**Were you ever employed here before?** □ No □ Yes, please explain:

**POSITION INFORMATION**

| **Position Applied For:** For which position do you wish to apply? | **Desired Salary** |
|---|---|

| **Employment Type Desired:** Mark all that apply. | **Shift Desired:** Mark all that apply. |
|---|---|
| □ Full time | □ Days |
| □ Part time | □ Evenings |
| □ Temporary | □ Nights |
| □ On-call | □ Weekends Only |
| | □ Alternating Weekends |

**Reasonable Accommodation:** Are you able to perform the essential functions of the job for which you are applying, with or without reasonable accommodation? □ Yes □ No

**Date Available:** When are you available to begin work?

## EDUCATION AND TRAINING

| Type of School | Name and Location (City, State) | Years Attended | | Graduated? | | Degree/Major |
|---|---|---|---|---|---|---|
| | | To | From | Yes | No | |
| High School | | | | ☐ | ☐ | |
| College | | | | ☐ | ☐ | |
| College | | | | ☐ | ☐ | |
| Graduate School | | | | ☐ | ☐ | |
| Nursing School | | | | ☐ | ☐ | |
| Vocational School | | | | ☐ | ☐ | |
| Technical School | | | | ☐ | ☐ | |
| Other | | | | ☐ | ☐ | |

**Skills and Training:** What skills or additional training do you have that are related to the job for which you are applying?

**Equipment:** Please list any machines or equipment you can operate that are related to the job for which you are applying?

**Foreign Language:** List any languages other than English in which you are fluent, and select whether written or spoken fluency.

| Language | Written | Spoken |
|---|---|---|
| | ☐ | ☐ |
| | ☐ | ☐ |
| | ☐ | ☐ |

**Occupational Licenses/Certifications:** Please list any licenses or certifications you have earned.

| Type | Number | Where Issued | Expiration Date |
|---|---|---|---|
| | | | |
| | | | |
| | | | |

**WORK EXPERIENCE** (List the most recent first, including any military experience.)

| Employer Name | Employer Phone<br>(   )   – | From (Month/Year) |
|---|---|---|

| Employer Address (Street number and name) | City | State | Zip Code | To (Month/Year) |
|---|---|---|---|---|

| Job Title | Reason for Leaving: Explain why you left this job. |
|---|---|

| Direct Supervisor | Supervisor Title |
|---|---|

| Starting Rate of Pay | Final Rate of Pay | May we contact this employer?<br>☐ Yes   ☐ No |
|---|---|---|

Responsibilities and Duties: Please briefly describe your specific responsibilities and duties.

| Employer Name | Employer Phone<br>(   )   – | From (Month/Year) |
|---|---|---|

| Employer Address (Street number and name) | City | State | Zip Code | To (Month/Year) |
|---|---|---|---|---|

| Job Title | Reason for Leaving: Explain why you left this job. |
|---|---|

| Direct Supervisor | Supervisor Title |
|---|---|

| Starting Rate of Pay | Final Rate of Pay | May we contact this employer?<br>☐ Yes   ☐ No |
|---|---|---|

Responsibilities and Duties: Please briefly describe your specific responsibilities and duties.

| **Employer Name** | | | | **Employer Phone** ( ) – | | **From** (Month/Year) |
|---|---|---|---|---|---|---|
| **Employer Address** (Street number and name) | | **City** | | **State** | **Zip Code** | **To** (Month/Year) |
| **Job Title** | **Reason for Leaving:** Explain why you left this job. | | | | | |
| **Direct Supervisor** | | | | **Supervisor Title** | | |
| **Starting Rate of Pay** | **Final Rate of Pay** | | | **May we contact this employer?** ☐ Yes ☐ No | | |
| **Responsibilities and Duties:** Please briefly describe your specific responsibilities and duties. | | | | | | |

| **Employer Name** | | | | **Employer Phone** ( ) – | | **From** (Month/Year) |
|---|---|---|---|---|---|---|
| **Employer Address** (Street number and name) | | **City** | | **State** | **Zip Code** | **To** (Month/Year) |
| **Job Title** | **Reason for Leaving:** Explain why you left this job. | | | | | |
| **Direct Supervisor** | | | | **Supervisor Title** | | |
| **Starting Rate of Pay** | **Final Rate of Pay** | | | **May we contact this employer?** ☐ Yes ☐ No | | |
| **Responsibilities and Duties:** Please briefly describe your specific responsibilities and duties. | | | | | | |

## Form 6.2    Application Form Affidavit

This is a sample affidavit template for your application form. Modify the template to fit your medical practice's needs. Consult with your legal counsel to ensure compliance with federal and state laws.

---

FORM 6.2                     **APPLICATION FORM**
**AFFIDAVIT**


Please read each statement carefully before signing.

**An Equal Opportunity Employer**
*[Practice]* is an equal opportunity employer. We do not discriminate on the basis of race, color, religion, national origin, sex, age, or disability. It is our intention that all qualified applicants be given equal opportunity and that selection decisions be based on job-related factors. Applicants requiring reasonable accommodation in the application and/or interview process should notify the recruiting specialists.

I certify that all information provided in this employment application is true and complete to the best of my knowledge and ability. I understand that any false information or omission may disqualify me from further consideration for employment and may result in my dismissal if discovered at a later date.

I authorize the investigation of any or all statements contained in this application. I also authorize, whether listed or not, any person, school, current employer, past employers, and organizations to provide relevant information and opinions that may be useful in making a hiring decision. I release such persons and organizations from any legal liability in making such statements. I understand that the employer may request a criminal background check and an investigative consumer report from a consumer reporting agency. These reports may include information as to my character, reputation, personal characteristics, and mode of living obtained from interviews with neighbors, friends, former employers, schools, and others.

I understand that if I am extended an offer of employment, it may be conditioned upon my successful passing of a complete pre-employment physical examination. I consent to the release of any or all medical information as may be deemed necessary to judge my capability to do the work for which I am applying. I understand I may be required to successfully pass a drug screening examination. I hereby consent to pre- and/or post-employment drug screening as a condition of employment, if required.

I understand that this application or subsequent employment does not create a contract of employment nor guarantee employment for any definite period of time. If employed, I understand that I have been hired at the will of the employer and my employment may be terminated at any time, with or without cause and with or without notice.

I have read, understand, and by my signature consent to these statements.


_____          _____
Signature                                        Date

**Form 6.3**        <u>**Reference Check Consent and Authorization Form**</u>

This is a sample template of a Reference Check Consent form for conducting reference checks during the selection process. Check with your legal counsel to ensure compliance with federal and state laws.

---

FORM 6.3              **REFERENCE CHECK**
**CONSENT AND**
**AUTHORIZATION FORM**

I have applied for employment with *[Practice]* and have provided information about my previous employment. My signature below authorizes my former and current employers and references to release the contents of my employment record and to provide any additional information that may be necessary for my employment with *[Practice]*, whether the information is positive or negative.

I authorize *[Practice]* and its agents to investigate all statements made in my application for employment and to obtain any and all information concerning my former and/ or current employment. This includes my job performance evaluations, wage history, disciplinary action(s), if any, and all other matters pertaining to my employment history. I knowingly and voluntarily release all former and current employers, references, and *[Practice]* from any and all liability of any kind, including but not limited to defamation, invasion of privacy, and breach of confidentiality arising from their giving or receiving information about my employment history, my academic credentials or qualifications, and my suitability for employment with *[Practice]*.

_____        _____
Applicant Signature                              Date

_____
Applicant Name (please print)

## Form 6.4     <u>Criminal Background Check Authorization and Consent Form</u>

This is a sample template of a consent form for conducting criminal background checks during the selection process. Check with your legal counsel to ensure compliance with federal and state laws.

---

FORM 6.4      **CRIMINAL BACKGROUND
CHECK AUTHORIZATION
AND CONSENT FORM**

I understand that in considering my application for employment, *[Practice]* may conduct a comprehensive investigation of my qualifications. I understand this investigation may include, but is not limited to, a criminal background check, credit report, and references from past employers and other sources *[Practice]* deems appropriate.

I consent to any authorized representative of *[Practice]* to obtain information pertaining to my law enforcement record including, but not limited to, any record of charge, prosecution, or conviction for criminal offenses. I authorize each law enforcement agency to which this form is presented to release any results, upon request of the authorized requestors as described above.

I understand that these searches will be used to determine employment eligibility under *[Practice's]* employment policies. Therefore, I release and discharge *[Practice]* and its agents to the full extent of the law from any claims, losses, liabilities, or any other charge or complaint arising from retrieving and reporting this information.

I hereby certify that the information provided on this Criminal Background Check Authorization and Consent Form is true, correct, and complete. I understand that any information which is proven to be incorrect or incomplete may disqualify me from further consideration for employment and may result in my dismissal if discovered at a later date.

| Applicant Signature | | | Date | |
|---|---|---|---|---|
| | | | | |

| **Printed Name** (Last, first, MI) | | | **Maiden Name** | |
|---|---|---|---|---|
| **Other Names Used** (Last, first, MI) | | | | |
| | | | | |
| **Current Address** (Street number and name) | | **Apt. #** | **Date of Birth** (Month/day/year) | |
| **City** | **State** | **Zip Code** | **Social Security #** | |
| **Driver's License #** | **State Issued** | **Expiration Date** | ☐ **Male** ☐ **Female** | |

**Form 6.5**         **Credit Report Authorization and Consent Form**

This is a sample template of a consent form for authorization to pull an applicant's credit report during the selection process. Check with your legal counsel to ensure compliance with federal and state laws.

---

**FORM 6.5**         **CREDIT REPORT AUTHORIZATION AND CONSENT FORM**

I understand that in considering my application for employment, *[Practice]* may conduct a comprehensive investigation of my qualifications. I understand that this investigation may include, but is not limited to, a criminal background check, credit report, and references from past employers and other sources *[Practice]* deems appropriate.

I hereby authorize and consent for *[Practice's]* procurement of a consumer credit report. I understand that, pursuant to the federal Fair Credit Reporting Act, *[Practice]* will provide me with a copy of any such report if the information contained in such report is, in any way, to be used in making a decision regarding my fitness for employment with *[Practice]*. I further understand that such report will be made available to me prior to any such decision being made, along with the name and address of the reporting agency that produced the report.

| Applicant Signature | | | Date |
|---|---|---|---|

| Printed Name (Last, first, MI) | | | Maiden Name |
|---|---|---|---|

| Other Names Used (Last, first, MI) | | | |
|---|---|---|---|
| | | | |

| Current Address (Street number and name) | | Apt. # | Date of Birth (Month/day/year) |
|---|---|---|---|

| City | State | Zip Code | Social Security # |
|---|---|---|---|

☐ Male      ☐ Female

## CHAPTER 7

# Employee Records

Policy 7.01   Record Retention

Employee records are a primary source of data for managing, evaluating, and documenting human resources (HR) and employment-related activities. Employee records contain facts for a myriad of applications, including required reports to government agencies, reports for employees, reports on the effectiveness of HR activities, and controls on operating expenses. In addition, records can highlight problem situations, such as complaints, and can also provide data on salaries and wages. The type of employee information collected and maintained by management depends on its need for specific information, the size of your practice, and applicable law.

Most organizations are subject to federal and state reporting regulations. Many of these regulations are employment related, but health, safety, and other types of regulations may also require reporting. Certain records are also kept to aid in employment decisions, such as hiring, promotions, training, discipline, layoffs, and terminations. Medical practices should determine which records must be created and retained, as well as how long to retain those records. Federal, state, or local laws may define how long certain documents must be retained. Employers should seek the advice of legal counsel on the requirements for retention of documents in relation to charges of discrimination, litigation, or if litigation is reasonably anticipated.

## Human Resources Information Systems

A human resources information system (HRIS), sometimes called a human resources management system (HRMS), is typically a hosted software solution that can help HR professionals track and maintain many HR functions, including employee records. In addition, many HRIS solutions offer features that allow employees to view and generate reports. Many small businesses, including medical practices, are finding that an HRIS is an inexpensive, yet highly valuable method to manage many HR functions.

HRISs range from advanced, enterprise-wide systems to simple solutions with limited features. They range from a "software as a service" solution to hosted solutions to in-house solutions. Prices range from inexpensive, encompassing only the basic HR functions, to expensive enterprise solutions. Many types of HRISs are available, and selecting one should be based on the needs of your medical practice. Your information technology (IT) department or IT advisor can help determine which solution is the best fit for your practice's needs.

Typical HRIS functionality includes:
- Payroll;
- Employee attendance and leave;
- Performance evaluations;
- Benefits administration;
- Employee records;
- Recruiting, including applicant tracking;
- Training, rewards, and bonus histories;
- Reporting; and
- Health and safety records.

## Employee Files

It is crucial for employers to carefully maintain employee files. It is important to know which documents to create, which documents to keep, where they should be kept, and how long to keep them. Most, but not all, employee records are kept in employee files, whether physical or electronic. Other policy issues that need to be addressed are destruction of files, employees' access to their files, and maintaining appropriate confidentiality.

**Documents Not Kept in Employee Files**
- Medical records
- Benefit-related documents
- Wage garnishment documents
- Child support documents
- I-9 forms and related documents
- Criminal background checks

### Employee File Contents

Typically, most employee files include the following:
- Pre-employment documents, including job application forms, résumés, results of pre-employment reference checks, and results of any nonmedical pre-employment tests;
- Job descriptions;
- Forms acknowledging receipt of an employee handbook;
- Personal and emergency contact information;
- Employment history, including date of hire, initial salary, dates of raises, explanations for raises, job classifications, work locations, layoffs, and terminations;
- Attendance records;
- Education and training records;
- Performance evaluations;
- Recognition and awards;

- Coaching, warning, and disciplinary records;
- W-4 forms; and
- Documents related to termination.

Employee file maintenance policies and practices should be developed keeping in mind applicable federal and state laws related to record-keeping, employee privacy, retention and destruction of records, and accessibility of employee files.

### Documents to Be Kept Separate from the Employee File
Certain types of employment records must be kept separately from employee files. A general rule is that any documentation that may not lawfully be considered when making personnel decisions (e.g., documents related to age, gender, race, disability) should not be kept in the employee file.

Medical records must be kept separately from employee files. Examples of medical records are:

- Information about drug use other than illegal drug use;
- Workers' Compensation claims and correspondence;
- Results for medical inquiries or examinations; and
- Claims submitted for medical, disability, or life insurance.

Records relating to benefits administration and insurance should also be kept separately because these may contain medical records. Self-identification forms from disabled employees, as well as requests for accommodation, should not be kept in employee files because such documents may also include medical records. Other documents that should not be kept in employee files include I-9 forms, any documents regarding an employee's eligibility to work in the United States, and documents related to child support or wage garnishment.

The Equal Employment Opportunity Commission (EEOC) recommends that any records of an employee's gender, race, ethnicity, or sexual orientation that may be required for reporting purposes be kept separately from the employee file.

### Accessibility and Confidentiality
Because employee files contain private and confidential information, great effort should be made to maintain the privacy and confidentiality of these files. A growing number of medical practices are using an HRIS to store and manage employee files. If your practice utilizes electronic employee files, ensure that the hosted solution is secure, employees have secure and controlled access to their employee files, and only designated HR professionals and supervisors have controlled access. If your practice chooses to use physical employee files, employees should have access to their own file at reasonable times and at reasonable intervals.

There is no federal law that requires private sector employers to provide employees access to their personnel files. However, some states have laws governing employees' access to their employee files. State laws differ but may explain rights and define procedures for employees who wish to inspect, copy, correct, and/or even expunge information contained in their employee file. These laws may also contain exceptions and limitations to access.

Regardless of whether there is an applicable state law, medical practices should have a well-defined policy on how and when employees have access to their employee files. Such a policy should comply with applicable state law and take into account the employer's and employees' interests. If your practice has physical employee files, you must ensure that the confidentiality of other files is not compromised when allowing an employee access to his or her employee file. In addition, your practice must provide supervision of employees while they have access to their files to guarantee that the contents are not removed or altered without consent. Practices may consider limiting access to specific days and times and requiring advanced notice so that the employee's file can be pulled and reviewed to remove any confidential materials. Policy 7.01 at the end of this chapter is an example of a policy about keeping records.

If your practice uses an HRIS solution to store and manage employee files, you must ensure that the employee cannot delete or alter documents or information in the file. Most systems do allow employees to update certain information within their employee files such as addresses, phone numbers, emergency contacts, and so on.

Be cautious about giving out employee information. Medical practices should refuse to release employment information to third parties without the employee's written authorization. If employee files are released without the employee's consent, the employee could claim an invasion of privacy.

## Record-Keeping, Reporting, and Government Requirements

State and federal laws require employers to create and maintain certain employment-related records. The following sections contain brief summaries of some of the laws governing record-keeping. Medical practices should work with legal counsel to ensure they are complying with all applicable laws regarding record-keeping.

### Federal Insurance Contributions Act

As mentioned earlier, several laws and regulations require employers to keep records regarding employee compensation and mandatory federal income taxes. Federal law, including the Federal Insurance Contributions Act (FICA), the Federal Unemployment Tax Act (FUTA), and the federal income tax withholding regulations, requires employers to keep employee records for at least four years. These records include but are not limited to:

- Name;
- Address;
- Social Security number;
- Gender;
- Date of birth;
- Occupation;
- Job classification;
- Total compensation;
- Tax forms;
- Hours worked;
- Wages subject to tax withholdings;
- Actual taxes withheld from wages; and
- Payments to annuities, pension, accident, health, and other benefits.

### Equal Pay Act

The EEOC requires employers covered by the Equal Pay Act (those covered by the Fair Labor Standards Act [FLSA]) to keep certain records required by the US Department of Labor (DOL). Covered employers must preserve records made in the regular course of business that relate to the payment of wages, wage rates, job evaluations, job descriptions, merit systems, seniority systems, and collective bargaining agreements. Covered employers must also keep records of any practice that explains the basis for payment of higher wages to employees of one sex than to employees of the other sex in the same establishment. These records may be important in determining whether a difference in wages is based on a factor other than gender. These records must be retained for at least two years.

### Occupational Safety and Health Act

The Occupational Safety and Health Act of 1970 requires most employers to maintain records of occupational injuries, illnesses, and deaths. The records consist of a log and summary of occupational illnesses and injuries, a supplementary record of each occupational injury or illness, and an annual summary of information contained in the log, all of which must be retained for five years following the end of the calendar year that the records cover. The log and annual summary must be completed for each location that is expected to remain in operation for one year or longer. For example, a medical practice with two offices must keep a separate log and annual summary at each office. An Injury and Illness Incident Report must be completed for each work-related injury or illness that occurs.

In addition, certain employers, including those with the potential for workplace exposure to bloodborne pathogens and other toxic substances, should prepare an Exposure Control Plan to eliminate or minimize employee exposure or provide documentation that demonstrates compliance. These documents usually include detailed records of training, exposure monitoring, medical monitoring, and others. The act also requires an employer to preserve and maintain employee medical and exposure records for the term of the employee's employment plus 30 years. Workers' Compensation laws in each state may also require similar reports.

### Title VII of the Civil Rights Act

Under Title VII and corresponding EEOC regulations, an employer who maintains employment records (any records having to do with hiring, transfer, demotion, promotion, layoff, termination, rates of pay, and selection for training programs) must keep the records for a period of one year from the date the records were made or one year from the date of the personnel action, whichever is longer. In the case of an involuntary termination, personnel records should be kept for one year following the date of termination. When a charge of discrimination has been filed, employers must preserve all records relevant to the charge until the final disposition of the charge.

### Americans with Disabilities Act

The Americans with Disabilities Act (ADA) incorporates Title VII's provision requiring certain records to be kept. If an employer keeps employment or employee records, including requests for reasonable accommodation, the employer must preserve those records for a period of one year from the date the record is created or one year from the date of the personnel action involved, whichever is longer. If a discrimination charge is filed, the employer must keep all records relevant to the charge until the final disposition of the charge.

Under the ADA, an employer must maintain all medical records for applicants and employees separately from employee files. In addition, the ADA requires confidential treatment of such medical files.

## Fair Labor Standards Act

Under the FLSA, employers are required to make and keep records generally including identifying information of employees and data about hours worked and wages earned. Records for nonexempt employees should generally include:

- Name, Social Security number, address, and zip code;
- Sex;
- Date of birth;
- Occupation;
- Time and day of the week on which the employee's workweek begins;
- Regular hourly rate of pay;
- Hours worked by the employee each workday;
- Total hours the employee worked each workweek;
- Total daily or weekly straight-time earnings;
- Basis on which wages are paid;
- Total overtime earnings for each workweek;
- Deductions from wages;
- Total wages per pay period; and
- Date of payment and pay period.

In addition, payroll and collective bargaining records must be retained for at least three years. Records on which computations are based must be retained for at least two years.

## Age Discrimination in Employment Act

Under the Age Discrimination in Employment Act (ADEA), a covered employer must keep records on each employee that include name, date of birth, address, occupation, rate of pay, and weekly compensation. These records must be kept for a period of at least three years.

The ADEA also requires employers to keep records of the following for one year after the date of the personnel action:

- Applications for employment, résumés, and any other form of employment inquiry in response to job advertisements, including records related to hiring decisions;
- Promotion, transfer, selections for training, demotion, layoff, recall, or discharge of any employee;
- Job orders submitted by the employer to an employment agency or labor organization for recruitment of employees for job openings;
- Test papers completed by applicants for any position that disclose the results of any employer-administered aptitude or other employment test considered by the employer in connection with any personnel action;
- Physical examination results considered in connection with any personnel action; and

- Any advertising related to job openings, promotions, training programs, or opportunities for overtime work.

Employers must also keep on file any employee benefits plan (such as pension and insurance plans) and any written seniority or merit system for the full period the plan or system is in effect and for at least one year after its termination.

### Immigration Reform and Control Act

Employers are required to have all new employees complete the I-9 form to verify they are eligible to work in the United States. As mentioned previously, these forms should be kept separately from the employee files in a designated file for the US Citizenship and Immigration Services or electronically. The forms must be completed within three business days after the first day of employment for pay and made available for inspection by the DOL or the US Department of Homeland Security. Employers must keep I-9 forms for either three years or one year after termination, whichever is longer. Some states also have laws related to verification of work eligibility, which may contain additional record-keeping requirements.

### Employee Retirement Income Security Act

Under the Employee Retirement Income Security Act (ERISA), covered retirement plans are subject to many reporting and disclosure requirements. Government agencies that require reporting under ERISA are the DOL, the Pension Benefit Guaranty Corporation, and the Internal Revenue Service. ERISA usually requires plan administrators to:

- Submit an annual return and report of the employee benefits plan;
- Provide plan participants a summary plan description upon enrollment, any changes to the plan, or every 10 years;
- Provide information about the plan upon written request of a plan participant or beneficiary;
- Submit the summary plan description to the DOL upon request; and
- Provide statements to employees who leave the organization and are eligible for benefits.

Check with your financial advisor and your accountant to determine your medical practice's specific reporting requirements.

### Employee Polygraph Protection Act

The Employee Polygraph Protection Act generally prevents most private employers from using lie detector tests. In the rare event that a polygraph test is permitted, the employer must provide certain notices to the examiner and the examinee. Employers requesting a polygraph test must retain records for a minimum of three years from the date of the polygraph test or from the date the test is requested if no test is conducted.

### Labor Relations and Union Reporting

Under the Labor-Management Reporting and Disclosure Act of 1959 (the Landrum–Griffin Act), private employers must report certain financial transactions to the DOL. For example, employers must report certain expenditures or arrangements that are made for the purpose of interfering with, restraining, or coercing employees in the exercise of their bargaining or representation rights. In addition, employers who engage a consultant to influence employees not to join a labor union must submit a record of the consultant's fee and expenses.

### Legal Hold Obligations

When a medical practice anticipates litigation, it must ensure that it retains all documents (including electronic documents) relevant to that potential litigation; otherwise it risks sanctions. This also applies in the context of threatened litigation or government investigations, audits, or proceedings. To prevent the accidental destruction of relevant information and documents, a medical practice must suspend their routine document destruction policies and notify all individuals who may have relevant documents in order to ensure the preservation of relevant documents and electronically stored information. Documents should be retained until the conclusion of the litigation, investigation, audit, or proceeding. Medical practices should consult legal counsel to develop a legal hold policy, and to comply with legal obligations in the event of potential litigation or a government investigation, audit, or proceeding.

## Summary

Record-keeping is an important activity for every medical practice. Employee records can be used as evidence during litigation. In addition, government agencies may require the creation and maintenance of certain employment-related records and may also have the right to inspect certain records. Every medical practice should have a policy regarding which records should be retained in each employee's file. These employee files should be confidential, but an employee should have access to their personal employee file. Careful documentation should be kept during the hiring and selection process as well as throughout a person's employment history, including any records related to disciplinary action and termination.

## Sample Policy

**Policy 7.01**      <u>**Record Retention**</u>

This is an example of a policy about keeping records.

---

POLICY 7.01           **RECORD RETENTION**

<u>Purpose:</u> To establish and maintain guidelines for employment-related record retention.

<u>Applies to:</u> Human Resources Department

<u>Policy:</u> The policy of *[Practice]* is to protect the confidentiality of certain confidential personal data that the organization may have. In addition, *[Practice]* creates and retains all records in accordance with applicable law.

<u>Procedures:</u>

1. *[Practice]* will maintain accurate, high-quality, and secure records electronically or on site for the duration of time provided by applicable law. Once the time period is complete, the records will be securely destroyed.

2. The oral response of *[Practice]* to verbal inquiries on employment data consists only of verification of employment.

3. *[Practice]* responds, in writing, to an appropriate inquiry on employee data only if that employee (or former employee) has signed a release that is part of the written inquiry.

4. Should an employee desire certain information to be released, he or she should submit, in writing, to the human resources director (or designee) precisely what information *[Practice]* is authorized to release and give permission to *[Practice]* to do so. *[Practice]* will only release such information that the employee specifically authorizes it to release.

5. *[Practice]* complies with all legal requests for employee data. If *[Practice]* is subpoenaed, it notifies the employee and gives him or her the opportunity to have the subpoena nullified before releasing the requested information.

6. Any retention periods do not apply to documents that are the subject of a legal hold. All records related to pending, threatened, or potential litigation or a government investigation, audit, or proceeding must not be destroyed during such litigation, audit, investigation, or proceeding.

<u>Approved by:</u> Practice Administrator

<u>Effective date:</u> 1/1/20__

CHAPTER 8

# Employee Development

Policy 8.01   Employee Development

Policy 8.02   Employee Orientation

Human resources (HR) remain our most important assets in the workplace. High-level employee performance is essential to the profitability and growth of medical practices. While customer service and information technology drive most organizations today, no advances can be made without having competent and motivated employees.

Training and development opportunities contribute to employee growth and greatly benefit not only the employee but the medical practice as well. With the uncertainty of the economy and the impact of the Patient Protection and Affordable Care Act, more emphasis should be placed on training and retaining top talent. Employee turnover can be very costly for medical practices; moreover, offering training and development opportunities for employees is a superior, lower-cost strategy, and a competent workforce increases productivity and reduces expenses and waste.

In addition, employees who believe they are denied opportunity for personal and/or professional growth eventually seek other employment opportunities where a more progressive and supportive organizational environment exists. The fast pace of change in healthcare technology, including electronic medical records and mobile health applications, requires a technology-savvy workforce that can provide the most efficient and up-to-date services. Goals of employee development programs may include increasing organizational efficiency, building and maintaining a workforce of highly skilled and efficient employees, and installing and implementing the best practices and techniques for performing job duties and responsibilities.

To provide high-quality patient care in a cost-efficient manner, healthcare organizations must create a work environment that develops competent employees. Because the quality of patient care is directly related to the knowledge, skills, abilities, and attitudes of your practice's staff, employee training and development programs should aim to improve performance and advance employee qualifications. Specific goals of training and development programs may include:

- Improve the knowledge, skills, and ability of employees;
- Transfer the acquired skills and accumulated knowledge of experienced staff to less experienced employees; and
- Train staff to accomplish current and future organizational requirements.

The specific training and development objectives and efforts of practices vary significantly, depending on management philosophy and group size. Regardless of size, management should plan and arrange for appropriate training and development opportunities for all employees.

Many training options are available, including on-site training, classroom training, college or vocational school instruction, apprenticeship training, internships, simulated training, and programmed instruction. The degree of commitment from top management to develop a highly functioning staff and your practice's available financial resources determines the amount and type of training and development offered.

### Types of Training and Development

- Employee orientation
- Technical and skills training
- Interpersonal training programs
- Career development programs

## Training and Development Policies

Training and development policies communicate to employees the importance your practice places on employee training, education, development, and job enrichment, along with optimizing productivity and profit. Such a policy must ensure that opportunities are available to all staff members.

A training and development policy should cover when and how to announce these opportunities, eligibility for attendance, required approvals, and types of programs endorsed by your practice. At the very least, your practice should offer training and development programs that increase existing employee knowledge and skills. A training and development policy should stress the importance of having supervisors encourage their staff to attend training programs and to groom competent employees for promotional opportunities. Building a pipeline of well-trained employees ready for the next step ensures productive succession. Policy 8.01 at the end of this chapter is an example of a training and development policy. Your practice may wish to adopt this policy, with modifications made to reflect specific management philosophy, organizational needs, and size.

## Employee Orientation and Onboarding

The goal of employee orientation and onboarding is to reduce turnover and increase retention. Effective orientation programs help newly hired employees learn not only about their individual job duties, benefits, and policies, but also which behaviors your practice values and how their jobs contribute to the overall success of your practice.

Your employees should understand that each of them is vitally important to effective and high-quality patient care.

Some medical practices orient new employees by spending a few minutes giving a tour of the facility, introducing coworkers, showing them their workspace, and then having someone show them how to do their job tasks. This type of orientation program fails to cover many critical elements that would normally help and encourage new employees to perform at their best. Others offer ½ day, 1-day, or 2-day new employee orientation programs, which provide a more thorough overview of your practice.

Onboarding is a growing HR trend advocating a comprehensive approach to bringing on new hires that goes beyond traditional orientation programs. Onboarding is the process of bringing new employees into the organization by providing information, training, mentoring, and coaching during their first 6 to 12 months of employment. It helps new employees more quickly contribute to the organization, increase their comfort level, reinforce their decision to join the organization, and enhance productivity, and it also encourages employee commitment, engagement, and retention. Research has also demonstrated that onboarding reduces stress and the chance of employees quitting soon after starting more than a traditional orientation program.

Onboarding and new employee orientation programs help employees develop a self-identity and a team spirit, which contribute to healthy attitudes toward your practice and can lower absenteeism and employee turnover. They are also a highly effective way to communicate not only that your practice demands full effort from its employees to maximize productivity and the quality of services, but also that your practice values and respects its employees. They also inform new hires about your practice's policy prohibiting unlawful discrimination and harassment. Keep in mind that your practice's Website gives the first impression of your practice, followed by the interview process and the type of new employee orientation program you offer. As mentioned previously, these all influence newly hired employees' long-term commitment to your practice.

To reinforce your practice's commitment to its employees, the HR department or administrator should consistently follow up with each new employee during the first few months of employment to see if there is a need for more information and/or training. Onboarding programs that include mentoring and coaching are more comprehensive and help to ensure a successful transition into your practice.

**New Employee Orientation Design**

At a minimum, your practice's orientation program should consist of two distinct parts: a general organizational overview and a departmental orientation. The organizational overview should provide information on your practice's history, mission, values, policies, and compensation and benefits. In addition, the general overview should introduce your practice's strategic plan and structure. This part should be given by the HR department or person responsible for these activities. The frequency of the orientation program depends on the size of your practice, employee turnover, and the number of new employees. In a small practice, employee orientation may be conducted on an individual basis as new employees are hired, and, usually, the person responsible for employee administration conducts the orientation. Medium-sized practices might offer this program once every few months, whereas larger practices may hold these programs more often. Ideally, orientation should be scheduled during the first week of work.

The second part of the orientation concerns information about essential functions and standards of performance. Generally, the immediate supervisor facilitates this departmental orientation to introduce new employees to their job duties and responsibilities, and the department's goals, performance standards, and policies. This orientation also familiarizes employees with the work area, coworkers, and work rules. The supervisor should follow up the orientation with effective, consistent communication with the employee, which should include making the employee feel welcomed and relaxed by greeting him or her each morning, and by encouraging questions. An assigned mentor can help facilitate this process.

**Onboarding Design**

Onboarding is intended to be a multi-faceted and customized approach and typically lasts from 6 to 12 months. It goes beyond the typical ½-day to 2-day new employee orientation program by facilitating social relations with the supervisor, managers, and coworkers. Most onboarding programs are designed to get feedback from new hires at the end of the first week, first month, first three months, and so on, asking different questions at each stage to learn how engaged or connected the new hire feels to your practice. Typical questions begin with asking about the recruiting process and whether the first few days met the employee's expectations. Later feedback inquires about any issues he or she might be struggling with, whether the employee has the necessary tools to complete his or her job, and then shifts focus to the employee's strategic goals. Many HR professionals develop a new employee onboarding checklist to ensure that new hires have adjusted to their organization and its culture. Many onboarding toolkits are available that your practice can customize and use. A sample Policy 8.02 about employee orientation is at the end of this chapter.

## Technical and Skills Training

Training helps create an atmosphere that encourages active employee participation and ensures maximum use of employees' skills and abilities. This type of training focuses on specific job skills, techniques, new medical knowledge, and new technologies. It provides employees with necessary technical training, promoting efficiency and competency. It often reduces learning time, errors, and improves the quality of service and productivity. The type of training that traditionally has been provided by healthcare organizations focuses on clinical skills, licensure, and credentialing. It is often conducted by medical professionals and coordinated through the HR department. An equal amount of time should be devoted to training employees how to efficiently use the organization's technologies, including information technology systems.

**Typical New Employee Orientation Topics**

- Welcome by practice administrator
- Overview of practice's mission, vision, values, and history
- Summary of policies and procedures
- Employee compensation and benefits
- Payroll procedures
- Shift and overtime scheduling
- Health, fire, and safety rules
- Overview of employee handbook
- Questions and answers
- Tour of facility
- Introduction to key people
- Job-specific information and requirements

## Team-Building Programs

Team-building training programs accompanied with skill-based exercises can be used to improve working relationships among coworkers, supervisors, and managers. By developing your staff's interpersonal skills, communication tends to flow more freely and effectively across and among departmental boundaries.

Often these workshops uncover internal working issues and misunderstandings among the employees, which result in less efficient patient care. Offering these types of workshops helps employees confront these small dissatisfactions among staff members. It is not unusual for practices to experience a disconnection among departments, management, and staff. Team-building workshops can enhance and build stronger camaraderie and team spirit. Effective teams work together more efficiently and result in higher patient satisfaction. Employees enjoy the opportunity to expand and develop their skills, which results in a more motivated, engaged, and effective workforce.

## Career Development Programs

Career development programs provide opportunities for employees to advance their careers and perform at their highest potential. The most common example of a career development program is supervisory training. These programs sometimes are considered nonessential, but they provide an extra benefit to employees. Career development programs should be offered within the constraint of your practice's needs for higher-level skills and the availability of resources to support these efforts. Devoting time and resources to developing staff positively affects bottom-line results. Career development programs can stimulate employee interest in their jobs, improve overall job performance, and provide management with a broader base to fill vacancies. In addition, employees with an outstanding work record perform better than new recruits.

### Career Pathing

Career pathing involves employees developing an organizational career path that includes career development. Career pathing examines what work experience, knowledge, skills, and personal characteristics are required for an employee to progress his or her career laterally, through promotions or transfers. It allows employees to gain new knowledge and skills while performing new jobs with different responsibilities.

Career pathing requires an employee to objectively assess his or her career goals, experience, skills, requisite knowledge, and personal characteristics. Employees then develop a written career path plan to obtain what is necessary in each of these areas to meet career goals. Usually, both the employee's immediate supervisor and an HR professional assist in reviewing and implementing the plan.

Some larger organizations have a formal process for the career-pathing process supported by management that involves creating a performance development plan. Otherwise, the performance evaluation process is another opportunity for career pathing.

Career-pathing programs are a retention tool, provide developmental opportunities, and help build critical leadership skills when management actively supports them. Overall, many workers leave their jobs for lack of career advancement and a lack of training.

Offering career-pathing programs to your top talent encourages retention and contributes to the continued success of your practice.

### Academic and Educational Programs

Academic programs are often offered to supplement other types of skills training and career development programs. They are designed to improve the overall competency in a specific area that may be outside the scope of the employee's present job. Academic and educational programs can be taught by colleges or vocational schools or other training companies, either in the classroom or online.

These programs also help employees maintain the essential knowledge and skills necessary for their duties and responsibilities. Employees can lose certain job knowledge and skills if they are not routinely used. Thus, academic and education programs can provide an opportunity for employees to reinforce their current skills or discover new skills that will contribute to their competency.

## Training and Development Laws and Regulations

Anti-discrimination laws cover employee training and development as well as other employment practices. Title VII of the Civil Rights Act of 1964, as amended, prohibits covered employers from discriminating against employees based on race, color, religion, sex, gender identity, sexual orientation, or national origin with respect to training and development. In addition, state and local laws may prohibit discrimination in training and development based on additional protected classes. However, employers are allowed to put some restrictions on employee training. For example, a training session may be limited to only employees who possess certain skills, have passed a certain exam, or who have demonstrated exceptional competence based on work history and performance.

The Fair Labor Standards Act specifies that attendance at lectures, meetings, training programs, and similar activities must be counted as paid working time unless the following criteria are met:

- Attendance is outside of the employee's regular working hours;
- Attendance is voluntary;
- The training is not job related; and
- The employee does not perform any work during such attendance.

## Summary

A medical practice's most valuable assets are its employees. It is important to train and develop employees so they can perform effectively and efficiently. There are several types of employee development programs that you can use to develop the skills and abilities of your employees. An onboarding or, at a minimum, a new employee orientation program should properly introduce all new employees to the medical practice as well as training and development opportunities.

### Sample Policies

**Policy 8.01**     ## Employee Development

This is an example of a policy about training and development programs.

---

**POLICY 8.01**                    **EMPLOYEE DEVELOPMENT**

Purpose: To establish and maintain guidelines for employee development.

Applies to: All *[Practice]* employees.

Policy: The policy of *[Practice]* is to conduct training and development programs that enhance the current skill level of the staff and develop the necessary skills required for efficient and productive job performance. *[Practice]* offers its employees the opportunity to improve their job skills, prospects for promotion, and their personal development.

Procedures:

1. Supervisors are responsible for encouraging employees to improve their skills and increase their job knowledge.

2. Management cooperates with employees in planning for further training and recommending additional training and development programs.

3. Employees are required to participate in training and development programs when it is considered necessary for satisfactory job performance.

4. *[Practice]* recognizes the need for all levels of management to constantly improve their skills. It provides training and development programs whenever feasible, based on available resources.

5. *[Practice]* offers safety and health programs to promote a safe and healthy working environment.

6. If continuing education and in-service programs are required for licensing or certification, *[Practice]* considers sponsoring and/or conducting such programs.

7. Employees may volunteer for training and development opportunities or management may recommend them. Regardless of the procedure, all employees must receive supervisory approval to attend such programs conducted during work hours.

8. All management-required training is provided without cost to the employee. Approval of payment fees for voluntary training and development programs is subject to the discretion of management.

9. Management encourages employees to take advantage of training and development opportunities whenever possible. However, completing such programs does not guarantee advancement.

10. All training and development programs sponsored or conducted by *[Practice]* are evaluated on the quality of instruction, content, and effectiveness. Participants in such programs may be required to take tests to determine the extent of their learning.

11. The designated human resources (HR) professional is responsible for announcing *[Practice]*-sponsored or *[Practice]*-conducted development programs. Such opportunities are posted on the employee bulletin board and online message board.

12. Certificates of completion are awarded to all employees who successfully complete any program sponsored or conducted by *[Practice]*.

13. The designated HR professional maintains records of training and development programs completed by each employee.

Approved by: Practice Administrator

Effective date: 1/1/20__

**Policy 8.02**     **Employee Orientation**

This is an example of a policy about new employee orientation programs.

---

POLICY 8.02          **EMPLOYEE ORIENTATION**

Purpose: To establish and maintain guidelines for employee orientation.

Applies to: All *[Practice]* employees.

Policy: The policy of *[Practice]* is to conduct new employee orientation programs to familiarize employees with the group, enable them to learn their assigned positions, and develop job skills required for productive and effective job performance.

Procedures:

1. An orientation program is conducted to acquaint new employees with [Practice's] policies, rules, and benefits. The designated human resources (HR) professional is responsible for designing, coordinating, and conducting this program.

2. The designated HR professional is responsible for the general orientation program that includes an introduction to *[Practice]*, and an explanation of policies and procedures, and employee benefits and incentives.

3. All supervisors are responsible for conducting a departmental orientation for new staff members to acquaint them with departmental rules and regulations. Supervisors are also responsible for teaching new employees how to perform their jobs and for training the current staff to teach new employees. On-the-job training is conducted during normal working hours.

4. Orientation programs are evaluated on their effectiveness and modified when appropriate.

5. The designated HR professional maintains records from the orientation programs.

Approved by: Practice Administrator

Effective date: 1/1/20__

# CHAPTER 9

# Employee Safety, Health, and Security

Employers realize how important occupational safety and health programs are to maintaining a productive and highly efficient workforce. The cost of unsafe and unhealthy conditions in the workplace is substantial considering the direct impact of such conditions on employee well-being, lost productivity, and morale issues due to accidents and illness. In addition, the cost of healthcare benefits to the employer will continue to rise, contributing to higher health insurance costs when employees are injured. The cost of providing safe and healthy work conditions and safety and training programs is low when compared to the cost of employee accidents, injuries and illnesses, and Workers' Compensation claims.

More important than the economic aspect of health and safety is the employee's right to work in an environment that does not pose a health hazard or an unreasonable risk of injury. An employer does not wish to see anyone harmed by its practice's everyday operations, but failure to establish and enforce strict health and safety policies may unintentionally encourage careless practices.

Today, the continuing rise of worldwide health disasters and the possible risks to healthcare workers and patients make such policies even more critical. Issues related to significant exposure to blood, body fluids, and tissues must be addressed, as well as exposure to contaminated needles, waste anesthetic gases, chemicals, hazardous materials, and drugs. Another continuing and growing concern is potential exposure to communicable diseases such as hepatitis B, influenza, and others. Policies should address the vaccination of those employees involved with direct patient care and supply handling.

Medical practices realize that they are a part of the community and society in which they work and must take a role in protecting it, enhancing it, and keeping it safe. Having a record of occupational health and safety problems is a detriment to the employer's public image and position in the community.

## Employee Safety

The physical condition of the workplace affects an employee's productivity, attitude, and organizational morale. For these reasons, most employers take aggressive steps to provide a pleasant, clean, friendly, and safe work environment. If working conditions are not safe, hygienic, and healthy, employees may suffer from lost time on the job due to occupational accidents or injuries. Therefore, personal health and safety are very important to your employees and impact their productivity. Overall Workers' Compensation claims in our country continue to increase and demand close oversight by management.

Safe work practices that are followed and enforced help to ensure not only that workers are kept out of danger, but also that the risk of damage to the medical practice's property and liability status is reduced. Thus, employers must establish policies to guide managers, supervisors, and employees in obeying health and safety regulations.

Employee health and safety areas to consider in a safety policy are:
- On-the-job injuries;
- Accident and injury reports;
- Medical emergencies;
- Posting emergency information and other required notices/information;
- Evacuation plans;
- First aid equipment;
- Weather-related alerts;
- Natural disasters;
- Care and use of equipment and chemicals/materials;
- Protective equipment and clothing;
- Safety inspections;
- Reporting certain injuries/illnesses (where applicable, such as in certain state plan jurisdictions);
- Reporting workplace hospitalizations and fatalities;

- Reporting unsafe conditions;
- Safety designated areas;
- Safety suggestions; and
- Safety incentive award programs.

Policy 9.01 at the end of this chapter is a sample policy on employee safety and health. Your practice can adopt this policy, with necessary modifications to reflect your practice's specific management philosophy, organizational needs, and staff size. *State laws vary in this area and affect the practice's legal requirements; the practice should be familiar with your state's laws.*

**Safety Laws and Regulations**

Most employee safety laws and regulations fall under the Occupational Safety and Health Act (the "act"). As mentioned previously, this law was passed in part to solve some of the inadequacies that were thought to exist in the states' Workers' Compensation laws. The law encourages employers and employees to work toward reducing the number of hazards in their workplace. It also stimulates employers and employees to develop new programs, or revise existing ones, to provide safe and healthy working conditions.

The act requires that every employer covered by the law must provide employees with a place of employment that is free from recognized hazards that could cause death or serious harm to employees. The act further requires that each employee abide by all legal standards, rules, regulations, and orders issued by the employer to comply with the law. An employer covered by the act is defined as any person who has employees and who is engaged in interstate commerce. The act provides for civil and criminal penalties for violation of the law or regulations issued thereunder. Some of the penalties can be at the employer as well as individual levels.

The following paragraphs discuss some of the key standards and regulations to which the Occupational Safety and Health Administration (OSHA) requires most medical practices comply. For more information, including downloadable fact sheets and posters, please see OSHA's Website at www.osha.gov. The federal standards that follow can all be found on the OSHA Website. Numerous states have their own regulations that also affect health and safety in the workplace. In some cases, such states' requirements go beyond minimum federal standards/requirements. As this manual only provides general information about compliance with these standards/requirements, you should carefully review the applicable standards and requirements to confirm compliance of your workplace.

*Bloodborne Pathogens Standard and Needlestick Prevention (29 CFR 1910.1030)*
OSHA issued this standard to help protect workers who are at risk of occupational exposure to bloodborne pathogens. These include HIV, hepatitis B, hepatitis C, and other potentially infectious materials. The regulation lays out what employers are required to do to protect employees and incorporates the Centers for Disease Control and Prevention's concept of universal precautions. This regulation requires employees to identify tasks and procedures and job classifications where occupational exposure to blood (i.e., human blood, human blood components, and products made from human blood) or other bodily fluids (i.e., semen, vaginal secretions, cerebrospinal fluid, synovial fluid, pleural fluid, pericardial fluid, peritoneal fluid, amniotic fluid, saliva, any

unfixed tissue or organ, etc.) occurs or may occur. The employer must prepare a written exposure control plan. The plan must be updated annually to reflect any changes.

In addition, employers must implement a policy for treating all human blood and other bodily fluids as if they are known to be infectious for bloodborne pathogens. Employers must also utilize engineering controls that isolate and/or remove the hazard from the workplace. These engineering controls can include disposal containers, sharps containers, and self-sheathing needles. Furthermore, your practice must establish policies to ensure the safety of work practice including handling and disposing of contaminated sharps, handling specimens and laundry, and cleaning surfaces and items. Personal protective equipment, such as appropriate gloves, gowns, eye protection, and masks, must be provided by the employer, and they must be cleaned, repaired, and replaced when needed.

The standard requires employers to make the hepatitis B vaccine available to all employees with exposure risk. Many employers choose to expand the vaccination offerings to other infectious diseases including influenza, H1N1 flu, and methicillin-resistant *Staphylococcus aureus* (MRSA). If an employee is exposed to a bloodborne pathogen, your practice must provide post-exposure follow-up evaluations at no cost to the employee.

Requirements of the Needlestick Safety and Prevention Act of 2000 are included in the Bloodborne Pathogens Standard. For example, employers must establish a sharps injury log for recording percutaneous injuries from contaminated sharps and protecting the injured employee's confidentiality.

In addition, medical practices should develop plans to handle and prevent tuberculosis (TB) transmissions. Although OSHA has not enforced any standards or regulations specifically on TB, medical practices should have a program to deal with the transmission of TB. A TB infection-control program should consist of a plan to ensure prompt detection, airborne precautions including respiratory protective equipment, and treatment of infected persons or those who are suspected of infection.

*Hazard Communication Standard (29 CFR 1910.1200)*
OSHA issued the Hazard Communication Standard providing employees with a "right-to-know" of hazardous materials in their workplace. Employers must have and keep updated a list of chemicals, such as alcohol, disinfectants, anesthetic agents, sterilants, and mercury used or stored in the facility. Employers must also have a written hazard communication program similar to the exposure control plan for bloodborne pathogens. In addition, employers must have a copy of the Material Safety Data Sheet from the manufacturer or distributor for each chemical.

In early 2012, OSHA updated the standard to align with the Globally Harmonized System of Classification and Labelling of Chemicals (GHS). Due to the update, chemical manufacturers and importers will have stricter requirements on labeling hazardous chemicals and data sheets will have a new, uniform format ensuring consistency. Medical practices will need to update their data sheet when the new ones become available and provide training to employees on the new label elements in addition to other training topics required by the standard.

*Ionizing Radiation Standard (29 CFR 1910.1096)*

OSHA issued the Ionizing Radiation Standard for all facilities that have radiation, including X-ray machines. The ionizing radiation sources can pose serious health risks to employees if certain safety precautions are not followed. The regulation requires the ionizing radiating machines to be in a restricted area to limit employee exposure. In addition, the restricted areas must be marked and equipped with caution signs. Regulated employers must undertake hazard surveys to evaluate radiation hazards and must also supply personal monitoring equipment to affected employees (and enforce use of such equipment). Storage of radioactive materials is also subject to requirements under the standard.

*Exit Route Standards (29 CFR 1910.33–1910.39)*

Finally, safety is an overriding concern in healthcare institutions because they have patients who are incapable of helping themselves in emergencies. Fire is one of the most dangerous emergencies. OSHA requires employers to have a written exit route plan for fire and other emergencies requiring evacuation. This OSHA standard requires employers to have exit routes planned out sufficiently for the number of people in a space and a posted diagram of evacuation routes. Evacuation training should be conducted for all employees. Your insurance company and/or local fire and police departments can help you develop evacuation routes.

In addition to the exit routes, your medical practice should have policies in place directing supervisors and employees on what to do and how to handle emergency situations, including natural disasters. Every employee should be notified about all emergency and disaster guidelines during orientation. Drills should be practiced at least once a year. The policies should also direct employees on how to help patients and visitors reach safety.

Different geographic regions in the country have different threats in terms of natural disasters. In California, for example, an earthquake emergency plan should be in place to protect employees and patients. Locations where tornadoes are common should have a plan for safety precautions when tornado warnings occur. Finally, coastal states should have evacuation plans for hurricanes and tropical storms.

*OSHA Posters*

OSHA requires all covered employers to post OSHA's posters in the workplace where employees can see them. The poster outlines the workers' rights and how to file a complaint with OSHA. Many states that have adopted their own workplace safety plans have poster equivalents. OSHA posters are available for download on OSHA's Website.

**Delegating Safety Responsibilities**

Most small practices choose to select an individual to be responsible for safety in the workplace. Larger medical practices may hire a safety officer for this role. Regardless of size, management should appoint a safety coordinator responsible for developing a comprehensive safety program suited to the group's particular needs and state and local laws.

Because much of safety and health compliance lies in providing educational safety and health training programs, oftentimes these safety functions must be combined with training. Safety incentive programs that encourage employee safe work practices are an effective way to ensure compliance with regulations. However, certain types of safety incentive programs that reward certain periods of time without workplace injury may result in the underreporting of workplace injuries and therefore violates the Occupational Safety and Health Act. Employees who do not follow the safety policies or do not report safety violations should be properly disciplined to ensure that safety regulations are followed.

## Employee Security

Because of vandalism, pilferage, theft, bomb scares, terrorism, and major incidences of workplace violence, most medical practices realize that securing their facilities and assets is very important. For example, the theft of business equipment, especially small items, is very costly to employers. Your medical practice's computers and networks present an entirely different area of security-related issues. In addition, workplace-related violence and other crimes have made security programs a top priority for employers.

Security programs involve taking precautionary measures to ensure adequate protection of the medical practice's property and assets, as well as those of its employees. Many healthcare managers have written and unwritten rules that range from "the last one out locks up at night" to contracting with security firms for surveillance. A medical practice's security needs vary depending on its location, the nature of its operations, and number of employees and patients. Some larger practices hire security consultants to develop and administer security programs.

To ensure the security of your practice's property and the safety of its employees and patients, employers should develop and maintain a security policy. The best security program cannot function effectively without the support of top management and the cooperation of all employees. At the very least, the medical practice should require employees to wear identification badges to prevent unauthorized entry and possible theft. Exterior doors should be secured at night, and doors to restricted areas should be secured at all times with a coded lock or a controlled-access badge programmed to unlock doors. All controlled substances kept at your practice must be kept in a secure place with only authorized individual access. Computer networking security should also be a top priority including controlled, authorized-only access for employees to protect sensitive information and scheduled automatic backups of data.

Issuing keys and access to any sensitive information stored in computers or on networks should be subject to tight security controls. Both should be issued only with management's approval and only to employees whose job duties require access. Employees should be reminded that all materials, including keys and practice and patient data, are the property of your practice and that they are responsible for safeguarding them. Keys should be returned and access to computers and networks should be discontinued immediately when an employee is terminated and before a final paycheck is issued. To be effective, security procedures must be periodically communicated to and reinforced with employees to keep them on alert.

Employee security policies generally include information technology (IT), computer security, and workplace violence. Many employers choose to have a policy focusing on appropriate use of the Internet and personal mobile devices, such as smartphones and tablets. Other areas to consider in your security policy are terrorism threats, bomb threats, and firearms. Policy 9.02 at the end of this chapter is a sample policy on security. A practice may adopt this policy, with necessary modifications to account for factors such as your practice's specific management philosophy, organizational needs, and staff size.

**IT and Computer Security**

One of the greatest security risks employers face today is around computer systems and data security. Although the threat of hackers and cyber terrorists is a major security risk, most computer system security breaches happen internally by unhappy or inattentive employees. It is very important to review your security software (e.g., antivirus and malware applications) and network security with your IT consultant to build a safety net against cyber criminals and human error.

Employee and patient privacy are also of high concern for medical practices as the prevalence of e-health and mobile health increases. Medical practices and healthcare organizations create and manage large amounts of highly sensitive and private data that needs to be protected at all costs. The Health Insurance Portability and Accountability Act (HIPAA) requires medical practices to protect the privacy and security of patient information. Therefore, medical practices must maintain secure and adequate IT systems and have management controls in place regarding system usage.

Medical practices can decrease their IT and computer security risks by developing strong policies, training staff on them, and ensuring consistent implementation. The computer systems security policies should include simple yet important protocols such as requiring employees to password-lock their computers when unattended. As mentioned previously, terminated employees should have system access revoked immediately. Policy 9.03 at the end of this chapter is a sample policy focusing on computer system security protocols. *Due to the sensitive and critical nature of this policy, it is highly advisable to require all employees to accept and sign this policy.*

*Personal Internet and Mobile Device Use*

The majority of employers have established policies that govern personal Internet usage. When employees use the Internet for personal reasons, productivity declines. Many employers use software that blocks employee access to certain Websites such as Facebook, Amazon, e-mail Websites, and so on. In addition, many employees now want to use their mobile devices, such as smartphones and tablets, to perform their job duties. Although this is not necessarily a negative transition, medical practices must protect themselves and their patients from security breaches and loss of productivity.

It is advisable to develop policies regarding acceptable Internet and mobile device usage. The social media explosion provides a new and unique method for medical practices to communicate with their patients; however, these networks have inherent risks. Policies regarding use of social media need to address the release of any potentially confidential information, including both private medical practice and patient information.

As mobile technology becomes more sophisticated and widespread, physicians, nurses, and other healthcare employees may wish to use their personal mobile devices in their jobs. Therefore, it is important for medical practices to update their human resources (HR) and HIPAA policies to ensure that employees are using their mobile devices for appropriate reasons and to ensure the security of the patient information and data exchanged. HIPAA regulations also apply to protecting patient privacy on mobile devices. Your policy for using mobile devices should include steps that must be taken to secure patient health information, including encryption and a plan if a device is lost or stolen. In addition, your practice should decide if it will provide mobile devices to employees who need them or allow those employees to use their personal mobile devices in the workplace. The use of personal mobile devices requires more security precautions than if your practice issues devices to employees specifically for work purposes.

The mobile device policy also needs to cover the use of cameras in the workplace. Because most, if not all, mobile devices have cameras, your practice must establish policies regarding acceptable use of them. For example, cameras should not be used to take pictures of private or confidential information. It is advisable to work with an IT consultant to determine which security measures should be in place before your medical practice allows the use of personal or practice-issued mobile devices when treating patients.

Policy 9.04 at the end of the chapter is a sample of an appropriate Internet use policy. In addition, Policy 9.05 is a sample policy for utilizing mobile devices for work-related purposes.

*Employee Monitoring*

As new technologies are introduced every day, finding the right balance between necessary monitoring and invasion of privacy is critical for employers. Employers have the right to monitor almost every aspect of an employee's communications. Employees want to believe that they and their personal information are protected, and they do not want to feel like they are being watched on the job every minute. However, employers want to know that their employees are properly preforming their jobs.

Different technologies allow employers to monitor virtually every communication channel at the employee's disposal. These include e-mail, voicemail, Internet usage, and telephones. There are a few laws and regulations restricting employee monitoring. The Electronic Communications Privacy Act of 1986 contains certain exceptions that have been interpreted to generally allow employers to monitor employees' e-mails as long as a policy for monitoring has been implemented informing employees of possible monitoring, and the monitoring is for a business-related purpose.

Employers generally monitor their employees because productivity decreases when employees use their computers and mobile devices for personal reasons. Medical practices should have a policy in place informing all employees of the types of media your practice will monitor. If no policy is in place, your practice may be susceptible to workplace privacy lawsuits by employees.

As with Internet and e-mail usage, employers may also monitor phone calls and voicemail. In most instances, employers monitor phone calls with customers for reasons of quality control. Some state laws, including California, require that the parties of the call be informed that the call is being recorded. However, federal laws do not require that any party be made aware of being recorded. It is critical to become familiar with your state laws to ensure compliance and reduce the risk of litigation.

Federal laws do provide privacy for personal calls. Federal laws may require employers to stop monitoring the call as soon as it is determined to be a personal call. However, if an employee has been informed to not make personal calls from work and the employer has a no-personal-calls policy, the employer may be able to monitor the call.

Employers may also monitor voicemail. Because the employer owns the voicemail system, the employer has the right to monitor it. The medical practice should inform all employees through a policy that your practice has the right to listen to an employee's voicemail. In addition, your practice should only use voicemail monitoring if it has a business-related reason for the monitoring. Employers should also inform employees in its policy that it has the right to and will monitor and record any conversation, voicemail, text message, or e-mail on any employer-issued device.

Employer monitoring rights and employee privacy rights recognized under the law are uncertain at this time due to constantly changing technology, laws, and court interpretations of such laws. Medical practices should consult with legal counsel to ensure that policies are up to date and in compliance with all applicable laws.

**Employee Privacy Protection**

Privacy is a person's right to keep personal information away from the world at large. However, an employee's desire for personal privacy sometimes conflicts with an employer's need to collect employment-related information and act on it. Workers do not want information about their private lives available to just anyone. They want control over what information an employer collects and who is able to examine it. Conversely, in an increasingly complex society, personal information is necessary to conduct business effectively.

This issue is particularly sensitive because the threat of cyber terrorism and hackers illegally accessing employee records kept on computer servers. Identity theft is a concern when protecting your employees' personal information, including names, addresses, Social Security numbers, and bank account information for direct deposit. Unprotected information can have a negative effect on employees.

Employee privacy protection is provided by a combination of federal and state legislation. The Fair Credit Reporting Act was passed in 1970 and allows employers to purchase credit reports from consumer reporting agencies for recruitment purposes with the consent of the job candidate. There is no federal law that dictates how a private employer protects its employees' personal private information. However, medical practices should cover privacy protection practices in their policies. As mentioned previously, employee personnel files should be kept securely with controlled access, and information from those files should only be released for a legitimate reason. All personal employee information should be considered private and confidential.

Developing and implementing the following strategies can help minimize the possibility for invasion of privacy claims.
- Develop a philosophy regarding employee privacy. Determine how you will be an appropriate protector of private employee information.
- Identify the competing interests of the employee, employer, and third parties concerning access to employee information, and work out a satisfactory balance among these interests.

- Determine which records and information will be kept in the employee files and by whom. In addition, consider which records will be kept in files outside the employee files.

- Understand your practice's legal duties with respect to employee privacy. Determine whether applicable state laws regulate employee access to employee files, what the applicable state laws are with respect to defamation and invasion of privacy, and what obligations your practice has to maintain confidentiality of employee health records.

- Examine access to employee information to ensure that only employees with a legitimate need to know have access to sensitive information. Review the procedures by which confidential information is verbally transmitted. Take steps to ensure that discussing private matters such as employee discipline take place only between the individuals who have a legitimate business reason to discuss the information.

Policies and procedures for handling employee records should be developed to attempt to reduce conflicts, litigation, and damage awards associated with privacy-related issues. See Chapter 7 for additional information on record-keeping issues. Policy 9.06 is a sample policy on employee data privacy protection. Because state and local laws vary and may affect the legal requirements, medical practices should be familiar with these laws as well.

### Patient Protected Health Information Privacy

Protecting patients' privacy and securing their health information is a critical component of the Medicare and Medicaid Electronic Health Records (EHR) Programs. Your practice is responsible and legally liable for the protection and security of protected health information (PHI). HIPAA established a set of rules and regulations regarding patient health information privacy and security. The HIPAA Privacy and Security Rules are a two-pronged approach to protecting patients' PHI. The Privacy Rule focuses on a patient's right to control use and disclosure of his or her PHI. The Security Rule addresses security safeguards and procedures necessary to protect a patient's electronic PHI from unauthorized access, use, or disclosure. The Health Information Technology for Economic and Clinical Health (HITECH) Act, part of the 2009 stimulus package (American Recovery and Reinvestment Act), amended and updated some of the requirements set out in HIPAA, including the "meaningful use" of EHRs as a requirement of Medicare and Medicaid reimbursement. Many states have adopted additional patient health information privacy and security legislation, so be aware of your state's specific laws and regulations. Following is a discussion of the HIPAA Privacy and Security Rules as they impact covered healthcare organizations and their security policies and procedures.

The HIPAA Privacy and Security Rules apply only to "covered entities" or healthcare organizations that bill or receive payment for healthcare in the normal course of business and transmit covered transactions electronically. These covered transactions include but are not limited to:

- Requests to obtain payment from a health plan for healthcare provided to a patient;

- Inquiries to a health plan to obtain information about a benefits plan enrollee involving eligibility, coverage, and associated benefits;

- Requests to obtain authorization for referring a patient to another healthcare provider;
- Requests for a claim status check; and
- Electronic transfers from a healthcare plan to a healthcare provider for an explanation of benefits and a remittance of advice.

The US Department of Health and Human Services (HHS) Website provides a Covered Entity Chart to help you determine whether your practice is a covered entity (www.hhs.gov).

The HIPAA Security Rule requires that covered entities ensure the confidentiality (i.e., PHI is neither accessible by nor disclosable to unauthorized persons), integrity (i.e., PHI is not alterable or destroyable in an unauthorized manner), and availability (i.e., PHI is accessible and usable as needed only to authorized persons) of all PHI they create, receive, maintain, or transmit. Secondly, covered entities must protect against any reasonably anticipated threats to the security or integrity of the PHI. Thirdly, your practice must protect against any reasonably anticipated, unpermitted use or disclosure of PHI. Lastly, your practice must ensure compliance among its employees.

**Protected Health Information includes:**

- Names;
- Contact information including addresses, phone numbers, e-mail addresses, etc.;
- Social Security numbers;
- Dates other than years such as date of birth;
- Medical record numbers;
- Health insurance beneficiary numbers; and
- Account numbers.

The Security Rule requires covered entities to develop and maintain policies and procedures documenting the security standards. The rule lays out 18 standards that must be implemented by covered entities and 36 implementation specifications. The key standards are highlighted here. Familiarize yourself with all of the standards and implementation specification requirements for your practice by using the HHS Website (www.hhs.gov). These requirements fall into three categories:

1. Administrative safeguards;
2. Physical safeguards; and
3. Technical safeguards.

Many of the required policies and procedures for PHI security are woven through all three safeguard categories. The key requirements that covered entities must develop and implement are discussed in the following paragraphs.

The administrative safeguards are the required policies and procedures to manage the security process, including the conduct of employees. The physical safeguards focus on the policies and procedures required to protect the PHI systems from natural and environmental hazards and intrusions, including hacking. Technical safeguards are the technologies and policies that protect PHI and control access to it.

All covered entities are required to perform a risk analysis to evaluate the likelihood and impact of potential risks to electronically stored PHI. Covered entities then must implement and maintain appropriate security measures to reasonably address the risks. Covered entities must document the implemented security measures and rationale for adopting the selected measures. This risk analysis is an ongoing process in which a covered entity must continuously track access to electronic PHI, detect security incidents, report to the appropriate authorities if necessary, periodically review the security measures' effectiveness, and regularly reevaluate potential risks.

A covered entity is required to designate an employee as the security official with the responsibilities of developing and implementing security policies, procedures, and protocols. In addition, covered entities must develop and implement security training and awareness programs for all employees, including management.

Additionally, the covered entity must develop and implement policies and procedures that address the following areas:
- Providing authorized employees access to PHI, including which employees will have access and which will not;
- Technology allowing only authorized users access to PHI;
- Specific functions that can be performed using PHI;
- Disciplinary actions if an employee does not comply with PHI policies;
- Plans to address and correct security incidents;
- Contingency plans for dealing with damaged systems containing PHI;
- Limited physical access to the information systems and the facility in which they are housed;
- Physical attributes of a workstation with access to PHI to restrict access to authorized users;
- Receipt, movement, and removal of hardware and/or electronic media that contains PHI; and
- Technological mechanisms that monitor and examine activity in systems to contain PHI.

For more detailed information regarding patients' PHI, go to the HHS's Office of Civil Rights Website (www.hhs.gov/ocr). Policy 9.07 at the end of the chapter is a sample Patient Protected Health Information Privacy policy.

### Workplace Violence and Harassment
Medical practices must commit to providing a safe and harassment-free workplace for employees to work. Obviously, a work environment free of violence and harassment is critical to employee safety, morale, and retention.

*Workplace Violence*
Although there is no single definition for workplace violence, violent behavior generally includes any physical touching that is intended to or does inflict injury on another, including but not limited to the use of a weapon against another individual. Violent behavior also includes stalking or intimidating a person, making physical or verbal threats, and intentionally destroying the property of another. Workplace violence can be

homicide, assault, physical abuse, and threats occurring in a place of work, jeopardizing a victim's safety, health, and well-being.

Experts warn that in most cases where violence has occurred, there were indicators of potential or impending violence before it actually happened. Ineffective or incompetent management contributes to workplace violence by:

- Not promptly responding to pre-employment warning signs or clues of future violence;
- Not admitting that a potentially violent situation has occurred;
- Not following up after warning behaviors;
- Not communicating an expectation of self-control to the involved employee; and
- Not communicating that the employee will be held responsible for his or her inappropriate and unacceptable behavior.

The emotional and psychological toll on employees subjected to workplace violence can be devastating. An employer's work effectiveness and productivity may be severely damaged. In addition to physical and emotional costs, workplace violence can have a dramatic impact on an employer's financial resources. Workplace violence also affects workers' morale and productivity, increases absenteeism, promotes worker turnover, and raises costs for security and Workers' Compensation.

Accordingly, practices should have a violence-free workplace policy strictly prohibiting violent or threatening behavior toward employees, patients, or vendors at any time while on a practice's property, during or after work hours, or while an employee is engaged in work. Medical practices should consider prohibiting the possession of weapons on company property to the extent permitted by law. Any violence-free workplace policy should encourage employees who are threatened, overhear a threat, or who observe any suspicious activity to immediately report the threat or suspicious activity.

*Workplace Harassment*
Practices should prohibit unlawful harassment, including unlawfully intimidating, hostile, or offensive conduct. Practices should also consider prohibiting conduct that might lead to unlawful harassment.

Prohibited conduct should include verbal, visual, or physical conduct that (1) relates to another person's sex, race, color, national origin, religion, disability, genetic information, age, or other status protected by law; or (2) is directed toward another person because of that person's sex, race, color, national origin, religion, disability, genetic information, age, or other status protected by law, where such conduct may have the purpose or effect of unreasonably interfering with an individual's work performance or creating an intimidating, hostile, or offensive working environment.

Some examples of prohibited harassment include telling racist or sexist jokes or making offensive or derogatory remarks about another person's race, ancestry, national origin, age, genetic information, or disability.

Prohibited conduct includes sexual harassment but is not limited to conduct that may constitute or lead to sexual harassment, such as use of suggestive sexual comments, jokes, or innuendo; persistent, unwanted flirtation or invitations for dates or other social activities; unwelcome sexual advances or passes; sexual remarks or questions about a person's body, clothing, or sexual activities; patting, pinching, or other offensive touching; or displays of sexually suggestive pictures or objects. Sexually harassing conduct may include conduct between persons of the same gender, regardless of the sexual preference of those persons.

Practices should understand that prohibited conduct may occur not only through personal contact, comments, visual displays, or observation, but also through exposure to media such as e-mail or display of Internet sites or other material or information on computer monitors.

Practices must have and enforce a harassment-free workplace policy. Such a policy must clearly define prohibited conduct as well as persons covered by the policy (including non-employees), outline a procedure for complaints, and strictly prohibit retaliation against any victim of or witness to harassment who makes a complaint or participates in an investigation of a complaint.

*Preventing Workplace Violence and Harassment*
On the whole, medical practices that have employees who enjoy their work, peers, patients, supervisors, and management usually have a lower occurrence rate of workplace violence and harassment.

Characteristics of at-risk work environments include medical practices with:
- A strict, authoritarian management style;
- Numerous grievances filed;
- Many disciplinary actions and/or terminations;
- Inconsistent, inequitable, or insensitive management;
- Chronic labor/management disputes;
- Multiple injury claims;
- Frequent layoffs and downsizing;
- Disgruntled employees;
- Interpersonal conflicts on the job; and
- Failure to recognize and intervene early in the cycle of violence.

Federal and state occupational safety and health agencies have taken an aggressive stance on enforcing an employer's statutory duty to provide employees with a working environment free of harm and violence. In addition, some states have implemented statutory mandates that ensure employers take precautions to minimize workplace violence.

As indicated previously, medical practices can protect the workplace by developing and enforcing strong workplace anti-violence and anti-harassment policies and procedures for anticipating, handling, and investigating potential violence or harassment. Such policies should provide proper guidance and communication channels for supervisors and employees who may be exposed to violence or harassment in the workplace.

When developing workplace violence and harassment prevention programs and policies, consider the following strategies:

- Designate a manager or managers who are responsible for creating, evaluating, and ensuring implementation of the employer's workplace violence and/or harassment prevention programs;
- Train supervisors and department heads on skills to anticipate and analyze potential problems, recognizing signs of potential conflict, and responding to potentially volatile situations to prevent escalation;
- Educate employees about the potential danger of workplace violence and the proper procedures for reporting or voicing concerns of violence and harassment;
- Develop procedures for investigating all complaints of employee indiscretions and work incidents that indicate a potential for violence or harassment;
- Establish procedures for pre-employment screening by conducting background and criminal checks of job applicants, if appropriate, and to the extent permitted by law;
- Implement procedures for alerting local law enforcement agencies when appropriate; and
- Consult legal counsel to ensure that all policies, procedures, and practices are in compliance with applicable law.

Supervisors and department heads should be specifically trained to recognize the signs of potential violence and harassment. Reporting procedures should be clearly known throughout your practice. All employees should know to whom to report violence, harassment, and/or threats within your practice. In addition, to comply with federal and state laws, your medical practice must not tolerate any type of retaliation against any employee who makes a good-faith report or complaint or participates in an investigation of a report or complaint of workplace harassment.

Policies 9.08 and 9.09 are sample workplace violence and harassment policies. Your practice can adopt these policies, with necessary modifications to take into account your practice's specific management philosophy, organizational needs, and staff size. Because state laws vary and may affect the legal requirements, your medical practice should be familiar with these laws. In addition, Forms 9.1 through 9.3 at the end of this chapter can be modified to suit your medical practice's needs when reporting and interviewing complainants and witnesses regarding workplace harassment.

*Employee Searches*
Employee investigations often become necessary when an employee has committed misconduct, exhibited poor work performance, engaged in violent or threatening behavior, or otherwise raised suspicions that they are unfit and possibly dangerous. Employers have a legal obligation to investigate all credible information indicating that an employee poses a potential risk of violence. This obligation might include conducting employee searches and using surveillance and monitoring of communications.

Managerial guidelines should clearly define when, where, and how your practice may conduct searches of an employee's person or personal property. Employees should be notified that their person and personal property may be subjected to search by the employer at any time. The employer should retain the right to search all computers, e-mail, voice messages, text messages, lockers, offices, filing cabinets, desks, or vehicles brought onto your practice's property to the extent permitted by law.

## Employee Health

Employee health programs are often overlooked for safety and security. However, the health of your practice's employees can be equally as important. When employees feel their best, they perform at their best. Furthermore, when something is bothering or troubling employees, it is difficult to focus on work. Medical practices should implement employee health programs and services that help employees live healthier lives, both at home and at work.

### Employee Wellness Programs

Employee wellness programs generally focus on promoting healthy lifestyle choices and physical activity. Effective wellness programs motivate, educate, and empower employees to make decisions that have a positive impact on the working environment. Wellness programs can be designed in any manner, depending on the size of your practice. Some large practices offer wellness programs in addition to the employee benefit plans. Small medical practices may offer the option of a wellness program as part of the benefits plan.

Workplace wellness programs cover a wide range of options. They may promote healthy lifestyles, provide personal trainers, offer health club memberships, provide volunteer or community service opportunities, or offer programs for fighting addictions. Practices may delegate the coordination of a wellness program to the designated HR professional or outside consultants as appropriate.

### Substance Abuse

It is becoming standard practice, particularly in healthcare, for employers to create a drug-free work environment. Drug and alcohol use at work can increase the risk of workplace violence. Nationwide we are facing increasing health problems associated with drug and alcohol use. Employees who use and/or abuse drugs and alcohol, including smoking, usually take more sick days, are involved in more accidents resulting in injury, and have an increased chance of making a mistake. Your medical practice should develop policies regarding the use of drugs and alcohol in the workplace. A substance abuse policy is critical because if an employee makes a mistake treating a patient while under the influence of drugs or alcohol, your medical practice could be held liable.

Policies on substance abuse, including alcohol, should cover the following items:
- Use of drugs or alcohol during work hours or in the workplace;
- Use of prescription medications or over-the-counter drugs that inhibit dexterity or thought processes;
- Disciplinary actions;
- Drug testing of current employees;
- Confidentiality of drug test results; and
- Consequences if an employee refuses a drug test.

Policy 9.10 at the end of the chapter is a sample policy focusing on substance abuse.

*Smoking Cessation Programs*

The right to smoke in the workplace is a controversial and compelling employment issue. Many state and local laws require public places, including workplaces, to be smoke free. Medical practices should have policies that outline when and where employees can smoke. Medical practices have the right to prohibit employees from smoking at work. However, medical practices should keep in mind that certain state and local laws prohibit employment discrimination against employees on the basis of participation in lawful off-duty activities, including smoking and tobacco use. No matter how your medical practice views this issue, an in-depth knowledge of state and local laws regarding smoking and lawful off-duty activities is essential to drafting an appropriate policy.

Employers are constantly fighting the increased cost of providing group health coverage and reducing the costs by trying to eliminate "high risk" employees. Smokers generally have higher-than-average health insurance premiums. Many insurance plans and organizations will offer a monetary incentive for nonsmoking employees or employees who quit.

Many employers also offer employees who smoke assistance when trying to quit. Medical practices can provide contact information for support groups or information regarding programs and seminars specializing in fighting nicotine addictions. Policy 9.11 is a sample policy about smoking while on the job.

## Employee Assistance Programs

Employee Assistance Programs (EAPs) were devised to help employees deal with personal problems that affect job performance and absenteeism. These programs positively impact employee morale and performance among staff. EAPs can refer employees to agencies outside of the workplace for treatment and rehabilitation. EAPs typically provide:

- Alcohol abuse rehabilitation;
- Drug abuse rehabilitation;
- Emotional counseling;
- Family and marital counseling;
- Legal counseling; and
- Many other employee benefits.

## Injuries on the Job

When employees are unable to work because of an accident or health-related problem, employers may offer short-term and long-term disability leave. In addition, various disability income continuation programs provide weekly or monthly payment instead of an employee's regular earned income. The level of disability benefits is set below an employee's normal rate of pay to provide an incentive for him or her to return to work upon recovery. Disability leave may also be impacted by the Family and Medical Leave Act or the Americans with Disabilities Act if your practice is a covered employer under either statute. State or local laws may also apply.

*Short-Term Disability*

Short-term disability insurance plans typically provide payment for as many as 26 weeks while the insured employee is absent from work due to an accident or illness. The benefits provided by these plans usually range from 50 to 80 percent of the employee's base pay, and most plans have a waiting period before payment begins. During this period, the employee typically uses sick leave. For example, many plans have a three- to seven-day waiting period for sickness. With a seven-day waiting period, the employee does not collect any benefits until the eighth day of absence due to illness. Frequently, no waiting period is necessary for an accident or Workers' Compensation claim. Some states require employers to provide short-term disability insurance for employees.

*Long-Term Disability*

Long-term disability insurance is a method of providing certain employees who cannot work for an extended period of time with partial income replacement. These employees probably are the most in need of assistance because they have the burden of additional medical expenses along with reduced or lost income.

Many long-term disability plans are funded in conjunction with the medical practice's pension plan, although some plans use self-insurance funding procedures. Long-term disability for a large practice averages three to five years of coverage. Long-term benefits usually replace 50 to 80 percent of the employee's base pay. Some practices offer this as a paid benefit. Others link employees interested in such a benefit with an insurance broker.

*Workers' Compensation*

Workers' Compensation laws were adopted to reduce the need for an employee injured on the job to litigate in order to receive monetary awards. All states have a Workers' Compensation law that applies to all employers with employees. Workers' Compensation benefits are the exclusive remedy for employees who are injured within the course and scope of employment. Workers' Compensation laws also provide benefits for surviving dependents of employees who are fatally injured on the job. State laws vary tremendously. Practices should become familiar with the state and local laws regarding Workers' Compensation.

## Summary

Medical practices should have policies that protect employees from dangerous environments, health threats, and security breaches. Safety is so important that your medical practice should appoint an individual to be responsible for workplace safety. Employees should be trained on all policies regarding workplace safety, on-the-job injuries, evacuation plans, and reporting security breaches.

Another area of concern that needs to be addressed is workplace violence and harassment. Each medical practice needs to have policies about how to handle workplace violence and harassment and provide supervisory training on how to recognize and manage threatening and harassing behaviors that could be a potential threat to maintain a safe and productive workplace environment.

Lastly, employee wellness programs are a proactive and positive approach to assisting employees to perform at their peak and to maintain a highly productive workforce.

Providing some kind of wellness assistance to your employees with health club member-ships, weight management programs, employee assistance programs, smoking cessation programs, and the like can increase employee loyalty and improve overall performance.

## Sample Policies

**Policy 9.01**    ### Employee Safety and Health

This is an example of an employee safety and health policy. *This suggested policy is for educational and illustrative purposes only. The particular laws of each state may differ, and this suggested general policy should not be implemented without considering applicable federal, state, and local laws. In addition, this suggested general policy should not be implemented without consulting your practice's attorneys and tailoring the policy to your specific needs and issues.*

---

**POLICY 9.01**       **EMPLOYEE SAFETY AND HEALTH**

Purpose: To establish and maintain guidelines for employee safety and health.

Applies to: All *[Practice]* employees.

Policy: The policy of *[Practice]* is to provide safe and healthful working conditions for all employees. To do so, *[Practice]* complies with all applicable safety and health laws as well as fire codes. *[Practice]* also develops the most feasible operating policies and procedures to provide such conditions. Employees are expected to comply with safety and health requirements, whether established by management or by federal, state, or local laws. Employees who violate this policy may be subject to disciplinary action, including termination of employment.

Procedures:
1. Management maintains ongoing programs at all levels to identify, mitigate, and/or eliminate occupational safety and health risks.
2. Management makes mitigating and eliminating such risks a top priority, including providing the necessary resources to implement safety and health programs.
3. Management limits and reduces employee exposure to occupational safety and health risks.
4. Top management appoints a manager as the Safety Coordinator responsible for coordinating safety-related activities. The Safety Coordinator is responsible for complying with applicable safety and health standards established by the Occupational Safety and Health Administration (OSHA) and other federal or state agencies. The Safety Coordinator investigates, evaluates, corrects, and minimizes and/or eliminates unsafe and unhealthy working conditions and also conducts periodic informal safety and health inspections of work areas. The Safety Coordinator is responsible for developing and communicating written safety guidelines to supervisors and investigating accidents. This person complies with OSHA requirements including, but not limited to, record-keeping and retention of records.

5. The Safety Coordinator develops training for employees and trains supervisors on health and safety guidelines, standards, and precautions. In addition, this person trains supervisors so they can in turn train their staff members.

6. The Safety Coordinator is responsible for implementing a written fire and evacuation plan and, at least annually, conducting emergency evacuation exercises with local fire and police authorities.

7. The Safety Coordinator is responsible for developing and implementing written plans and training programs for natural disasters (earthquake, flood, tornado, hurricane, landslide, etc.) and medical emergencies.

8. The Safety Coordinator is responsible for implementing and annually updating a written bloodborne pathogens exposure control plan (which must be updated annually) and a written hazard communication program.

9. Supervisors are responsible for protecting the health and safety of their staff members by inspecting the work area under their control, being familiar with safety and health guidelines and procedures, and training employees in health and safety precautions.

10. Management establishes a safety idea program and creates appropriate rewards and recognition for employees whose ideas significantly improve the safety of the workplace.

11. It is *[Practice's]* philosophy that health and safety is the responsibility of each employee. Therefore, the following behaviors or items are prohibited or restricted to the areas indicated below:

    • Portable heaters are prohibited;

    • Coffee makers, refrigerators, microwave ovens, slow cookers, and other heat- or cold-producing appliances are prohibited except in break areas, kitchens, or conference rooms set up for serving meals;

    • Candles, lanterns, incense, and open flames are prohibited;

    • Holiday decorations made of combustible materials, including but not limited to natural trees or wreaths, are prohibited; and

    • Decorations of any kind must not be hung from or in any way impede the operation of fire sprinklers.

12. All employees whose job duties involve direct patient care, handling used medical equipment, or exposure to bodily fluids including but not limited to blood, tissue, and waste are offered the hepatitis B vaccine within 10 days of employment at no cost to them. Employees who refuse the vaccine must sign a waiver and affidavit verifying their refusal.

13. The Safety Coordinator is responsible for developing a written tuberculosis control plan in accordance to the National Institute of Occupational Safety and Health (NIOSH) guidelines.

14. Every employee is responsible for immediately reporting violations of health and safety procedures to the Safety Coordinator.

15. Every employee is responsible for immediately reporting any accidents resulting in injury to the injured employee's supervisor and to the Safety Coordinator. Injuries include any incidents or contaminated needle/instrument punctures, lacerations, or significant exposure to blood, body secretions and fluids, or tissue from employees or patients.

Approved by: Practice Administrator

Effective date: 1/1/20__

**Policy 9.02**      **Security**

This is an example of a security policy. *This suggested policy is for educational and illustrative purposes only. The particular laws of each state may differ, and this suggested general policy should not be implemented without considering applicable federal, state, and local laws. In addition, this suggested general policy should not be implemented without consulting your practice's attorneys.*

---

**POLICY 9.02**                  **SECURITY**

<u>Purpose:</u> To establish and maintain guidelines for *[Practice]* and employee security.

<u>Applies to:</u> All *[Practice]* employees.

<u>Policy:</u> The policy of *[Practice]* is to provide appropriate security for its employees and *[Practice]* property.

<u>Procedures:</u>

1. Management develops a security program that protects employees and patients, as well as *[Practice]* property and assets.

2. Top management appoints a manager as the Security Coordinator responsible for *[Practice's]* security program and initiatives.

3. Management provides employee training and retraining on security policies and procedures and on employees' security responsibilities.

4. Employees are required to comply with all security policies and procedures.

5. Employees are issued identification (ID) badges, which must be visibly worn at all times while on the premises during working hours.

6. *[Practice]* keys are issued only to employees whose duties require the use of keys. Employees must return all keys, ID badges, and other *[Practice]* property before they are issued a final paycheck.

7. Only authorized employees are allowed to enter the facilities during nonworking hours.

8. Management discourages visits to *[Practice]* by family and friends of employees. Management prohibits personal visitors in work areas.

9. Possession of any weapons on *[Practice]* property, including parking areas, is prohibited. Weapons include any object capable of causing serious bodily harm or death to another and may include but are not limited to all firearms, air pistols or air rifles, knives, or any other weapon or device that could be used as a tool of violence.

10. Hazardous materials and toxic agents on site must be securely locked with authorized-only, controlled access. Employees without access to hazardous materials or toxic agents are prohibited from possessing them.

11. Unauthorized opening of or tampering with locks, duplication of keys issued by *[Practice]*, or unauthorized access to a facility, or restricted or locked areas is prohibited.

12. Tampering with electronic security or life safety equipment (e.g., security cameras, security detection devices, fire extinguishing and fire detection equipment) is prohibited.

<u>Approved by:</u> Practice Administrator

<u>Effective date:</u> 1/1/20__

**Policy 9.03**      **Computer System Security**

This is an example of a computer system security policy. *This policy is separate from your practice's HIPAA privacy and security policies. This suggested policy is for educational and illustrative purposes only. The particular laws of each state may differ, and this suggested general policy should not be implemented without considering applicable federal, state, and local laws. In addition, this suggested general policy should not be implemented without consulting your practice's attorneys.*

---

**POLICY 9.03**                 **COMPUTER SYSTEM SECURITY**

Purpose: To establish and maintain guidelines for computer system security.

Applies to: All *[Practice]* employees.

Policy: *[Practice's]* policy is to protect the security of *[Practice]*-owned computer systems and equipment, including but not limited to computers, computer systems, e-mail systems, network equipment, storage devices, computer files, operating systems, and databases. All employees must read, accept, and agree to this policy prior to accessing *[Practice's]* computer or e-mail systems.

Procedures:

1.  Users of *[Practice's]* computer systems and other resources are expected to access systems, databases, or other information only to the extent required to perform work-related duties.

2.  It is the responsibility of each employee to ensure that *[Practice's]* computer systems are used for proper business purposes and in a manner that does not compromise the confidentiality of protected health information or proprietary or other sensitive information.

3.  *[Practice]* will allow minimal personal use of *[Practice]*-issued desktops, laptops, telephones, printers, faxes, and other office equipment to the extent that its use does not interfere with or limit *[Practice's]* operations, the employee's ability to perform their job duties, or does not violate any *[Practice]* policy.

4.  Users should never disable antivirus or malware programs, click on a link or open an attachment in an unfamiliar e-mail, or open an e-mail from an unknown sender to avoid malware or viruses from loading unexpectedly onto computers. If a user suspects their computer or system has been infected, the user should notify his or her supervisor immediately and stop using the system.

5.  All users are required to use a user ID and password to access *[Practice's]* computer systems. Users are accountable for any activity associated with their user IDs and passwords. Users may not under any circumstances provide their password to another person or use another person's user ID or password. Users must change their passwords every 60 days or at any time a compromise of the password is suspected. Users must not write down or store passwords. Passwords should not include any word found in the dictionary or any easily guessable word.

6. To avoid theft or unauthorized access to *[Practice]* computer systems, users must activate a password-protected screen saver by locking their computer when stepping away from their workstation. Users must log or sign off at the end of each workday.

7. Users may not access, research, or change any account, record, file, or application that is not required to perform their job duties.

8. Users are prohibited from installing any software or hardware on *[Practice]* systems without the approval of management.

9. Users may not modify or tamper with hardware or software provided by *[Practice]*.

10. Users may not modify or destroy any information required to be retained for legal purposes or which is subject to a legal hold.

11. Users using computer systems to access, use, or disclose patient information must also follow the Health Insurance Portability and Accountability Act (HIPAA) and other data privacy and security policies of *[Practice]*.

12. Employees do not have a personal privacy right or expectation of privacy in any matter created, received, viewed, sent, or stored on a *[Practice]* computer, or from using *[Practice's]* e-mail system or network, whether or not the matter is designated as private or confidential.

13. *[Practice]* monitors its computer systems and may read and copy any and all files or data contained on any computer, including but not limited to e-mail messages and personal file directories, at any time and without prior notice.

14. *[Practice]* maintains full access to all computer systems for the purpose of ensuring compliance with legal requirements as well as *[Practice]* policies, supporting the performance of internal investigations, and assisting with the management of *[Practice's]* information systems.

15. An employee's failure to comply with this policy may lead to disciplinary actions including but not limited to restriction of access, revocation of privileges, termination, or legal action.

I have read, understand, and hereby consent to this policy.


_____          _____

 Employee Signature                                              Date


Approved by: Practice Administrator

Effective date: 1/1/20__

**Policy 9.04**      **Appropriate Internet Use**

This is an example of an Internet use policy. *This suggested policy is for educational and illustrative purposes only. The particular laws of each state may differ, and this suggested general policy should not be implemented without considering applicable federal, state, and local laws. In addition, this suggested general policy should not be implemented without consulting your practice's attorneys.*

---

POLICY 9.04                          **APPROPRIATE
                                      INTERNET USE**

Purpose: To establish and maintain guidelines for appropriate Internet use.

Applies to: All *[Practice]* employees.

Policy: *[Practice]* is dedicated to providing its employees with the most technologically advanced tools to perform their job functions. Along with this goal comes the need for restrictions for appropriate usage of the Internet. All employees must read, accept, and agree to this policy prior to accessing *[Practice]* information and Internet resources.

Procedures:
1.  Access to the Internet is provided to facilitate and further the following objectives:
    *   *[Practice]* business activity and communications;
    *   Research and development;
    *   Employee education related to job duties; and
    *   General information gathering associated with being well informed about medical, business, governmental, and public affairs.
2.  Acceptable uses of the Internet are:
    *   Accessing Websites containing business-related data;
    *   Exchanges of e-mail messages with a patient, vendor, or business partner for *[Practice]*-related matters; and
    *   Minimal use of Internet for personal reasons, as long as the use does not violate any other part of this policy or any other *[Practice]* policy. All Web and e-mail traffic is subject to monitoring and retention.
3.  *[Practice]* will allow minimal personal use of *[Practice]*-issued desktops, laptops, telephones, printers, faxes, and other office equipment to the extent that such use does not interfere with or limit *[Practice's]* operations or the employee's ability to perform their job duties, and such use does not violate any *[Practice]* policy.
4.  Employees do not have a personal privacy right or expectation of privacy in any matter created, received, viewed, sent, or stored on a *[Practice]* computer, or using *[Practice's]* e-mail system or network, whether or not the matter is designated as private or confidential.
5.  *[Practice]* monitors Internet usage, e-mails, voice messages, and phone calls at its discretion in the ordinary course of business.
6.  Employees may not send any e-mail, unless encrypted, that contains private, sensitive, or confidential information, including but not limited to *[Practice]* information or specific patient data.

7. The use of computer systems or e-mail accounts not provided by *[Practice]*, for use in conducting *[Practice]* business, is prohibited.

8. Employees are prohibited from using instant messaging systems not provided by *[Practice]* and accessing non-*[Practice]* e-mail accounts from *[Practice's]* computer system.

9. Using e-mail or any other electronic communications to send offensive, threatening, or otherwise inappropriate information is strictly prohibited. E-mail should not be used to solicit outside business ventures or for any political or religious purpose, unless approved in advance by *[Practice]*.

10. Use of social media Websites are blocked for *[Practice]* employees. Social media refers to any Internet communication that may be accessed publicly such as social networking sites, bulletin boards, blogs, microblogs, chat rooms, and so on. Unless required by job or work assignment duties, employees are prohibited from:

    - Using *[Practice]* resources to connect to social networking sites such as Facebook, Twitter, etc.;

    - Using *[Practice]* resources for personal bulletin board messaging, updating wikis, or blogging, including audio and video blogs, podcasts, and video podcasts; and

    - Using *[Practice]* resources to join Internet chat-room conversations, forums, mailing lists, etc.

11. Employees who must access social media Websites for job-related duties must receive approval from management.

12. Employees who engage in the use of online social media are expected to adhere to all applicable *[Practice]* policies at all times. Further, employees must comply with the following rules whenever using social media:

    - Do not use or disclose protected health information;

    - Do not misuse *[Practice]* time and resources;

    - Do not make false statements;

    - Do not make unauthorized statements on behalf of *[Practice]*; and

    - Be professional and respectful.

13. Employees may not access Websites deemed by *[Practice]* to be inappropriate for the workplace. Such sites include, but are not limited to, pornography or other sexually explicit material, hate speech and other potentially violent or other criminal activity, and gambling. *[Practice]* may block without notice any sites deemed inappropriate. Employees should avoid attempting to access blocked Websites as *[Practice]* may monitor user attempts to access blocked sites and may initiate disciplinary action as deemed appropriate. Some Websites that include inappropriate or objectionable content may not be blocked. Employees are expected to exercise good judgment in evaluating whether particular Website content is appropriate for the workplace.

14. Failure to comply with this policy and the policies and standards derived from it may lead to disciplinary action up to and including termination or legal action.

I have read, understand, and hereby agree to follow this policy.

_____        _____
Employee Signature                                               Date


Approved by: Practice Administrator

Effective date 1/1/20

**Policy 9.05**     ### Appropriate Use of Mobile Devices

This is an example of a mobile device policy. *This policy is separate from a practice's HIPAA privacy and security policies. This suggested policy is for educational and illustrative purposes only. The particular laws of each state may differ, and this suggested general policy should not be implemented without considering applicable federal, state, and local laws. In addition, this suggested general policy should not be implemented without consulting your practice's attorneys.*

---

POLICY 9.05             **APPROPRIATE USE OF
                        MOBILE DEVICES**

<u>Purpose:</u> To establish and maintain guidelines for usage of mobile devices.

<u>Applies to:</u> All *[Practice]* employees.

<u>Policy:</u> *[Practice]* is dedicated to providing its employees with the most technologically advanced tools to perform their job functions. To do this, *[Practice]* may issue mobile devices, including but not limited to iPhones, Blackberries, Android devices, iPads, tablets, and so forth. In addition, under certain circumstances, *[Practice]* may allow employees to use their personal mobile devices for work-related purposes with restrictions. Along with this goal comes the need for restrictions for appropriate usage of *[Practice]*-issued and personal mobile devices.

<u>Procedures:</u>
1. *[Practice]* will only issue mobile devices to employees on a case-by-case basis as approved by management.
2. Employees who choose to use a personal mobile device for *[Practice]*-related purposes must obtain prior approval from management. If approval is given, employees must agree to all security measures required by *[Practice]* including the possible deletion of personal data, pictures, music, videos, and other private property should the device be lost or stolen.
3. Employees with a *[Practice]*-issued mobile device may not use a personal device to conduct *[Practice]* business. Employees should limit the use of *[Practice]*-issued mobile devices to work-related purposes.
4. All mobile devices used for *[Practice]*-related purposes must be protected with a password or passcode.
5. All mobile devices and services purchased by *[Practice]* will be billed directly to *[Practice]*. Employees should incur only necessary, appropriate, and reasonable expenses on *[Practice]*-issued devices.
6. Conversion of personal phone numbers to *[Practice]*-issued mobile devices and conversion of work phone numbers to personal mobile devices are prohibited.
7. All *[Practice]* policies, including but not limited to policies regarding personal data privacy, confidential information, patient protected health information, appropriate Internet and e-mail use, computer security, workplace violence, and harassment, apply to all mobile devices used in the workplace.
8. Information exchanged using a *[Practice]*-issued mobile device may be reviewed by *[Practice]* (e.g., e-mail, text or chat messages) in accordance with the Appropriate Internet Use and Computer System Security policies.

9. Employees are prohibited from downloading applications to their *[Practice]*-issued mobile devices unless approved by management.

10. The use of cameras in the workplace is restricted, including camera phones or other handheld devices containing camera functions. Under no circumstances is an employee authorized to use a camera to capture, store, or transmit confidential or private *[Practice]* data, including patient health information. Personal devices with a camera function should not be used or be visible in the workplace and must be stored accordingly.

11. Under no circumstances may an employee use a mobile device to capture, store, or transmit confidential or private *[Practice]* data, including patient protected health information.

12. Employees are solely responsible for their *[Practice]*-issued devices and for actions taken while operating the devices. *[Practice]* requires employees with *[Practice]*-issued mobile devices to protect them from loss, damage, or theft.

13. If a *[Practice]*-issued mobile device or a personal mobile device approved for work-related use is lost or stolen, the employee must immediately notify management to report the loss and suspend the service.

14. Employees are expected to use a hands-free device or refrain from using mobile devices while driving on *[Practice]* business and/or during working hours. Under no circumstances are employees allowed to place themselves at risk to fulfill business needs. Employees charged with traffic violations, including those resulting from use of their mobile devices while driving, will be solely responsible for all liabilities arising from such actions.

15. *[Practice]* is not liable for personal mobile devices brought into the workplace.

16. Employees should not use personal mobile devices during working hours except as approved by *[Practice]*, and they should ensure that friends and family members are aware of this policy. Flexibility will be provided in emergencies or other circumstances demanding immediate attention.

17. Failure to comply with this policy and the policies and standards derived from it may lead to legal liability and disciplinary action.

Approved by: Practice Administrator

Effective date: 1/1/20__

**Policy 9.06**        **Personal Data Privacy**

This is an example of a personal data privacy policy. *This suggested policy is for educational and illustrative purposes only. The particular laws of each state may differ, and this suggested general policy should not be implemented without considering applicable federal, state, and local laws. In addition, this suggested general policy should not be implemented without consulting your practice's attorneys.*

---

POLICY 9.06                        **PERSONAL**
                                   **DATA PRIVACY**

Purpose: To establish and maintain guidelines for personal data privacy.

Applies to: All *[Practice]* employees.

Policy: The policy of *[Practice]* is to protect the confidentiality and security of personal data that *[Practice]* may have so as to provide privacy for the individual employee. In addition, it is the policy of *[Practice]* to create and retain all records according to applicable federal, state, and local laws.

Procedures:

1. *[Practice]* will collect, create, and maintain personal employment-related data in compliance with applicable employment and data protection laws.

2. *[Practice]* will collect personal data from applicants and employees through employment applications, employee information forms, Websites, the telephone, e-mail, facsimiles, background checks, and various other sources.

3. Personal data includes but is not limited to name, address, phone number, Social Security number, birth date, marital status, bank account information, wage and salary information, performance reviews, disciplinary reports, and other records regarding job-related events during and after employment.

4. *[Practice]* collects and processes personal data for many reasons including:
   - Payroll administration;
   - Administration of all human resources, employee compensation and benefits, and employment programs;
   - Recruitment, staffing, and selection of individuals for positions;
   - Planning changes in organizational structure and managerial roles;
   - Leaves of absence and attendance records;
   - Contact with next of kin;
   - Performance evaluation and management;
   - Disciplinary and/or grievance proceedings;
   - Training and development;
   - Access control and other security measures;

- Compliance with applicable laws, policies, guidelines, and contracts, including obtaining legal advice and the provision of information as required by any government or other authority, pursuant to legal process or otherwise; and

- Protection of *[Practice]*, the workforce, or the public against injury, theft, legal liability, fraud, abuse, and other misconduct.

5.  *[Practice]* may disclose personal data to a third party but only when required by law or for business purposes. Third parties may include:

- Payroll administration;

- Medical benefits plan administrators;

- Retirement benefits plan administrators;

- Other benefits administrators;

- Accountants;

- Consultants;

- Law firms representing *[Practice]*;

- Banks; and

- Social Security organizations.

6.  Where *[Practice]* has disclosed personal data to a third party through an outsourcing agreement, *[Practice]* requires the third party to have adequate security measures in place and will only process personal data for the purposes identified in the agreement.

7.  An employee's access to his or her employee file is dictated by applicable state law. Employees upon reasonable request and after providing proof of identity may have access to view his or her employee file a maximum of two times per year.

8.  Employees may request that incomplete or inaccurate personal data be corrected, amended, or deleted.

9.  Employees may not review letters of reference, confidential information concerning other individuals, and management planning information. The human resources professional is responsible for removing such documents prior to the employee reviewing his or her file.

10. Employees may request copies of documents in their files and may be charged for copying costs.

Approved by: Practice Administrator

Effective date: 1/1/20__

**Policy 9.07**      **Patient Protected Health Information Privacy**

This is an example of a patient protected health information privacy policy. This sort of high-level policy is not sufficient to meet the requirements of HIPAA, and practices should carefully consider whether this type of HR policy will conflict with existing and other compliance policies. *This suggested policy is for educational and illustrative purposes only. The particular laws of each state may differ, and this suggested general policy should not be implemented without considering applicable federal, state, and local laws. In addition, this suggested general policy should not be implemented without consulting your practice's attorneys.*

---

POLICY 9.07           **PATIENT PROTECTED HEALTH INFORMATION PRIVACY**

Purpose: To establish and maintain guidelines regarding patient protected health information privacy.

Applies to: All *[Practice]* employees.

Policy: It is the policy of *[Practice]* to protect the confidentiality, integrity, and availability of our patients' protected health information (PHI). It is the policy of *[Practice]* to assess on an ongoing basis potential risks and implement security measures to address potential risks. *[Practice]* will also continuously track access to PHI, detect security incidents, report security breaches as necessary, and periodically review the effectiveness of security measures. Any employee's behavior that compromises a patient's privacy or PHI is subject to discipline under this policy. Violation of this policy may result in disciplinary action up to and including termination of employment.

Procedures:
1. All employees have the responsibility to comply with HIPAA (Health Insurance Portability and Accountability Act) and HITECH (Health Information Technology for Economic and Clinical Health) regulations.
2. *[Practice]* will maintain any and all PHI of all patients, whether oral, written, photographic, or electronic, in a private and secure manner and will use and disclose such information only to authorized individuals or entities and only when required to do so by law or to complete business activities.
3. Where *[Practice]* has disclosed PHI to an authorized business associate, *[Practice]* requires the associate to have adequate security measures in place.
4. *[Practice]* will designate a qualified employee as the security officer whose responsibilities include but are not limited to developing and implementing security policies, procedures, and protocols.
5. Employees will be granted access to PHI only if access is appropriate to the employee's job duties. Authorized users have the responsibility to safeguard all PHI including but not limited to using and disclosing PHI to those who are allowed permission, by authorization, and/or by law.
6. *[Practice]* will establish appropriate technical, administrative, and physical safeguards to prevent PHI from intentionally or unintentionally being used or disclosed in violation of HIPAA's requirements. Technical safeguards include limited access to information by creating firewalls, and physical safeguards include locking doors and file cabinets.

7. Employees may not send any e-mail, unless encrypted, that contains private, sensitive, or confidential information including but not limited to *[Practice]* information or PHI.

8. Under no circumstances may an employee use a mobile device to capture, store, or transmit confidential or private *[Practice]* data including patient PHI.

9. Any employee who commits, observes, or becomes aware of unauthorized or inappropriate access, use, or disclosure of PHI has an affirmative obligation to report the incident(s) to a supervisor and/or the designated security officer. The supervisor, security officer, and *[Practice]* management will investigate the suspected breach of security, mitigate any harmful effect that may result from the breach, and determine appropriate disciplinary actions and/or sanctions concerning the breach. All corrective actions will be documented in writing and maintained in the appropriate employee file.

10. *[Practice]* will make all reasonable efforts to keep any investigation as confidential as possible. However, in many cases, it will be necessary to interview some employees, the accused employee, members of management, and other possible witnesses.

11. Under certain circumstances related to the HITECH provisions of HIPAA, *[Practice]* may be required to notify individuals, the Department of Health and Human Services, and, in some cases, the media if a security breach has occurred.

12. Neither *[Practice]* nor any employee may intimidate, threaten, coerce, discriminate against, or take other retaliatory action against individuals for exercising their rights, filing a complaint, participating in an investigation, or opposing any improper practice under HIPAA.

13. No individual shall be required to waive his or her privacy rights under HIPAA as a condition of treatment, payment, enrollment, or eligibility.

14. PHI is only to be altered or destroyed when authorized and only by authorized employees. PHI removal, whether physical or electronic, should be conducted in the following ways:

    - Papers containing PHI should be shredded; and
    - Electronic files containing PHI should be deleted and/or permanently removed from server files, in-boxes or e-mail archives, file directories on hard drives, USB/flash drives, or external hard drives.

15. All PHI should be stored on *[Practice]* servers and should never be stored on laptops, desktops, and/or mobile devices.

16. The *[Practice's]* privacy policies and procedures shall be documented and maintained for at least six years. Policies and procedures must be changed as necessary or appropriate to comply with changes in the law, standards, requirements, and implementation specifications (including changes and modifications in regulations). Any changes to policies or procedures must be promptly documented.

17. Management educates and trains all employees on how to secure and protect patients' PHI and on all HIPAA regulations.

18. *[Practice]* shall document certain events and actions (including authorizations, requests for information, sanctions, and complaints) relating to an individual's privacy rights.

19. The documentation of any policies and procedures, actions, activities, and designations may be maintained in either written or electronic form. Covered entities must maintain such documentation for at least six years.

Approved by: Practice Administrator

Effective date: 1/1/20__

**Policy 9.08**   <u>**Workplace Violence**</u>

This is an example of a workplace violence policy. *This suggested policy is for educational and illustrative purposes only. The particular laws of each state may differ, and this suggested general policy should not be implemented without considering applicable federal, state, and local laws. In addition, this suggested general policy should not be implemented without consulting your practice's attorneys.*

---

**POLICY 9.08          WORKPLACE VIOLENCE**

<u>Purpose:</u> To establish and maintain guidelines regarding workplace violence.

<u>Applies to:</u> All *[Practice]* employees.

<u>Policy:</u> It is the policy of *[Practice]* to provide a safe and secure workplace environment for its patients, visitors, and employees, as well as security for the property of employees and *[Practice]*. To prevent workplace violence, it is the responsibility of each employee to report any threats, displays of aggressiveness, assault, or a weapon within *[Practice's]* facilities.

<u>Procedures:</u>

1. *[Practice]* prohibits the possession of a weapon, threatened violence, and any type of violent or threatening behavior toward employees, clients, or vendors at any time while on *[Practice]* property, during or after working hours, or while an employee is engaged in *[Practice]* business, regardless of the employee's location.

2. Weapons, for purposes of this policy, include any object capable of causing serious bodily harm or death to another and may include but are not limited to all firearms, air pistols or air rifles, knives, or any other weapon or device that could be used as a tool of violence.

3. Violent behavior for purposes of this policy generally includes any physical touching that is intended to or does inflict injury on another, including but not limited to the use of a weapon against another individual. Violent behavior also includes stalking or intimidating a person, making physical or verbal threats, and intentionally destroying the property of another.

4. *[Practice]* will designate a manager who is responsible for developing, evaluating, and implementing *[Practice's]* workplace violence prevention program.

5. Employees who observe or witness or feel that they have been victims of threatened violence or any type of violent behavior have an affirmative obligation to report the incident(s) to a supervisor and/or the designated workplace violence manager immediately.

6. If the supervisor or member of management is alleged to be engaged in violent conduct or behavior, the employee can report the incident to the designated workplace violence manager and/or the Practice Administrator.

7. Employees must also report any weapons, suspicious behavior, unusual incidents, or unauthorized persons on the premises to the workplace violence manager immediately.

8. All workplace violence reports are promptly and thoroughly investigated by the designated workplace violence manager and reported to the Practice Administrator who will take appropriate action.

9.  Management educates and trains all employees on how to identify behaviors that may indicate the possibility of workplace violence and how to respond to violent or potentially violent situations.

10. *[Practice]* prohibits any retaliation against individuals who make a good-faith complaint, file a complaint, or who assist or otherwise participate in an investigation. If, at any time, an employee feels that he or she is being retaliated against or that a complaint is not being handled properly, he or she should contact the designated workplace violence manager.

11. *[Practice]* will make all reasonable efforts to keep any investigation as confidential as possible. However, in many cases, it will be necessary to interview the complainant, the alleged perpetrator, members of management, and other possible witnesses. The Practice Administrator will inform the complainant of the completion of the investigation.

12. To ensure that *[Practice]* successfully provides a work environment that is free of violence, *[Practice]* will impose appropriate disciplinary action for violations of this policy up to and including termination of employment.

Approved by: Practice Administrator

Effective date: 1/1/20__

**Policy 9.09**          <u>**Workplace Harassment**</u>

This is an example of a workplace harassment policy. *This suggested policy is for educational and illustrative purposes only. The particular laws of each state may differ, and this suggested general policy should not be implemented without considering applicable federal, state, and local laws. In addition, this suggested general policy should not be implemented without consulting your practice's attorneys.*

---

POLICY 9.09                              **WORKPLACE**
                                         **HARASSMENT**

<u>Purpose:</u> To establish and maintain guidelines prohibiting workplace harassment, inappropriate conduct, and offensive behavior.

<u>Applies to:</u> All *[Practice]* employees.

<u>Policy:</u> *[Practice]* is committed to providing a working environment in which its employees, visitors, and patients are free from unlawful discrimination and harassment and intimidating, hostile, or offensive conduct. *[Practice]* does not tolerate harassment and other inappropriate conduct or offensive behavior that is based on or directed toward someone because of sex, race, color, national origin, religion, disability, genetic information, or any other unlawful basis. Voicemail and electronic communications, including e-mail and Internet usage, are covered by this policy in the same manner as other communications and actions.

<u>Procedures:</u>

**Prohibited Conduct**

1.  For the purpose of this policy, prohibited conduct includes verbal, visual, or physical conduct that: (1) relates to another person's sex, race, color, national origin, religion, disability, genetic information, age, or other status protected by law; or (2) is directed toward another person because of that person's sex, race, color, national origin, religion, disability, genetic information, age, or other status protected by law, where such conduct may have the purpose or effect of unreasonably interfering with an individual's work performance or creating an intimidating, hostile, or offensive work environment.

2.  Prohibited conduct may include, among other things, telling racist or sexist jokes or making offensive or derogatory remarks about another person's race, ancestry, national origin, age, genetic information, or disability. Prohibited conduct includes, among other things, sexual harassment as discussed below.

3.  Prohibited conduct includes but is not limited to conduct that may constitute or lead to sexual harassment, such as use of suggestive sexual comments, jokes, or innuendo; persistent, unwanted flirtation or invitations for dates or other social activities; unwelcome sexual advances or passes; sexual remarks or questions about a person's body, clothing, or sexual activities; patting, pinching, or other offensive touching; or displays of sexually suggestive pictures or objects. Sexually harassing conduct may include conduct between persons of the same gender, regardless of the sexual preference of those persons.

4. Prohibited conduct may occur not only through personal contact, comments, visual displays, or observation, but also through exposure to media such as e-mail or display of Internet sites or other material or information on computer monitors.

**Persons Covered**

5. Unlawful discrimination and harassment is prohibited whether it is committed by managers, supervisors, coworkers, or non-employees, including patients, vendors, and visitors. Employees must not engage in prohibited conduct against other *[Practice]* employees, patients, vendors, or visitors.

**Complaint Procedure**

6. Employees who observe or witness or feel that they have been victims of harassment have an affirmative obligation to report the incident(s) to a supervisor and/or the designated workplace violence manager immediately. If the supervisor or member of management is alleged to be engaged in harassing conduct or behavior, the employee can report the incident to their manager, the designated workplace violence manager, and/or Practice Administrator.

7. All employees are expected to be truthful, accurate, and cooperative during any *[Practice]* investigation.

8. All workplace harassment reports are promptly and thoroughly investigated. Based on its investigation, *[Practice]* will take prompt and appropriate action as warranted.

9. *[Practice]* prohibits any retaliation against individuals who make a good-faith complaint, file a complaint, or who assist or otherwise participate in an investigation. If, at any time, an employee feels that he or she is being retaliated against or that a complaint is not being handled properly, he or she should contact his or her manager, the designated workplace violence manager, or the Practice Administrator.

10. *[Practice]* will make all reasonable efforts to keep any investigation confidential to the extent possible, consistent with the need for a thorough investigation.

11. To ensure that *[Practice]* successfully provides a work environment that is free of unlawful harassment, *[Practice]* will impose appropriate disciplinary action for violations of this policy up to and including termination of employment.

12. Management educates and trains all employees on this policy.

Approved by: Practice Administrator

Effective date: 1/1/20__

**Policy 9.10**      **Substance Abuse**

This is an example of a substance abuse policy. *This suggested policy is for educational and illustrative purposes only. The particular laws of each state may differ, and this suggested general policy should not be implemented without considering applicable federal, state, and local laws. In addition, this suggested general policy should not be implemented without consulting your practice's attorneys.*

---

POLICY 9.10                              **SUBSTANCE ABUSE**

Purpose: To establish and maintain guidelines regarding substance abuse.

Applies to: All *[Practice]* employees.

Policy: *[Practice]* is dedicated to maintaining a drug- and alcohol-free workplace. *[Practice]* recognizes that drug and alcohol use in the workplace can have serious consequences in terms of safety, security, and productivity. Employees are required to report to work physically and mentally able to perform their duties and carry out their responsibilities without endangering their own health or safety or that of patients, other employees, and visitors. Employees are strictly prohibited to use, possess, manufacture, distribute, sell, or be under the influence of illegal drugs or alcohol while working or conducting *[Practice]*-related activities on or off *[Practice]* premises.

Procedures:

1. Illegal drugs are any controlled substance, medication, or other chemical substance that is illegal under federal law or is a substance, either over-the-counter or prescription, that is not being used for its intended purpose(s) or for which it was prescribed.

2. No employee shall report for work or remain on duty while under the influence of alcohol or illegal drugs.

3. The use, possession, manufacture, distribution, dispensation, or sale or any alcohol or illegal drugs during working hours, including rest and meal periods or while on *[Practice]* property, is prohibited.

4. It is not a violation of this policy if an employee with a current and valid prescription for a drug uses, possesses, or is under the influence of such drug in the manner and for the purposes prescribed as long as the drug is not illegal under federal law and such use does not affect the employee's performance or create a risk to the safety of the employee, patients, or others.

5. It is not a violation of this policy for an employee to use, possess, or be under the influence of an over-the-counter drug if such use does not affect the employee's performance or create a risk to the safety of the employee, patients, or others.

6. *[Practice]* reserves the right to require a drug or alcohol screening of the employees at any time and on any employees based on reasonable cause.

7. If there is reasonable suspicion that an employee is under the influence of drugs or alcohol or if the employee has been observed possessing, selling, or using a prohibited substance on the job, *[Practice]* may, subject to applicable laws and without advanced notice, conduct searches for drugs and alcohol on *[Practice]* premises and property including but not limited to personal effects, desks, briefcases, lockers, purses, baggage, and vehicles to the extent permitted by law. All employees are required to cooperate in the conducting of such searches.

8. An employee who is perceived to be under the influence of drugs or alcohol will be removed immediately from the workplace, and *[Practice]* may require the employee to submit to a drug screening.

9. An employee has the right to refuse drug or alcohol testing. However, such refusal will result in immediate termination to the extent permitted by law.

10. If information available to *[Practice]* indicates that an employee reported to work or was working under the influence or intoxicated due to drugs or alcohol, the employee will generally be terminated. *[Practice]* reserves the right to terminate any employee based on this indication with or without a positive drug or alcohol test.

11. Drug screening tests will be conducted on a specimen provided by the employee.

12. An employee who fails a drug screening may discuss with the Practice Administrator, in confidence, any reasons he or she believes may explain the test results. The employee has the right to request and obtain all information related to his or her test.

13. All information, interviews, reports, statements, memoranda, and drug test results, written or otherwise, will be treated as confidential by *[Practice]*. This confidential information will only be released to outside parties pursuant to written consent from the person tested, unless such release is compelled by an agency hearing officer, a court, or when required by law.

14. *[Practice]* encourages employees to seek help for addiction or drug or alcohol abuse before performance problems or other violations of this policy occur and directs employees to its Employee Assistance Program.

15. Employees working on certain federal contracts or grants will be subject to additional policies and requirements in accordance with the Drug-Free Workplace Act of 1988.

Approved by: Practice Administrator

Effective date: 1/1/20__

**Policy 9.11**     <u>**Smoking**</u>

This is an example of a smoking policy. *This suggested policy is for educational and illustrative purposes only. The particular laws of each state may differ, and this suggested general policy should not be implemented without considering applicable federal, state, and local laws. In addition, this suggested general policy should not be implemented without consulting your practice's attorneys.*

---

**POLICY 9.11**                                  **SMOKING**

<u>Purpose:</u> To establish and maintain guidelines for smoking.

<u>Applies to:</u> All *[Practice]* employees.

<u>Policy:</u> It is the policy of *[Practice]* to prohibit smoking or use of all tobacco products, including cigarettes of any kind, cigars, pipes, chewing tobacco or snuff, in all indoor practice work areas. Smoking is prohibited in all outdoor areas on *[Practice]* property except in designated smoking areas.

<u>Procedures:</u>
1. Designated smoking areas must be located in an area within 50 feet of an entrance or exit to the building.
2. Smoking is prohibited within 100 feet of flammable liquids or other highly combustible materials.
3. In keeping with preventive health measures, *[Practice]* encourages employees to break the smoking habit, and it provides assistance through the Employee Assistance Program in such efforts.

<u>Approved by:</u> Practice Administrator

<u>Effective date:</u> 1/1/20__

**Sample Forms**

**Form 9.1**   **<u>Workplace Harassment – Report of Prohibited Conduct</u>**

This is a sample Workplace Harassment – Report of Prohibited Conduct form template. You can modify the template to fit your medical practice's needs.

---

FORM 9.1      **WORKPLACE HARASSMENT – REPORT OF PROHIBITED CONDUCT**

*[Practice]* takes all reasonable steps to ensure an employee's right to a safe and healthy workplace environment. *[Practice]* does not tolerate any incidents of unlawful harassment against employees, patients, or visitors. This form is used by *[Practice]* to initiate an investigation concerning an incident or incidents of workplace harassment. Submit the completed and signed form to the Administrator or the designated human resources professional.

| Complainant - Name, Position, Phone Number | Date(s) of Incident(s) |
|---|---|
| | |

**Complainant's Relationship to the Practice**

☐ Employee             ☐ Patient             ☐ Visitor

| Complainant Recipient - Name, Position, Phone Number | Date Complaint Received |
|---|---|
| | |

**Description of Event(s):** Explain in detail the situation you are reporting, including a description of what happened, where it occurred, who else was present, and what action was taken at the time. Attach additional pages if necessary.

**Name(s) of Witnesses and/or Others Involved**

**Complainant's Response to Incident:** How did the complainant respond? For example, did the complainant confront the person engaging in the behavior or report it to anyone else?

| **Other Related Incidents:** Has the conduct happened to anyone else? |
| --- |
| |
| **Affect on Complainant:** How is this matter affecting the complainant? |
| |
| **Other Relevant Information:** Does complainant have any other relevant information, documents, or evidence? |
| |

*[Practice]* takes every complaint of harassment very seriously. You can assist in the investigation of the incident(s) by providing as much information and as many details as possible. *[Practice]* will hold this report and all investigative findings confidential to the extent possible.

| **Certification:** I hereby certify that all information provided by me in this report is true, complete, and accurate to the best of my knowledge and made in good faith. | |
| --- | --- |
| **Complainant Signature** | **Date** |
| | |

## Form 9.2 **Workplace Harassment Interview Form**

This is a sample Workplace Harassment Interview Form template. You can modify the template to fit your medical practice's needs and the particular investigation.

---

FORM 9.2      **WORKPLACE HARASSMENT INTERVIEW FORM**

| Complainant - Name, Position, Phone Number | Date of Interview |
|---|---|

**Description of Event(s):** As described in detail by the complainant.

| Alleged Harasser - Name, Position, Phone Number, Relationship to Complainant | Date of Interview |
|---|---|

**Description of Event(s):** As described in detail by the respondent(s) including what happened, where it occurred, who else was present, and what action was taken at the time.

**Name of Witnesses and/or Others Involved:** Identified by the alleged harasser(s).

| Name of Witness and/or Others Involved (Last, first, MI) | Date of Interview |
|---|---|

**Description of Event(s):** As described in detail by the witnesses, including what happened, where it occurred, who else was present, and what action was taken at the time.

## Form 9.3 Workplace Harassment – Summary of Investigation Form

This is a sample Workplace Harassment – Summary of Investigation Form template. You can modify the template to fit your medical practice's needs and the particular investigation. Your practice representative must use his or her discretion, based on experience and the circumstances, to determine the level of detail to include in the investigation summary. For example, in some circumstances, it may be inappropriate to disclose disciplinary information about third parties or to identify witnesses.

---

FORM 9.3                **WORKPLACE HARASSMENT –
SUMMARY OF INVESTIGATION FORM**

| Practice Representative Completing This Summary | Date |
|---|---|
|  |  |

**Nature of Complaint**

**Investigation of Complaint:** What steps did you take to investigate the complaint?

**Investigation Findings**

**Actions in Response**

| Date Reviewed with Complainant/Employee | |
|---|---|
| **Practice Representative Signature** | **Date** |
| I acknowledge that I have reviewed this form. | |
| **Complainant Signature** | **Date** |

CHAPTER 10

# Managing Employee Relations

Policy 10.01  Outside Employment

Policy 10.02 Dress Code and Appearance

One of the most important interpersonal relationships within a medical practice is the one between the employee and the supervisor. Management reflects its culture through the supervisors' attitudes toward employees in the workplace. Therefore, healthy relationships are critical to the success of your medical practice. Your practice should strive to provide not only a healthy work environment but also be known in the community as a great place to work and encourage employees to perform their best.

Management decisions affect the cost of delivery of healthcare services, which ultimately affects patients. The whole purpose of employee relations is to attract, develop, and retain high performers as well as improve working conditions and increase employee productivity. This chapter addresses key issues regarding the critical aspects of employee relations such as employment contracts, dress and appearance, outside employment, employee organization and representation, employee files, and so on.

## Employment Contracts

Many employers use written contracts, rather than application forms, to establish the terms and conditions of employment relationships. Historically, medical practices and clinics have used employment contracts with physicians and some other healthcare professionals. For example, a written employment contract may be used when a senior-level manager has bargained for a unique form of compensation (i.e., a set of benefits different from the typical ones provided to employees).

### Elements of Employment Contracts

To be legally binding, an employment contract must contain certain elements. First, both parties (i.e., the medical practice and the candidate) must agree to the terms of the contract. Usually the employment offer contains an express limit to the duration of time the offer must be accepted or rejected. It also must define the duration of the job, which could be one year, five years, indefinitely, and so on. The employment contract must also include detailed descriptions of the employee's duties and responsibilities. A thorough job description reduces any ambiguities between job duties listed in the employment contract and the job description. MGMA's *Job Description Manual for Medical Practices, 3rd edition*\*, includes sample job description templates. It is critical when utilizing employment contracts to ensure that the description of the duties and responsibilities matches those in the respective job description and on performance evaluations and, most importantly, that it reflects what the employee is actually doing in his or her job.

> ## Critical Elements of Employment Contracts
>
> - At-will disclaimer (if employment is at will)
> - Duration of employment (if the employment is not at will)
> - Amount of compensation
> - Benefits
> - Responsibilities and duties
> - Termination
> - Confidentiality and privacy clauses
> - Non-compete agreement

Often, employment contracts will define reporting relationships within your practice. Clearly defining the amount of compensation and the benefits the employee will receive is a critical element of employment contracts. The employment contract should outline vacation leave, disability leave, and other leaves of absence. In addition, health, dental, and vision insurance coverage, retirement benefits, and the employee's contribution to such plans should be detailed. Other benefits that the employee will receive should also be outlined in the contract. Some of the critical yet often missing elements are describing the grounds for termination, conflict resolution, patient and practice privacy and confidentiality clauses, non-compete agreements, and liability insurance coverage.

### Non-Compete Agreements

Medical practices should consider whether to have an agreement with the employee in which he or she promises and is legally not allowed to compete with your practice for a specific amount of time after the employment relationship is terminated. Enforceability of non-compete agreements varies greatly from state to state. Consult with legal counsel to determine under what circumstances a non-compete agreement may be enforceable in the state in which your medical practice is located.

A non-compete agreement may contain a provision that the employee will not begin a competing business or work for a competitor within a specific geographic area or for a specified period of time after leaving your practice. These non-compete agreements are typically used with senior-level managers or employees with access to trade secrets.

If a non-compete agreement is absent from the employment contract, the employee is free to compete with his or her former employer by working for a competitor or establishing his or her own business. A former employee may also be free to solicit the former employer's patients.

---

\*   Written by Courtney H. Price and Alys Novak (Englewood, CO: Medical Group Management Association, 2008).

Non-compete agreements should include the following components:
- A reasonable geographic area in which the employee will not compete;
- A reasonable time period during which the employee will not compete;
- An appropriate limit on the type of professional activity in which the employee will not compete.

Form 10.1 at the end of this chapter is a Sample Physician Employment Contract and should be used for educational and illustrative purposes only. As mentioned previously, the particular laws of each state may differ in terms of employment contracts, non-competition, and other agreements.Accordingly, the suggested general template should not be used without considering applicable state laws and the philosophy of your practice, and review by legal counsel.

## Outside Employment

Moonlighting, when an employee holds two or more jobs, is a way of life for many workers. Reasons for moonlighting range from economic needs to short work weeks that leave employees free time to devote to multiple career interests. Also, many healthcare professionals enjoy teaching. But sometimes employees with more than one job can pose problems for their primary employer. These may include fatigue, poor performance, absenteeism, and tardiness. A conflict of interest may arise between the outside employment and the employee's primary job. In sum, although employers do not have the right or legal standing to tell employees how to use their off-work hours, practice management does have a right to require the effective performance of the primary job and to ensure patient safety.

Medical practices can have a policy requiring employees to notify their supervisor if they have or plan to get a second job. Managers should handle discussions about outside employment on a case-by-case basis. Supervisors may discuss the challenges of holding multiple jobs, including fatigue, reduced commitment to practice, higher accident and absentee rates, and neglect of routine job duties and scheduled overtime, as applicable to each situation.

As mentioned previously, medical practices generally must allow employees the opportunity to work at outside employment Activities and conduct away from the job must not compete with, conflict with, or compromise practice interests or adversely affect job performance and the employee's ability to fulfill all responsibilities to your practice. Outside employment should not be considered an excuse for poor job performance, absenteeism, tardiness, leaving early, refusal to travel, or refusal to work overtime or different hours.

Medical practices should establish a policy regarding outside employment. When developing an outside employment policy, first consider the needs of your practice and then try to meet the employee's needs when possible. Your outside employment policy should prohibit employees from moonlighting with a practice's competitor in a position that could create a conflict of interest, including being harmful to the practice's public image. The policy should require employees to report any additional jobs they work to their direct supervisor. If a medical practice determines that an employee's outside work interferes with his or her performance, hinders his or her ability to meet the requirements of your practice, or creates a conflict of interest, the employee may be asked to terminate the outside employment if he or she wishes to remain employed with your practice.

Policy 10.01 at the end of this chapter is a sample outside employment policy. Your practice should adopt this policy and modify it to reflect your practice's specific management philosophy, organizational needs, and staff size. State laws vary in this area and may affect your practice's legal requirements; your practice should become familiar with your state's laws. Form 10.2 is a sample template of an outside employment request form.

## Employee Dress and Appearance

How your employees dress and their appearance can affect the culture, brand, and reputation of your medical practice. Employees who look and dress professionally can have a positive impact on patients and their families, vendors, referring physicians, providers, and regulators and how they perceive your practice. Professional dress and appearance can inspire employee pride and confidence in their work.

The dress code, appearance, and personal hygiene requirements for a medical practice are slightly different from a business's dress policies. Although a conservative and professional style should be expected, safety should also be taken into consideration. Employees who have direct contact with patients and those who use complex medical equipment should have clothes that protect them from bodily fluids, chemical spills, or other accidents such as slipping or tripping.

### Common Dress Code and Appearance Guidelines

A dress code and appearance policy should address all aspects of an employee's appearance, including clothes, footwear, uniforms, piercings, tattoos, perfumes and colognes, and security badges, if required. A medical practice should expect all employees to appear and dress in a professional, neat, clean, and well-groomed manner. Some medical practices also include a specific list of what is not appropriate, such as jeans, t-shirts, sweatshirts, shorts, miniskirts, midriff-baring shirts, halter tops, flip-flops, sandals, hats, and so on. Establish a dress code and appearance policy that corresponds with your practice's culture, brand, and vision. The following paragraphs contain some guidelines to use when developing your dress code and appearance policy.

#### Dress and Clothes

Most likely, each medical practice will have a slightly different philosophy about employees' dress. Regardless, clothing worn by employees should be neat, clean, and appropriate for the duties employees perform. Some medical practices may have a business casual dress code while others may have "casual Fridays." Typical business casual for women encompasses tailored trousers or dresses, skirts, or capri pants of appropriate length. Some medical practices require female employees to wear socks, nylons, or tights. Appropriate shirts, blouses, blazers, and sweaters are usually acceptable. Sleeveless dresses and tops may be allowed as long as they look professional. Business casual for men usually includes dress slacks or tailored pants, and a pressed, collared-shirt. Men may be required to wear a tie. Some business casual allows for men to wear golf or polo shirts and short-sleeved dress shirts.

Many medical practices require shirts to cover the employee's back and midriff. Often, spaghetti straps, halter tops, and t-shirts with writing or characters are prohibited as well as exposed cleavage. In general, skirts and dresses should have hemlines no shorter than three inches above the knee. Medical practices should require undergarments be worn at all times and should not be visible above, below, or through any clothing.

*Medical Uniforms*

In a medical practice, dress code and appearance policies typically include a provision for uniforms or scrubs. All employees having direct contact with patients should be required to wear scrubs or an appropriate medical coat. Some medical practices will provide their employees with these medical uniforms, yet others require their employees to purchase their own uniforms to the extent permitted by law, and some will reimburse employees for purchasing scrubs. Medical practices usually require solid-colored scrubs and some require employees to wear a specific color. Other medical practices, such as a pediatrics practice, may allow employees to have patterns, color schemes, or characters on their medical uniforms.

*Jewelry and Accessories*

With the prevalence of body piercing increasing among the younger generation, medical practices should address visible accessories and jewelry worn at the workplace. Employees should wear jewelry and accessories in moderation. Often, medical practices will only allow jewelry in ear piercings and prohibit employees to wear jewelry in piercings at other locations, such as the tongue. Other practices may allow employees to wear a small nose piercing. Be cautious with jewelry requirements because in some religions and cultures, women wear nose piercings or a forehead decoration called a *bindi*. Employers should generally allow employees who want to wear religious and cultural symbols to do so under Title VII of the Civil Rights Act. However, jewelry worn to work should not interfere with the employees' ability to perform their duties, nor compromise patient care, or impact employee or patient safety.

Buttons, pins, badges, or trinkets should also be considered in a dress code and appearance policy. Medical practices should prohibit any employee from wearing any potentially offensive trinkets, including political buttons and stickers. Many medical practices will allow their employees to wear up to a certain number of trinkets as long as they are professional in nature and reflective of a professional organization or have been approved by practice management.

*Grooming, Hygiene, and Tattoos*

Medical practices must also address the grooming standards and hygiene of their employees. All employees should maintain good personal hygiene including clean and well-manicured, short fingernails; proper oral hygiene; and absence of any body odor. Some practices may prohibit employees from wearing nail polish on their fingernails while others prohibit only cracked or peeling nail polish. Some healthcare organizations have also prohibited employees who have direct patient contact from chewing gum and/or tobacco during working hours.

In addition, medical practices should require employees to have their hair clean and neatly styled. Employees who provide patient care should have long hair tied back or styled in a manner that won't easily touch the patient or have to be pushed out of the face with the hands. Men with facial hair, including sideburns, mustaches, goatees, and beards, should have them neatly trimmed, combed, and clean. Often, medical practices will not allow their employees to wear their hair in an unnatural hair color such as purple, blue, pink, and so on.

Your medical practice should consider limiting the use of perfumes, colognes, and other fragrances. Some patients may be allergic to these scents or strongly bothered by them. Usually medical practices allow employees who are not involved with direct patient care to wear minimal perfume or cologne. In addition, employees should be required to wear all make-up in moderation.

As with body piercings, tattoos and other body art should be covered as much as possible at the workplace. Tattoos could be offensive to some patients. Employers often allow employees to cover their tattoos with clothing such as long-sleeve shirts or turtlenecks, or they may require employees to use make-up or other materials to physically cover visible tattoos.

*Footwear*

Medical practices should consider employee and patient safety when developing their dress code and appearance policies. Open-toed shoes such as sandals or flip-flops could create a safety issue in a medical office due to the large amount of live electrical wires and the potential for spills such as bodily fluids and hazardous chemicals. Many practices require their employees to wear clean, low-heeled, sturdy shoes that are conducive to a lot of time standing and walking, including tennis shoes and medical clogs for employees who wear medical uniforms.

*Identification/Security Badges*

Medical practices may require employees to wear an identification (ID) or a security badge. Although ID badges are usually covered in your practice's security policies, it is important to have employees wear badges in a specific place. For example, the ID badge must be worn above the waist on either a collar clip or medical lanyard in clear view. Additionally, some medical practices will include a provision that all badges must remain free of stickers or anything else that alters the badge's appearance.

**Legal Implications**

Although there are no employment laws that directly govern dress codes, each medical practice has the right to institute its own policies as long as the dress code policy is based on sound reasoning and does not discriminate based on age, gender, race, ethnicity, religion, disability, or any other protected status. Title VII of the Civil Rights Act and many state laws require covered employers to make reasonable accommodations to employees with sincerely held religious beliefs. Employers are required to provide such an accommodation as long as it does not create an undue hardship on the employer such as compromising the safety of patients or employees.

A common accommodation request is an employee requesting to wear religious headwear such as a yarmulke or head-covering when the dress code prohibits it. In this case, the employer would have to determine if granting the employee's request would create an undue hardship for the employer. For example, consider whether the employee would be unable to perform his or her responsibilities and duties effectively. Could the safety of patients or other employees be compromised if he or she wore the headwear. As mentioned previously, nose piercings and bindis may be religious symbols that employees should be allowed to have as long as they are related to an employee's sincerely held religious belief and they do not affect safety or otherwise cause an undue hardship for your practice.

Generally, dress codes will distinguish between certain dress for men and women. Practices can have different policies for men and women as long as the policies are not discriminatorily different for either sex. For example, the practice cannot allow men, but not women, to wear jeans when they are performing the same job. The dress code and appearance policy must be job related and a business necessity.

In addition, racial discrimination claims can arise if a dress code and appearance policy is not applied equally to all races or if it disproportionately burdens one race over another. For example, courts have upheld racial discrimination claims against employers requiring all employees to be clean shaven because a unique condition, pseudofolliculitis barbae, found exclusively among African-American males, can be aggravated by shaving. Some courts have also ruled in favor of complainants in this situation based on disability discrimination.

It is highly advisable to consult with your practice's attorney before denying a request for reasonable accommodation on your practice's dress code and appearance policy to ensure compliance with anti-discrimination laws. Policy 10.02 is a sample dress code and appearance policy that should be adapted to reflect your practice's specific needs and philosophy.

## Employee Organization and Representation

While employee organization through unions in the United States has remained static in the last few years overall, the healthcare industry has seen an uptick as healthcare organizations struggle with the economic downturn. The healthcare industry now employs more people than any other industry, making it more desirable for unions to target as manufacturing jobs decrease in the United States. Most unionizing efforts occur to garner higher wages, more employee recognition, and greater employee respect. Hospitals continue to see the highest numbers of unionized employees where medical practices see almost no union presence. For the purposes of this book, employee organization and representation will only be briefly overviewed. It is important for medical practice administrators and physician owners to understand the laws and regulations regarding unionization. In addition, it is critical to protect your practice from claims under these laws.

Union organizing activity in the healthcare industry has increased in proportion to the increasing number of employees in this industry. This is combined with recent decisions by the National Labor Relations Board (NLRB) removing certain barriers that may have prevented healthcare employees to unionize. Although unionization in medical practices is rare, you can prepare for a potential unionizing effort by considering the following questions that are the foundation of most unionizing efforts.

1. Is there a gap between the pay, benefits, and working conditions received and wanted by your employees?
2. If there is a gap, is it large enough to motivate employees to change it via union membership?

The medical practice's goal is to maintain a nonunion status by providing good working conditions, developing and maintaining good working relationships between management and employees, establishing complaint procedures for resolving employees' dissatisfactions, and offering competitive wages and benefits. Practice management must also treat employees consistently and without unlawful discrimination. Most practices that are able to do these things are usually able to avoid union organizing attempts and to benefit from employee participation in quality improvements and other joint efforts.

## Federal Laws Governing Labor Relations in Healthcare

As mentioned in chapter 2, three primary federal laws govern labor relations:

1. Wagner Act of 1935 (National Labor Relations Act);
2. Taft–Hartley Act of 1947; and
3. Landrum–Griffin Act of 1959.

In 1974, the Wagner Act was amended to extend its coverage to not only proprietary healthcare institutions but also to nonprofit healthcare facilities. In addition, several provisions were adopted applicable only to healthcare institutions, known as the Health Care Amendments of 1974. These amendments specifically extended jurisdiction of the NLRB to:

- Hospitals;
- Convalescent hospitals;
- Health maintenance organizations (HMOs);
- Health practices;
- Nursing homes;
- Extended-care facilities; and
- Other institutions devoted to the care of sick, infirm, or aged people.

The diverse pressures affecting the healthcare industry, including the economy, reduced payments from Medicare and Medicaid, and the impact of the Patient Protection and Affordable Care Act of 2010 could increase the prevalence of unionization not only in large hospitals and clinics but also in medical practices.

## Employee Committees

Employee committees are a good way to get employees to participate in matters affecting their jobs and quality of work life. Employee participation improves efficiency and effectiveness, and creates a more satisfactory work environment. Participation also gives employees a voice in work policies and procedures that affect them, fosters teamwork, and improves morale.

Employee participation can take many forms. The most common is a committee of management and nonsupervisory employee representatives (although it can consist of only one or the other) who address workplace issues. These issues could range from quality of patient care, to workplace and patient safety, to vacation scheduling, and many other variations. Some of the more common examples of employee participation are safety committees, advisory groups, and employee communication committees.

Properly structured committees give employees a meaningful voice in important practice decisions that directly affect them. Involved employees tend to be dedicated employees and are less likely to file complaints about how they are treated or the way things are done. They are less likely to leave your practice, resulting in lower employee turnover and lower costs associated with training new hires. Employee committees establish an atmosphere of open communication, which is beneficial to the entire workforce. In addition, employees can provide innovative ideas on productivity, quality, incentive plans, patient care, safety, and other areas because they usually know the practicalities of their jobs better than management.

If employee input results in work changes that are consistent with the employer's ideas, employees will be happier and more productive. They are more likely to accept or buy-in to changes that are made based on their input. However, even if employee committees are formed, management runs the risk of disgruntling employees if committee ideas and recommendations are not implemented or taken seriously. If this happens, employees who offer their time and energy to participate in a committee may believe that your practice is wasting their time or has even been dishonest with them.

There is not a single description of the perfect employee committee structure that can be used in all medical practices. Every practice is unique in its needs and goals. Committees need to be created to fit an employer's need at that time. Your medical practice should follow these guidelines for establishing an employee committee:

- Create committees with the limited purpose of performing essentially a managerial or adjudicative function such as scheduling, evaluating, or disciplining.

- Have employees make ad hoc proposals that are either accepted or declined by management with no explicit promise or expectation of a particular response.

- Consider establishing an employee communications committee where all employees participate on a rotational basis and give input to help solve managerial problems.

- Establish committees that deal only with permissive subjects, such as quality issues of patient care, patient safety, workplace safety, patient care delivery systems, acuity systems, or supervisory duties.

- Establish committees to generate new ideas for or share information with management but do not make proposals to management.

- If your practice prefers to have management involved with a committee, have a management facilitator who doesn't have a vote. Alternatively, ensure that managers have a minority representation on the committee.

If your medical practice is unionized, the employer should inform employees that bargainable issues cannot be discussed because they are matters between the management and the union. Whether a medical practice is unionized or not, practices can build successful employee committees by following the guidelines mentioned previously and also protect your practice against potential unionization efforts.

**Employee Organization and Representation**
Hospitals, medical and dental offices, and residential care centers with a gross annual volume of at least $250,000 are under NLRB jurisdiction. For nursing homes and visiting nurses associations, the minimum is $100,000. The NLRB recently proposed a new rule to require all covered employers to post employees' rights under the National Labor Relations Act. This Employee Rights Notice-Posting rule was supposed to take effect in early 2012, however, a court ruling has temporarily prevented the posting requirement, and there is no requirement or deadline for posting at this time. Employers should

watch developments and upcoming court rulings regarding this rule. Should the rule be implemented, employers will be required to download, print, and post the Employee Rights under the NLRB poster.

## Summary

Interpersonal relationships among managers and staff are very important to any medical practice. Practices should strive to encourage, build, and maintain strong working relationships between supervisors and employees. This chapter discusses the critical employee relations issues of outside employment, employment agreements, and dress codes.

## Sample Policies

**Policy 10.01**        <u>**Outside Employment**</u>

This is an example outside employment policy.

---

**POLICY 10.01            OUTSIDE EMPLOYMENT**

<u>Purpose:</u> To establish and maintain guidelines regarding outside employment.

<u>Applies to:</u> All *[Practice]* employees.

<u>Policy:</u> The policy of *[Practice]* is to allow its employees to hold multiple jobs as long as those activities do not adversely affect performance of their duties at *[Practice]*, do not create a conflict of interest or the appearance of such, and do not violate applicable laws and regulations. Because outside employment can cause problems, the employee must discuss the possibility of outside employment before accepting any position for such work. Difficulties may occur when employees work in any job beyond their position with *[Practice]*. Under all circumstances, *[Practice]* is considered the employee's primary employer.

<u>Procedures:</u>

1. Employees can be allowed to work outside or hold other jobs, subject to certain restrictions. Activities and conduct away from the job must not compete with, conflict with, or compromise *[Practice's]* interests or adversely affect job performance and the ability to fulfill all responsibilities to *[Practice]*.

2. Employees may not use any *[Practice]* tools or equipment or disclose any confidential information when engaging in outside employment.

3. Employees may not solicit or conduct any outside business during paid working time.

4. Employees are cautioned to carefully consider the demands that additional work activity will create before accepting outside employment.

5. If *[Practice]* determines that an employee's outside work interferes with his or her performance or the ability to meet the requirements of *[Practice]*, as modified from time to time, the employee may be asked to terminate the outside employment if he or she wishes to remain employed with *[Practice]*.

6. Employees must report to their direct supervisor interest in accepting outside employment by completing the Outside Employment Request Form. This form is reviewed by the employee's immediate supervisor, who determines its appropriateness after a discussion with the employee. The supervisor submits the form to the designated human resources professional to file in the employee's file.

7. Employees are responsible for notifying their supervisor of any changes in their outside employment status. Employees document the changes on a new form and submit to their immediate supervisor.

8. When considering outside employment, the following criteria may be considered:
   - Will the outside employment in any way reduce the employee's productivity?
   - Does the outside employer do business with *[Practice]*, or is the outside employer a competitor of *[Practice]*?
   - Does the outside employment in any way create actual or perceived conflicts of interest?
   - Will the nature of the outside employment adversely affect the group's image?

9. Outside employment is not considered an excuse for poor job performance, absenteeism, tardiness, or refusals to work overtime. If management determines that an employee's outside employment is causing or contributing to any of these conditions, the employee is expected to either discontinue his or her outside employment or resign from *[Practice]*.

10. Violations of this policy may result in discipline up to and including termination.

Approved by: Practice Administrator

Effective date: 1/1/20__

**Policy 10.02**       **<u>Dress Code and Appearance</u>**

This is an example of a dress code and appearance policy.

---

**POLICY 10.02**          **DRESS CODE AND
APPEARANCE**

<u>Purpose:</u> To establish and maintain guidelines for employee dress and appearance.

<u>Applies to:</u> All *[Practice]* employees.

<u>Policy:</u> *[Practice]* believes appropriate dress and hygiene are important in ensuring patient and employee safety and promoting a positive image to our patients and our community. Therefore, employees are expected to maintain a professional, business-like appearance while in the workplace, appropriate for their working environment and the requirements of their position. Employees are expected to dress in accordance with accepted social, business, and medical standards at all times. Department leadership may establish a reasonable standard of attire appropriate for their department depending on its function. Reasonable accommodations may be made in regard to religious, cultural, or disability requests on a case-by-case basis and in accordance with applicable laws.

<u>Procedures:</u>

1. Supervisors are responsible for ensuring their employees are dressed and appear appropriately. Supervisors will consider safety and physical requirements of the position as well as contact with patients, families, referring physicians, regulators, and others when interpreting this policy. *[Practice]* management will make the final decision regarding appropriateness since this policy is not and cannot be all-inclusive.

2. Employees who arrive to work inappropriately dressed will be sent home immediately and directed to return to work in proper attire. Under such circumstances, employees will not be compensated for their time away from work.

3. Employees whose appearance is not appropriate will be asked to immediately rectify or fix their appearance. If the remedy requires 30 minutes or more or if the employee has to leave work and return later, he or she will not be compensated for time away from work.

4. Violations of this policy may be subject to disciplinary action up to an including termination.

5. Guidelines and basic expectations for clothing and dress are:

   • All employees are expected to wear appropriate business casual attire or, if required, medical uniforms that are clean, neat, and properly fitted. Business casual includes:

      – Dress slacks or tailored pants;

      – Dresses or skirts with hemline no shorter than three inches above the knee;

      – Capri pants;

      – Shirts with collars, blouses, and sweaters;

      – Sleeveless dresses and shirts are allowed as long as they look professional;

      – Blazers and ties for men are optional; and

      – Socks or hosiery, in a conservative color and lacking design or seams, must be worn when appropriate for the work environment.

- Employees required to wear medical uniforms must wear solid color scrubs in standard blue or green, earth tones, or soft pastel colors. A scrub shirt may have a pattern or design as long as it color-coordinates with a solid pant. A medical coat is also permitted as an appropriate medical uniform when worn over appropriate business casual dress or scrubs. The medical coat must be white in color and clean. Shoe covers, masks, gloves, hats, or other personal protective wear must be discarded before leaving the area where they are used treating a patient. Employees will be reasonably reimbursed by *[Practice]* for their medical uniforms.
- Undergarments should be worn at all times and may not be visible above, below, or through clothing.

6. Guidelines and basic expectations for footwear are:

- All employees are expected to wear appropriate footwear for their work environment that is clean, neat, and in good repair.
- Employees required to wear medical uniforms may wear leather tennis shoes or medical clogs.
- Employees must wear low-heeled, close-toed, and sturdy shoes.
- Shoes must be worn at all times.

7. Guidelines and basic expectations for jewelry and accessories are:

- Employees may wear conservative jewelry including earrings, necklaces, and bracelets as long as they do not interfere with duties and responsibilities.
- No visible piercings are acceptable other than on the ear.
- Employees may wear up to three pins or buttons on their clothing. The pins or buttons must be of a professional nature and may not be offensive or political in nature.
- All tattoos and body art must be covered by clothing while at the workplace.

8. Guidelines and basic expectations for grooming and personal hygiene are:

- Good personal hygiene should be evident at all times, including but not limited to:
  - Body cleanliness including the absence of body odor;
  - Limiting the use of perfume, cologne, perfumed lotion, and other fragrances; and
  - Proper oral hygiene;
- Fingernails must be clean, short, and well-manicured. Nail polish is acceptable but only in a single, solid color with no cracks, chipping, or designs. Employees who provide direct or indirect care to patients may not use artificial nails.
- Employees must have clean and neatly styled hair. Employees who provide patient care must keep their hair pulled back or styled in a manner that won't touch a patient or interfere with care or patient safety.
- Facial hair including mustaches, goatees, beards, and sideburns must be neatly trimmed, combed, and clean.
- Employees with patient contact may not chew gum or tobacco during working hours.

9. All *[Practice]*-issued identification and security badges must be visibly worn above the waist attached by a clip or medical lanyard. Stickers or any other object that alters the badge's appearance may not be placed on the badge.

10. Inappropriate and prohibited attire items and appearances include but are not limited to:
   - Shorts, sweatpants, spandex, leggings, athletic pants, and wind suits;
   - Jeans and t-shirts;
   - Hats, bandanas, or other head-coverings unless approved by management;
   - Spaghetti straps and halter tops;
   - Shirts that don't cover the back or midriff and are revealing;
   - Miniskirts or skirts shorter than three inches above the knee;
   - Flip-flops, sandals, and other open-toed shoes;
   - House slippers;
   - Visible body piercing such as tongue, nose, facial or others unless approved by *[Practice]* management;
   - Visible tattoos and body art;
   - Unnatural-appearing makeup;
   - Unnatural hair color such as green, blue, purple, pink, and so on; and
   - Wild or extreme hair styles such as Mohawks.

Approved by: Practice Administrator

Effective date: 1/1/20__

**Sample Forms**

**Form 10.1**     **Sample Physician Employment Contract**

This is a Sample Physician Employment Contract template. Modify the template to fit your medical practice's needs. The particular laws of each state may differ, and this template should not be used without considering applicable federal, state, and local laws. In addition, this template should not be implemented without attorney review.

---

FORM 10.1          **SAMPLE PHYSICIAN**
                   **EMPLOYMENT CONTRACT**

This Employment Agreement (herein "Agreement") is effective as of the ____ day of _____, 20____, (herein "Effective Date") by and between {*PRACTICE*} (herein "Employer"), a {*CITY, STATE*} {*CORPORATION, PC, LLC, LLP*} and _____ (herein "Employee").

In consideration of the terms, conditions, and provisions contained in this Agreement, Employer and Employee agree as follows:

1. EMPLOYMENT

   1.1. Employer shall employ Employee as a physician engaged in the practice of {specialty or medical focus of practice such as cardiology, family medicine, etc.} and related medicine, and Employee accepts employment with Employer under the terms and conditions set forth in this Agreement.

   1.2. Such employment shall commence on the ____ day of _____, 20____, and end on the ____ day of _____, 20____. The Employee's employment thereafter continues for successive one (1) year terms, unless either party gives at minimum ninety (90) days' prior notice that the employment will not be renewed.

2. SERVICES

   2.1. Pursuant to this Agreement, Employee is employed as a full-time employee by {*PRACTICE*}. The Employee agrees to devote his or her full energy, interest, ability, and skills, on a full-time basis, to the performance of his or her duties hereunder exclusively for and on behalf of Employer. Full-time means a minimum of forty (40) hours each week (plus such additional hours, if any, as Employer may require consistent with the demands of the practice) attending to patients of Employer. Employee will observe and conform to all applicable laws and reasonable customs of the medical profession and comply with all general policies and standards of performance regarding the services performed.

   2.2. Employee will: (i)maintain an unrestricted license to practice medicine in the State of _____; (ii) maintain eligibility to practice in the Medicare and Medicaid programs; (iii) maintain good standing active or associate staff privileges, with appropriate credentials, on the medical staff of hospitals as reasonably required by Employer; (iv) maintain registration with the Drug Enforcement Administration ("DEA"); (v) be and remain insurable by malpractice liability in accordance with the requirements of applicable {*STATE*} laws; and (vi) maintain certification by such credentialing agencies as shall be reasonably determined by Employer.

2.3. During the term of this Agreement, Employee shall not, directly or indirectly, on behalf of him or herself or any other person, firm, partnership, corporation, or other business entity: (i) engage in the practice of medicine other than as an employee of Employer pursuant to this Agreement; (ii) conduct any professional practice or activity, other than the professional practice and activities conducted as an employee of Employer pursuant to this Agreement; or (iii) be involved in any other duties or pursuits for monetary gain that interfere with the performance of Employee's duties and responsibilities on behalf of Employer pursuant to this Agreement.

3. DUTIES

3.1. Employee shall perform the professional, administrative, and other duties and services described below, all as and when requested by, on behalf of, and under the general direction, control, and supervision of Employer.

3.1.1. Interviewing and evaluating the medical needs of patients of Employer; and providing medical services and treatment to such patients if, in the reasonable discretion of the Employee, such services are in the medical best interests of the patient;

3.1.2. Participating in all call coverage programs as Employer may implement to satisfy patient coverage needs. Employee agrees to cooperate with other physicians and employees of Employer to provide such coverage services in accordance with the policies established by Employer including, without limitation, coverage during and after office hours, and on weekends and holidays. Employer retains the exclusive right to set and modify the coverage assignments from time to time;

3.1.3. Supervising healthcare services provided by physician assistants, nurse practitioners, or other service providers to patients who are evaluated and treated by physician assistants or nurse practitioners of Employer;

3.1.4. Generating and completing in a timely manner adequate, legible, and proper medical and other records in form and content consistent with the policies and procedures of Employer, for all patients treated by Employee while employed by Employer;

3.1.5. Assisting Employer in billing for all services provided by Employee on behalf of Employer;

3.1.6. Performing other such duties as required by Employer or as described in Employer's job description.

3.2. Employee agrees to render services for Employers in a competent, professional, and ethical manner and in accordance with prevailing standards of practice, and otherwise act in a manner consistent with all applicable professional and ethical requirements and standards established by applicable federal, state, and local licensing or accrediting agencies and bodies and professional organizations.

3.3. Employee agrees to comply with all applicable federal, state, and local laws and regulations and all Employer's policies and procedures.

3.4. Employee agrees to maintain his or her skills through continuing education and training.

4. COMPENSATION AND BENEFITS

    4.1. Commencing with the Effective Date for all services rendered by Employee under this Agreement, Employer shall compensate as follows:

        4.1.1. Employer shall pay Employee a base salary of $_____ per year, less applicable required deductions, including payroll taxes, to be paid in accordance with Employer's normal payroll practice.

        4.1.2. Employer may pay Employee a _____% productivity bonus on the 15th of each month for the productivity of the previous month. Any productivity bonus must meet applicable legal requirements, including the Stark law.

    4.2. In accordance with Employer policies and procedures, the Employee shall be entitled to the following benefits:

        4.2.1. Employee shall have the right to participate in the qualified retirement plans offered by Employer. Such participation is subject to the eligibility, vesting, benefit accrual, and other requirements as set out in applicable policies and procedures of Employer. Employer shall have the right to amend, limit, reduce benefits, or terminate any such plans.

        4.2.2. Employee shall be entitled to participate in Employer benefit plans such as medical, dental, and vision coverage it provides to all regular full-time employees including coverage for Employee, his or her spouse, and children as long as Employee meets the eligibility requirements of such plans and requirements set forth in Employer policies and procedures.

        4.2.3. Employee shall be entitled to up to _____ days of paid time off, five (5) days for attendance at Employer-approved medical conventions, seminars, and meetings, and the _____ paid holidays recognized by Employer for its general staff during each year including holidays on which Employee is scheduled for call coverage. Such paid time off must be scheduled in accordance with Employer policies and procedures.

    4.3. During the term of this Agreement, Employer shall pay for, or reimburse Employee for, the amount of (i) Employee's medical staff dues and related fees at hospitals and other healthcare facilities where Employer requires Employee to obtain and maintain medical staff privileges, (ii) Employee's {STATE} medical licensure costs and Drug Enforcement Administration registration fees, (iii) pre-approved out-of-pocket expenses incurred by Employee for CME taken by Employee during the term, and (iv) any other costs or expenses that Employer, in its sole discretion, determines are reasonably necessary to the performance of Employee's services.

    4.4. Employer shall provide professional liability insurance coverage for patient care services performed by Employee within the scope of Employee's duties under this Agreement. Employee may obtain, at his or her sole expense, such primary, supplemental, or additional professional liability insurance coverage as Employee desires. If Employee voluntarily terminates this Agreement or Employer terminates this Agreement for cause and professional liability coverage for Employee has been provided to Employer on a claims-made basis, Employee, at his or her sole expense, shall obtain a reporting endorsement or tail coverage to continue and maintain coverage protection of Employer for acts or omissions committed by Employee under this Agreement. Employee must provide Employer with evidence of such tail coverage.

5. BILLING AND REPORTING

    5.1. Employer retains the exclusive right to establish and modify the amount of all fees to be charged for professional services rendered by Employee under this Agreement. All such fees shall be charged on behalf and in the name of Employer, and all such fees shall be the sole property of Employer. Employee agrees not to bill any patient or third-party payor for those services performed and to remit to Employer all payment he or she receives on account of professional services performed as an employee of Employer. Employee hereby assigns to Employer his or her right to bill for the medical services performed by him or her as an employee of Employer and to receive payments from any patients or other third-party payor, including but not limited to any managed care payor, Medicare or Medicaid programs, with respect to those services.

5.2. Employee shall keep and maintain, or cause to be kept and maintained, appropriate records relating to all professional services rendered by him or her under this Agreement, and shall prepare all reports and correspondence necessary or appropriate under the circumstances. All records, reports, correspondence, case histories, X-ray films, and other files or records concerning patients consulted, interviewed, treated, or cared for by Employee during the term of this Agreement shall belong to and remain the property of Employer, and Employee hereby assigns to Employer all right, title, and interest, if any. Upon termination of this Agreement, and at any other time upon demand by Employer, Employee will deliver to Employer all such records, histories, films, or files that are directly, or indirectly, in his or her control or possession. However, upon termination, Employer shall furnish Employee, at a reasonable reproduction cost, and at agreeable times, any such records, histories, films, or files, subject to applicable {STATE} and federal confidentiality and/or privacy laws.

## 6. TERMINATION

6.1. This Agreement shall be terminated without cause on the happening of any one or more of the following events, without the necessity of delivery of any notice of termination or any other action except as expressly stated below:

6.1.1. *Mutual Consent.* Upon written consent of the parties to terminate this Agreement. The effective date of termination under this clause shall be the termination date specified in such notice or the ninetieth (90th) day after such notice is received.

6.1.2. *Death.* Death of Employee.

6.1.3. *Dissolution of Employer.* Employer is dissolved or the business of the Employer is otherwise terminated.

6.1.4. *Incapacity/Disability.* Chronic illness, disability, or failing health of Employee that prevents Employee from performing his or her duties and responsibilities under this Agreement for thirty (30) consecutive days or for forty-five (45) days in a six-month period. The effective date of termination under this clause shall be the end of the applicable thirty (30) days or six-month period.

6.2. At the election of Employer, the occurrence of one or more of the following events shall constitute grounds upon which Employer may immediately terminate this Agreement and Employee's employment hereunder for cause effective upon the giving of written notice of termination to Employee:

6.2.1. *Loss of License.* If Employee shall cease to be licensed in the State of {STATE}, or any medical license, permit, registration, or other license or certification of Employee, including but not limited to Medicare and Medicaid, is suspended, restricted, revoked, or canceled, or Employee is otherwise subject to professional discipline or censure, or any representation made by Employee herein is at any time false or inaccurate.

6.2.2. *Loss of Staff Privileges.* Employee's medical staff membership or privileges at any hospital or other healthcare facility where Employee provides any services or where Employer requires Employee to obtain and maintain medical staff membership and privileges are denied, revoked, lost, restricted, or suspended.

6.2.3. *Quality of Service.* Employer determines in good faith that Employee is negligent in the performance of healthcare services.

6.2.4. *Illegal or Unethical Actions.* Employee commits or permits any act or conduct which, in the good faith determination of Employer (i) endangers the health, life, or safety of any patient, coworker, or any other person; (ii) may place Employer into public ill-repute or in noncompliance with any federal, state, or local law, rule, or regulation; (iii) adversely affects, or is likely to adversely affect, Employer's relationship with any payor, hospital, or other healthcare facility or patient, or with any third party contracting with Employer; or (iv) constitutes professional misconduct, or fraudulent, oppressive or criminal behavior, or alcoholism or substance abuse.

6.2.5. *Failure to Comply with Employer Policies and Procedures.* Employee fails to substantially comply with any of the certificate of formation, bylaws, policies, procedures, standards, requirements, compliance plans, or other rules and regulations of Employer as may be established and modified from time to time by Employer.

6.2.6. *Failure to Satisfy Performance Goals.* Employee fails to satisfy the performance and productivity goals established for and communicated to Employee by Employer.

6.2.7. *Breach of Contract.* Employee breaks any term or provision of this Agreement, and the breach, if rectifiable and not otherwise cause for termination, is not rectified to the reasonable satisfaction of Employer within ten (10) days after written notice of the breach is given to Employee.

6.2.8. *Termination by Employee for Cause.* Employee may immediately terminate this Agreement and his or her employment hereunder for cause effective upon the giving of written notice of termination to Employer if (i) Employer fails to pay any base salary payment due to Employee hereunder and such failure continues for more than five (5) days after the scheduled date of such payment; or (ii) Employer breaches any other term or provision of this Agreement, and the breach, if rectifiable and not otherwise cause for termination, is not rectified to the reasonable satisfaction of Employee within ten (10) days after written notice of the breach is given to Employer.

6.3. Unless otherwise expressly provided herein or in any other applicable notice of termination, the expiration or any termination of this Agreement and Employee's employment hereunder shall be effective from and after the expiration of any notice period expressly stated herein or when the termination notice is deemed given, whichever is applicable.

6.4. Upon the expiration or any termination of this Agreement, Employee shall be entitled to all base salary earned up to the expiration or termination date prorated by days, and any outstanding and unpaid expense reimbursements owed to Employee hereunder. Upon payment of such amounts to Employee, Employer shall have no further liability or obligation of any kind to Employee hereunder or as a result of the expiration or termination of this Agreement or the termination of the employment of Employee pursuant to this Agreement unless otherwise required by law. The expiration or termination of this Agreement shall not affect the liability of either party for any breach of this Agreement.

7. REPRESENTATION AND WARRANTIES OF EMPLOYEE

7.1. Employee represents and warrants to Employer the following:

7.1.1. Employee holds a valid and unrestricted license to practice medicine in the State of {*STATE*} issued by the {*STATE*} Medical Board. Employee has never had any physician license held by him or her limited, withdrawn, suspended, curtailed, or revoked in any state or jurisdiction, nor has Employee ever been placed on probation by any medical licensing board.

7.1.2. Employee possesses all appropriate certifications, registrations, and approvals from the Federal Drug Enforcement Administration, {*STATE*} Department of Public Safety, and any other applicable federal or state agency necessary to prescribe and dispense drugs under applicable federal and state laws and regulations, and no such certification, registration, or approval now or previously held by Employee has ever been limited, withdrawn, suspended, curtailed, placed on probation, or revoked.

7.1.3. Employee is duly enrolled in the federal Medicare program and the {*STATE*} Medicaid program and eligible to seek reimbursement under such programs for covered services rendered by Employee to beneficiaries of such programs. Employee's enrollment and eligibility to participate in any such program or in any other third-party payment system has never been curtailed, suspended, revoked, or otherwise been the subject of any proceeding that can result or could have resulted in the same.

7.1.4. Employee has never been convicted of a felony or any crime involving moral recklessness.

7.1.5. Employee has never been a party to or the subject of any litigation relating in any way to medical services provided or omitted by Employee. To the best of Employee's knowledge, there is no litigation, investigation, or proceeding whether civil, criminal, or administrative in nature, pending against Employee as of the Effective Date.

7.1.6. None of the execution, delivery, or performance of this Agreement by Employee will violate, conflict with, or constitute a breach or default under any agreement (whether written or oral) to which Employee is a party or by which Employee is bound.

8. RESTRICTIVE COVENANTS

8.1. *Confidential and Proprietary Information. Confidential information* for purposes of this Agreement means any and all information, in any form whether written, oral, electronic or otherwise, of Employer relating to Employer or Employer's medical practice or business including, but not limited to, the name and address of any patient of Employer, patient records, medical records, charts, files, books, other records, fee schedules, methods of operation, business plans, strategies, strategic plans, software, databases, existing or complemented managed care or other relationships with payors, financial information, trade secrets, employee matters, and any other information of any kind of Employer relating to Employer or Employer's medical practice or business. *Proprietary information* for purposes of this Agreement means any and all trademarks, trade names, service marks, and copyrighted or patented materials, including, but not limited to, Employer's names and logos, acquired by Employer or used in the medical practice or business of Employer.

8.1.1. Employer agrees to disclose Confidential Information to Employee during the term of this Agreement and in the course of performance of this Agreement.

8.1.2. Employee agrees:

8.1.2.1. The Confidential Information and the Proprietary Information are vital to the business and financial success of Employer and that unauthorized disclosure or use of Confidential and/or Proprietary Information would seriously and adversely affect the medical practice and business of Employer.

8.1.2.2. All Confidential Information and all Proprietary Information are and shall remain the sole property of Employer and that Employee does not and shall not have ownership interest therein.

8.1.2.3. All Confidential Information is confidential to and trade secrets of Employer.

8.1.2.4. To maintain the confidentiality of all Confidential Information and to not disclose, divulge, communicate, or otherwise use any Confidential Information or Proprietary Information except solely as necessary for the performance of Employee's duties and responsibilities under and in accordance with the terms of this Agreement or as otherwise expressly consented to in writing by Employer.

8.1.2.5. If a dispute arising from or relating to this Agreement is submitted for adjudication to any court, arbitration panel, or other third party, the preservation of the secrecy of Confidential Information and Proprietary Information may be jeopardized, and accordingly all pleadings, documents, testimony, and records relating to any such adjudication will be maintained in secrecy and will be available for inspection by Employer, Employee, and their respective attorneys and experts, who will agree, in advance and in writing, to receive and maintain all such information in secrecy, except as may be limited by them in writing.

8.2. *HIPAA Compliance.* Employee agrees not to use or disclose any protected health information or individually identifiable health information, as defined by 45 CFR Part 164, other than expressly permitted by this Agreement and the requirements of the federal privacy regulations and security standards. Employee further agrees to comply with all policies, procedures, and directives of Employer regarding the use and disclosure of protected health information.

8.3. [NOTE: THIS NON-COMPETE MAY NOT BE ENFORCEABLE IN CERTAIN STATES] *Non-Compete Agreement.* Employee agrees that during the _____-year period immediately after the end of the term of this Agreement, he or she shall not engage in any business or practice that competes with the business of Employer. For the purposes of this Agreement, this means the Employee engaging in the practice of medicine: (i) as an individual practitioner anywhere, whether at a physician office, hospital, ambulatory surgical center, or any other healthcare facility, in a restricted area; or (ii) directly or indirectly as a proprietor, owner, partner, principal, agent, member, director, manager, employee, consultant, independent contractor, service provider, lender, affiliate or stockholder of any entity, group, or person that comprises or engages in a medical practice anywhere, whether at a physician office, hospital, ambulatory surgical center, or any other healthcare facility, in a restricted area, whether directly or indirectly through one or more parent, subsidiary, or other entities.

8.3.1. *Restricted area* means:

8.3.1.1. The physician office location currently utilized by Employer at {*ADDRESS*}, and all areas within a five (5) mile radius of such physician office or within such areas at any time during the term of this Agreement and thereafter;

8.3.1.2. Any other physician office location hereafter established by Employer at any time during the term of this Agreement, and all areas within a five (5) mile radius of any such physician office hereafter established by Employer at any time during the term of this Agreement, irrespective of whether Employer ceases to conduct operations at any such office or within any such areas after such office is established by Employer.

8.3.1.3. If Employee acts in violation of this provision, Employer shall be entitled to preliminary and permanent injunctions restraining Employee from such violations as well as other remedies available at law or in equity.

8.4. Employee shall not, directly or indirectly, during any portion of the term of this Agreement or the _____-year period immediately after the end of the Agreement: (i) call on or solicit, or attempt to call on or solicit, any Employer's past or present patients in any manner that is competitive with Employer's business as conducted as of the expiration or termination of this Agreement; (ii) solicit, employ, or otherwise engage as an employee, independent contractor, or otherwise, any person who is or was an employee or independent contractor of Employee at any time during the term of this Agreement or in any manner induce or attempt to include any such employee or independent contractor of Employer to terminate his or her employment or engagement as such with Employer.

8.5. Limitations on these restrictive covenants are:

8.5.1. Employer shall grant Employee access to:

8.5.1.1. A list of patients whom Employee has seen or treated pursuant to this Agreement within one year of the effective date of expiration or termination;

8.5.1.2. The medical records of patients treated by Employee pursuant to this Agreement upon written authorization of the patient and any copies of medical records for a reasonable fee as established by the {*STATE*} State Board of Medical Examiners.

8.5.2. Employee shall not be prohibited from providing continuing care and treatment to a specific patient or patients during the course of an acute illness even after this Agreement or Employee's employment hereunder has been terminated.

9. MISCELLANEOUS PROVISIONS

9.1. This Agreement shall be governed by and construed and interpreted in accordance with the laws of the State of {*STATE*}, without regard to conflicts of laws or principles that might require the application of the laws of any other state.

9.2. Except as otherwise expressly provided in this Agreement, any controversy or claim arising out of or relating to this Agreement, or any breach thereof, shall be settled by arbitration, in the city of {*CITY*} in the State of {*STATE*}. The prevailing party with respect to any controversy or claim arising out of or in connection with this Agreement shall be entitled to recover reasonable attorney's fees and costs incurred in connection with such claim or controversy.

9.3. If any provisions in this Agreement shall be deemed to be invalid or unenforceable by a court having jurisdiction, the remainder of this Agreement, and the application of such provision to circumstances other than those as to which it is deemed invalid or unenforceable, shall not be affected thereby.

9.4. This Agreement, including the Exhibits hereto, sets forth and constitutes the entire agreement, and supersedes any prior or contemporaneous agreements whether written or oral between Employer and Employee relating to the subject matter of this Agreement. There are no representations, warranties, covenants, promises, agreements, arrangements, or understandings, written or oral, express or implied, between the parties with respect to the subject matter of this Agreement that are not set forth in this Agreement.

9.5. No amendment to any provision of this Agreement shall be valid or effective unless such amendment is in writing and signed by both parties.

9.6. Neither party shall have the right to assign this Agreement or any right hereunder, or to delegate all or any of its duties or obligations hereunder, without prior written consent of the other party; provided that Employer may assign this Assignment to any entity that is wholly owned by Employer or by any or all of the owners of Employer, or in connection with the sale of all or substantially all of the assets of Employer, to the purchaser of such assets in such sale transaction.

IN WITNESS WHEREOF, EMPLOYER, by EMPLOYER's duly authorized representatives, and EMPLOYEE, have signed this Agreement as of the day and year first written above.

EMPLOYER:                          EMPLOYEE:
{NAME OF PRACTICE}

By: _____      By: _____

Name: _____      Name: _____

Title: _____

Date: _____      Date: _____

## Form 10.2        <u>Outside Employment Request Form</u>

This is a sample template of an outside employment request form. Modify the template to fit your practice's needs.

---

FORM 10.2                **OUTSIDE EMPLOYMENT REQUEST FORM**

Employee name _____ Date _____

Department _____ Date _____

Job title _____ Supervisor _____

Medical group employment date _____

I have an interest in working in a second job. I understand that the practice is my primary employer. I do not believe that this second job will be a conflict of interest or affect my current position.

Name of outside employer _____

Job title _____

Job duties and responsibilities _____

_____

_____

Work schedule (list the exact work schedule and number of hours assigned each week)

_____

_____

Additional comments _____

_____

_____

I understand that any changes occurring in my outside employment must be amended and recorded on a new form submitted to my supervisor. This form will become part of my employee record and is subject to review by the Practice.

_____        _____
Employee Signature                                                                         Date

_____        _____
Employee's supervisor                                                                     Date

_____ Approved        _____ Disapproved

Comments _____

_____

_____

# CHAPTER 11

# Managing Performance

The performance management system, which includes performance planning, evaluation, and rating, is a vital component of human resources (HR) management. It is perhaps the most important and sometimes most troublesome aspect of the employer/employee relationship.

The outcomes of the performance management process are used in setting individual goals and objectives; awarding salary increases; identifying promotional, transfer, and training opportunities; and determining potential disciplinary and termination actions. Often this aspect of managing is the most vulnerable point of the employment relationship, generating the most complaints about management functions. These complaints occur because many performance evaluation systems are too subjective and result in poor management decisions based on arbitrary judgments and evaluations. Vague and poorly defined performance criteria lend themselves to biased judgments and evaluations, and litigation. Therefore, it is critical for employers to have a performance management system that accurately measures and improves employee performance and is legally defensible.

Many medical practices have not developed or used a formal performance evaluation system; however, the impetus to do so is very clear. Salaries and wages comprise as much as 60 to 70 percent of a healthcare organization's total operating costs. There is a clear link between the successful organizational operation and the effective and efficient performance of its employees. A comprehensive performance management system can help employers attract and retain highly qualified employees to ensure quality and cost-effective service and patient care. The result helps both employers and employees better achieve their personal and professional goals.

Managers and staff often have misguided thinking and may have counterproductive beliefs about why organizations should use performance management systems in the first place. Many of these beliefs result from managers and supervisors using poorly designed performance evaluation forms that focus on judging the employee as a person, rather than evaluating the employee's job performance and

**Effective Performance Management Systems have:**

- Organizational goals and objectives;
- Individual's performance and planning;
- Employee performance measurements;
- Performance reviews;
- Ongoing feedback and coaching; and
- Recognition and rewards.

behavior. Some employees believe that their performance reviews reflect more of a parent–child relationship where the supervisor scolds the employee for poor performance. This awkward situation causes tension and distress for both the employee and the supervisor. Another typical problem with performance appraisal forms is using poorly defined performance evaluation criteria that can inadvertently tie performance to administrative issues, such as compensation, rather than to the development of the employee, the supervisor, and the organization.

An effective performance management system involves management planning, organization, leading, and controlling performance. It results in increased productivity and more engaged employees. Supervisors are expected to have insights into which goals to set, how to achieve those goals, how to organize work efforts appropriately, how to lead workers in the right direction, and how to monitor and control performance so that it stays on target to reach practice goals.

Your medical practice should emphasize performance expectations up front with all employees, reinforce them consistently, and reward results regularly. Your practice should provide a uniform framework for performance management that ensures employees know exactly what is expected of them and supervisors know how to establish a job-related basis for planning, managing, and evaluating performance.

## Performance Planning

Federal and state statutes do not mandate performance evaluations for private employees, and an employer generally cannot be held liable for failure to give an employee a performance assessment. There are expectations though. If an employer makes a promise, either oral or written, to an employee that he or she will receive an evaluation but the employee does not receive an evaluation, the employer could, in theory, be found liable under a breach of contract. The employee relied on the employer's promise but the employer broke the promise and therefore the employee was harmed.

Most often, promises of performance evaluations are written in an employment offer letter, an employment contract, or in the employee handbook. Likewise, during new employee orientation or onboarding, employees are orally informed that their performance will be evaluated by their supervisor. Either way, the medical practice has promised to evaluate an employee's performance.

If your employee handbook states, "Employees will receive annual performance evaluations," that statement could create an enforceable right to a performance evaluation. On the other hand, a slight wording change can have important legal ramifications. If the employee handbook states, "Employees should receive annual performance evaluations," a court is much more likely to rule that an annual performance review is not a right of the employee but rather a goal of the employer. You should review your practice's employment offer letters, employment contracts, and employee handbooks to eliminate any language that may obligate your practice to give performance evaluations.

There are several pitfalls that your practice's management and supervisors can avoid to protect your practice from legal issues regarding performance management issues. Management can protect your practice by:

- Developing, implementing, and maintaining a sound performance system;
- Providing training about the system;
- Enforcing the use of the system;
- Ensuring appropriate use of the system and relevant policies and procedures; and
- Requiring legal consultation and advice before discharging an employee.

Supervisors can to help protect your practice from any legal ramifications by:

- Paying careful attention to performance planning;
- Giving adequate performance feedback to employees regularly, not just during the official performance evaluation process;
- Observing and correcting performance problems immediately;
- Thoughtfully and thoroughly completing the required performance evaluation forms;
- Completing regular evaluations in a timely manner;
- Being honest and thorough in performance feedback;
- Not inflating performance ratings; and
- Taking the performance management systems seriously.

## Evaluating Performance

Measuring and evaluating an employee's performance enables practice management to determine if he or she achieved or even exceeded expectations and goals. Managers and supervisors can use this information to better understand, manage, and help improve the employee's performance. Evaluating employees gives supervisors the information about how their employees are doing and what, if any, issues need to be resolved in order to increase performance and productivity. In addition, this information helps supervisors make intelligent decisions about recognition and rewards, promotions, development opportunities, employee discipline, if needed, and possible termination.

**Performance Evaluation Tools**

- Critical Incident Rating
- Peer Review
- 360-Degree Evaluation
- Performance Standard
- Criterion-Based Method
- Goal Setting

Evaluating performance also gives employees a chance to receive constructive feedback about their performance and make changes if necessary. It also provides employees with the opportunity to discuss with their supervisor any possible issues, challenges, or problems that might be hindering their performance.

Some of the more common performance evaluation tools are described in the following list. For a more detailed explanation, please refer to MGMA's book, *The Medical Practice Performance Management Manual: How to Evaluate Employees*[*].

- **Critical incident rating.** This approach is based on a reviewer's written observation of an employee's performance throughout a designated time period. It relies heavily on the supervisor's communication skills and on which events the supervisor chooses to record that tend to be skewed toward unsatisfactory performance incidents. This approach provides valuable job-specific examples that can be helpful to employees. The documents of critical incidents is a vital step in developing a performance improvement plan or when preparing to discipline or terminate an employee.

- **Peer review.** This method is frequently used in healthcare organizations to evaluate professionals such as physicians. This approach involves a panel of colleagues who confidentially rate a physician's performance. It is also being used for other employees in the medical field. Ratings from highly sophisticated people are providing insight into the physician's performance; however, this approach tends to foster a sense of camaraderie rather than providing objective and constructive feedback.

- **360-Degree evaluation.** This approach is very popular and used by almost all types of businesses. It involves obtaining feedback from a variety of raters who interact with the employee on a regular basis, including supervisors, coworkers, staff from different departments, direct reports, suppliers, and others. The employee also completes a self-assessment using the same format as other raters. This method can achieve a more accurate assessment of the employee's overall performance. The supervisor should discuss the results with the employee.

- **Performance standard.** Employees are rated on common job-related factors that are applicable across specific groups or all employees. This method is useful in reinforcing the performance factors that are important to the medical practice. Supervisors provide employees with the ratings on each factor and an explanation of that rating. Although this approach takes quite a bit of time to develop and implement, it is easy to use and is a common-sense approach that facilitates effective communication between the supervisor and employee.

- **Goal setting.** A goal-setting system involves negotiation between the supervisor and employee to establish performance goals and objectives for a set time period. The supervisor and employee then develop performance standards that the employee will strive to achieve before the next performance review. This method is directly tied to your practice's strategic plan, so employees become very aware of how their performance will affect your practice's success. This approach tends to focus too heavily on results, ignoring the methods required to achieve the objectives. It can also be time-consuming because the supervisor must negotiate goals and objectives with each employee.

---

[*]  By Courtney H. Price and Alys Novak (Englewood, CO: Medical Group Management Association, 2002).

Some practices choose to use the same evaluation tool for all employees, regardless of job function or exempt/nonexempt status. Other practices will identify key performance factors that are mandatory for all employees (e.g., patient satisfaction) and then add other performance factors for specific job duties and responsibilities. Using separate evaluation forms for management and nonmanagement is strongly recommended. This is an effective way of reinforcing performance factors that pertain to management such as leadership, creativity, innovation, decision making, fiscal responsibility, and strategic planning.

Policy 11.01 at the end of this chapter is a sample performance evaluation policy that your practice may want to adapt to your specific management philosophy and organizational needs.

**Physician Performance Evaluation**

In many healthcare organizations, physicians and practice managers either ignore evaluating physician performance or talk about it but never implement it. Little is published in medical literature about the design and implementation of physician performance evaluation systems. It's almost as if physician performance evaluation is a taboo topic and/or a legacy of the autonomy that physicians have enjoyed in the past. This could be because physician performance evaluation is challenging and multidimensional due to the complexity of their job responsibilities, their skepticism about the process, and the difficulties of critiquing peers with whom they work closely.

However, there is an increasing emphasis on evaluating physician performance since physicians directly impact the quality and cost of patient care, which affects the success and profitability of any healthcare organization. In our rapidly changing environment, the demands for high-quality care and physician accountability is an essential core component of effective healthcare management. These trends, along with the increasing number of employed physicians, is why more healthcare providers are beginning to focus on assessing the complex components of physician performance.

Healthcare organizations that do evaluate physician performance frequently use some type of a peer review process. However, peer performance reviews have an underlying philosophy of camaraderie rather than providing objective and constructive feedback. Physician performance evaluation forms have primarily concentrated on assessing clinical competencies rather than behavioral competencies. Clinical competencies include knowledge and proficiency of technical skills, billing and chart analysis to assess patient outcomes, the number of procedures performed, physician adherence to procedural guidelines, and so on.

A more effective approach for evaluating physician performance is using a blended approach that addresses both clinical and behavioral competencies. Behavioral competencies focus on interpersonal skills and fit with the organization's vision, mission, and culture. They include effective communication skills, clinical reasoning, using good judgment, managing emotions, showing empathy, and establishing good relationships with patients and their families. Rarely does a physician performance evaluation form reflect the importance of behavioral skills, which are more difficult to evaluate and often ignored.

To address this issue, MGMA published the *Physician Job Descriptions Toolkit** to help practices and other healthcare organizations develop or redesign a physician performance evaluation system. It includes a Physician Performance Self-Evaluation template and a Physician Performance Evaluation template.

## Promotions and Transfers

Employees are often an overlooked resource to fill internal positions. Your practice knows more about its current staff's work history, performance, and potential than it does about new recruits. Often the high costs of recruiting, orienting, and training new employees can be saved by promoting competent employees – those who have already demonstrated their loyalty, stability, and work performance – to higher-level jobs.

The hope of a promotion to a better job and a chance for a salary increase are very important to most employees, so a promotion-from-within policy can be an effective motivator. Employees will strive to do their best and often obtain additional training and/or education to increase their chances of being promoted. Sample policy 11.02 at the end of this chapter can help increase employee morale, improve productivity, and reduce turnover while being cost-effective. Depending on the level of the vacant position, it can take six months to a year for a new employee to become fully productive. Since current employees are already familiar with your practice and its staff, they must only learn the new job duties and responsibilities.

When current employees are promoted, they are able to perform the duties of several jobs, which creates a more flexible and cross-trained workforce. Also, when they are promoted, their lower-level vacant job may be easier to fill. Your practice should fill each position with the best qualified person. Keep in mind that promoting from within builds morale and usually increases productivity. However, in today's climate of high unemployment and economic uncertainty, employees are more reluctant to leave their jobs, so promotional opportunities may not be as available as they were in the past. Therefore cross-training, job enhancement, and promoting from within have become a major focus for employers.

Transfers are another good way to fill vacant positions. Transfers can happen in one of two ways:
1. Management-mandated transfers; and
2. Employee-requested transfers.

A medical practice can require employees to move to a different department or a different role within the organization. Any practice management may mandate a transfer due to:
- Fluctuations in department workloads;
- Variations in department production flow; and
- More efficient use of employees' skills and abilities.

Usually, an employee will accept a transfer to a new position at the same salary, assuming that the same skills or previously acquired skills are used. In all cases, management

---

* *Physician Job Descriptions Toolkit: Defining Roles for Success* by Courtney Price (Englewood, CO: Medical Group Management Association, 2013).

should retain the right to transfer employees, regardless of whether they agree with the transfer. Three criteria that should be considered when deciding whether to transfer an employee are:

- The employee's ability to perform the new job;
- Whether his or her performance was satisfactory in the former job; and
- The salary grade of the new position compared to the former one.

Sometimes an employee has difficulty performing his or her present duties because of personality differences with the present supervisor, the working dynamics of the department, or a conflict with another staff member. Under these circumstances, the employee can request a transfer to another position. If approved, management should determine if the previous supervisor, coworkers, or surroundings were the cause of the work difficulties rather than a lack of ability to perform the job. In this way, turnover can be reduced and, ultimately, the employee will be happier and more productive in his or her new position.

When an employee requests a transfer, the designated HR professional or your practice administrator should determine the reason for the request. If the reason is due to personality conflicts with supervisors or coworkers, practice management and the HR professional should work with the employee and his or her supervisor to see if a compromise can be reached, keeping the employee in his or her current position.

In other cases, the employee may believe he or she needs a change of atmosphere, an opportunity to advance in a different type of work, or a different set of working conditions that may be available in another department. It is in your practice's best interest to try to help an employee find a new position within your practice. If there is a vacant position, the employee requesting a transfer should apply to the open position just as any other employee or applicant would. An employee-requested transfer may not be possible if there is not an open position for which the requesting employee is qualified.

**Promotion/Transfer Program Elements**
The designated HR professional or practice administrator should coordinate your promotion/transfer program. Supervisors and managers may be unaware of qualified employees who might be eligible for and interested in a promotional opportunity in their department. To be effective and respected by staff, top management must actively support the group's promotion program.

Promotion/Transfer programs begin by establishing a process to post job vacancies on message boards, bulletin boards, online, or through e-mail to inform current employees of openings. The job posting should include a brief description of the job duties, responsibilities, qualifications, and the hiring supervisor/manager. The employee should submit their résumé and complete your practice's application form to be considered for the position.

### Promotion/Transfer Program Elements

- Job Posting
- Job Bidding
- Skills Inventory
- Staff Coordination
- Good Record-Keeping
- Employee Development

Job bidding is another procedure that may be used where interested employees complete an employee job bid form and submit it to the designated HR professional or the administrator. The job bidding system should be open to all full- and part-time employees working at least 20 hours per week. In most cases, employees should be employed by your practice for at least six consecutive months before being considered for a promotional opportunity. A current skills inventory of your present staff is an effective method of locating internal employees eligible for promotion/transfer and is coordinated by the designated HR professional. Information on employees' skills, education, training, and interests can be pulled from a database or from employees' records and evaluated.

Assign someone to be responsible for coordinating your practice's promotion/transfer program. This person can counsel employees who are interested in transfers or promotions, or who are considering resigning to obtain a position outside your practice.

An effective promotion/transfer program relies on good employee records. This helps practices report results to the Equal Employment Opportunity Commission, if necessary. Managers should also publicize any efforts to promote employees. Your practice should keep statistics on the number and kinds of employees who are either transferred or promoted each year. Reviewing and analyzing the results contributes to the continual success of the program.

Highly motivated, productive, and efficient employees are a valuable commodity. Supervisors should urge outstanding employees to seek promotions. Your practice should also do its best to accommodate employees requesting a transfer to keep top talent in your practice. Your practice should encourage its supervisors and managers to endorse your promotion/transfer program and refrain from blocking transfers and promotions of qualified employees. A supervisor or manager who permits and encourages upward mobility builds a motivated and productive staff.

## Legal Considerations

Employment policies concerning the promotion or transfer of employees must comply with Title VII, the Americans with Disabilities Act (ADA), the Age Discrimination in Employment Act, the Genetic Information Nondiscrimination Act, and state and local nondiscrimination laws. Thus, promotion/transfer policies should be written to ensure that they do not have the intent, purpose, or effect of unlawfully discriminating against any employee because of race, color, religion, national origin, gender, disability, age, genetic information, or any other status protected by federal, state, or local law. In addition, a transfer may be considered a reasonable accommodation for a qualified individual with a disability under the ADA.

## Promotion/Transfer Policy

Your medical practice's promotion/transfer policy needs to establish promotion guidelines to follow when a position becomes vacant. Promotion decisions should generally be based on merit, work record, and selected examinations when appropriate. Seniority should be considered only if two or more applicants for the same job are equally qualified. The right to transfer or reassign employees when reasonably necessary is management's decision. In the absence of a written policy establishing transfer procedures, employees often will attempt to negotiate a transfer directly with a supervisor rather than with the appropriate manager. An employee requesting a transfer should follow the same procedures when applying for open positions as employees seeking promotions.

Temporary transfers may be necessary to meet temporary work overloads, address a staff shortage, avoid overtime, and prevent the need to hire temporary help. Transfers may include a change in the workdays, hours, or location.

If an employee refuses to be transferred, he or she may be subject to disciplinary action for insubordination. *However, under no circumstances should an employee be transferred as a disciplinary measure.* Any disciplinary action related to insubordination should be described in your practice's policies and procedures manual and be appropriate to the offense. In addition, frequent employee requests for transfer should not be permitted. This recurring activity is a clear warning that potential performance problems exist.

A time limit for accepting applications or job bids should be set for every job opening. When promoting or transferring employees, your practice runs the risk of the employee being unable to satisfactorily perform the job. For this reason, many implement a six-month training period. If the employee fails to perform the new job satisfactorily, your policy should state whether he or she will be reinstated to the former position or to a comparable position, if one is available. Policy 11.02 is an example of a promotion and transfer policy that can be adapted to reflect a practice's specific management philosophy, organizational needs, and staff size.

## Retaining and Motivating Employees

The ability to retain and motivate your most talented employees is directly related to the success of your medical practice. The cost of recruiting and training new employees is easily double that of a departing employee's salary. Because of the shortage of qualified applicants in many healthcare fields, retaining your top talent is crucial to your practice's success. Build a practice culture that promotes employee involvement and encourages top talent to stay with your practice for the long term. Your goal should be to become an employer of choice in your community.

### Elements for Retaining and Motivating Top Talent

- Employee Engagement
- Continuing Education
- Recognition and Rewards
- Employee Development

Many talented employees seek to work for a high-performing and well-managed medical practice. They want an opportunity to grow within their jobs, increase their responsibilities, and obtain promotions. Top talent wants competitive pay and fringe benefits based on a performance- and merit-based reward system. Motivation starts at the top of your medical practice. Motivated managers have more motivated employees. Management should be proactive in anticipating any dissatisfaction from their top employees. To motivate and retain top talent, determine what these employees want and then decide whether to give it to them, how to give it to them, or how they can earn it.

**Employee Engagement**

Organizations with engaged employees are more successful, productive, and cost-effective. Labor is the largest expense in most medical practices, so finding a way to retain and motivate your high-qualified employees increases your practice's productivity and profitability. Many studies have shown a strong correlation between employee engagement and productivity.

Engagement begins by providing your employees with everything and anything, within reason, they need to do their jobs and be successful. Employees should have all the materials they need within arm's reach to be as productive as possible. Your supervisors should be sure that new hires have the necessary resources to start working in their new positions immediately and to continue their work throughout the year.

Your medical practice should clearly communicate to all employees what is expected of them, what the vision of your practice is, what your practice values are, and how the medical practice measures success. This process begins with your new employee orientation and/or onboarding process. Employees cannot be engaged or productive if they do not know what is expected of them and how they will be evaluated. Your medical practice's vision should be shared by all top-level managers, and you should encourage your employees to help your practice achieve its vision. Lastly, employees become more motivated and engaged when the rewards they receive are memorable and meaningful. Getting to know each of your employee's personality, behavioral traits, and needs, as well as providing employee-specific rewards can increase productivity, engagement, motivation, and retention.

One way to increase employee engagement is through providing continuing education opportunities as discussed in Chapter 8, Employee Development. Continuing education adds to an employee's job satisfaction. It can also be used to train your most talented employees to become the next generation of managers, or it can be used as a reward incentive. Continuing education is a must for many of your employees to keep their technical skills and knowledge current. However, offering a continuing education program to uncertified or nonlicensed employees is also a good practice to enhance employee motivation and retention.

Most employees want to believe that their skills are being used to the optimal level in their jobs. Managers should be aware of which employees have which skills and place them in job functions that optimize those skills. Employees should also be given responsibilities that they find challenging but not overly stressful, when possible.

**Recognition and Reward Programs**

The goal of recognition and reward programs is to positively reinforce the desired on-the-job behavior, improve employee morale, and contribute to employee retention. Medical practices with a highly participatory work environment that recognize and reward top performers outperform practices that do not. Some may rationalize that salaried employees who earn a competitive

**Recognition and Reward Programs:**

- Stimulate performance;
- Create a positive environment;
- Increase employee retention;
- Improve employee morale; and
- Improve patient care.

wage are paid enough and their salary should be a sufficient source of motivation and recognition. But in reality, money sometimes does little to encourage employees to do their best work or exceed job expectations.

Extra effort and increased commitment are more a function of how workers are treated than what they are paid. Studies dating as far back as the 1940s support this assertion, with employees consistently ranking factors such as interesting work, supervisors' appreciation, job security, and participation in decision making as being more important than their salaries. Although money can be effective in some situations, it usually provides only a brief stimulus, whereas personal recognition and appreciation have longer-term, positive effects. Today, recognition and reward programs have replaced the traditional monetary reward system of the past.

This section briefly discusses ways to recognize and reward employees to build engagement and loyalty. For a more in-depth discussion about recognizing and rewarding employees, please refer to MGMA's book, *Acknowledge! Appreciate! Applaud! 172 Easy Ways to Reward Staff for Little or No Cost*.

There are four distinct types of recognition and reward programs:

1. **Awareness.** Awareness focuses on being sensitive to coworkers and colleagues in the workplace. Welcoming body language such as direct eye contact when speaking with someone and smiling can help employees feel more valued. In addition, simple greetings at the beginning of the shift and pleasantries at the end of the shift can also encourage employees to perform at their best.

2. **Acknowledgment.** Acknowledging employees for hard work and contribution to your practice can easily motivate employees. Just simple praise from a supervisor for exhibiting a behavior that your practice values can make an employee's day. Thank-you notes or a pat on the back can likewise increase morale.

3. **Appreciation.** Appreciation involves tangible, but not always monetary, rewards for achieving goals and excellent performance. These include traditional rewards such as certificates, tickets to sporting events, and gift cards. These rewards should be given only for a very clear reason such as achieving a performance goal, exceptional attendance, or outstanding service to patients and should be tailored to the recipient's personal tastes.

4. **Applause.** Applause rewards are a more public recognition and include rewards of exemplary performance. These should be saved for truly exceptional performance. These types of rewards might be acknowledged in a ceremony or event to honor the employee. As with appreciation rewards, the applause reward should be given for a very clear reason and commensurate with the accomplishment.

Many medical practices are implementing informal recognition and rewards where supervisors have the authority to give small, instantaneous tokens of appreciation without the approval of management. This type of recognition and reward should also reward special performance or achievement of a goal. These programs can be very inexpensive, and they also can be quickly implemented and easily managed. The philosophy is that it is the little things that count the most.

---

* By Alys Novak and Courtney H. Price (Englewood, CO: Medical Group Management Association, 2011).

How best to establish an incentive program that fits the desires of your medical practice's needs depends on your practice's size and its philosophy on compensation, recognition, and rewards. You can start by identifying employee preferences through employee surveys or by holding small focus groups. If your practice already has a recognition and rewards program, this is a good time to ask employees if the current program is still effective and meaningful and how it could be improved. By obtaining this information, you can develop more realistic goals for the program and identify what types of behaviors, achievements, and accomplishments will be recognized and rewarded.

Policy 11.03 at the end of the chapter is a sample recognition and rewards policy. Practices should modify this policy to fit the needs and philosophy of the practice's employee recognition and reward program. Because each medical practice's recognition and rewards program will vary drastically, this sample policy is meant to be generic.

*Recognition and Reward Guidelines*

Below are a few recommended guidelines to use for designing or redesigning an effective recognition and rewards program.

1. **Design rewards that match your group's culture.** Rewards and incentives should reflect your practice's culture and value system.

2. **Link rewards to business goals.** Rewards should be closely aligned to practice goals and support your practice's overall strategy and mission.

3. **Allow for flexibility.** Be flexible enough to respond to change in your practice's strategic direction, economic conditions, and staff needs. Give supervisors latitude in how they recognize outstanding performance achievements and encourage on-the-spot recognition.

4. **Keep the program simple and easy to understand.** Communicate the structure and benefits of the recognition and rewards program so that managers and staff can easily understand and embrace it.

5. **Match the reward to employees' performance outcomes.** Employees need to understand exactly why they are being recognized or rewarded. Otherwise, they will only experience a short-term glow without lasting impact.

6. **Be consistent in how you recognize outstanding performance.** Avoid favoritism among employees and recognize everyone who produces targeted goals. Inconsistent feedback sends confusing messages and contributes to low morale.

7. **Tailor your rewards to the recipient.** Ask recipients, as well as their colleagues, what rewards they value the most. Then let employees choose among several options. Avoid rewards that might embarrass an employee, and be sensitive to individual needs and personalities.

8. **Ensure that recognition is timely.** Timely and equitably distributed rewards are essential to stimulating outstanding performance. Very little time should lapse between the desired behavior and the corresponding recognition. The value of timely recognition is its immediacy and the likelihood that it will lead to the repeated, desired behavior.

9. **Track employee achievements.** Include in the employee's file a record of outstanding performance and recognition. Notify the employee's family of any special recognition.

10. **Recognize and reward often.** Allow employees to build on achievements and continue improving by using small perks on a regular basis, thereby creating lasting value.

11. **Review and revise your reward program.** Solicit ongoing feedback from staff, making adjustments as necessary. Communicate new changes once they are approved for implementation.

## Employee Conduct

Certain rules and regulations governing employee behavior are necessary for the orderly operation of your medical practice and for the protection and safety of your employees and patients. These rules and regulations may be outlined in an employee Code of Conduct. These rules should communicate your sincere interest to protect, assist, and guide employees in performing their job duties and responsibilities, especially in how they interact with patients, visitors, and coworkers. A Code of Conduct can help guide your employees' behaviors and ensure the proper image for your practice.

A Code of Conduct should state what is expected of employees in general terms. Regulating employee conduct is a matter that should be handled with the utmost sensitivity. Employees should be treated with respect and dignity. Most organizations avoid specific rules that could be seen as too restrictive or unnecessary. A Code of Conduct should clearly define prohibited conduct. Should the need for disciplinary action arise, your decision will be more readily accepted by employees if a comprehensive conduct policy has been established and communicated to your employees.

Although most organizations have written employment policies and procedures concerning employee conduct, the scope of these policies varies greatly. A Code of Conduct may cover many different areas and depends on your practice's philosophy. A practice's Code of Conduct may include the following topics:

- Absenteeism;
- Business travel;
- Carelessness and negligence;
- Collections of money and gifts;
- Conflicts of interest;
- Coworker relations;
- Destruction or vandalism of property;
- Disorderly conduct;
- Employee attitude;
- Falsification of time sheets;
- Fraudulent statements;
- Gambling;
- Gratuities and gifts from patients or vendors;
- Housekeeping;
- Insubordination;
- Intent to harm;
- Personal belongings;

- Maintenance of equipment;
- Media relations;
- Offensive language;
- Patient/Employee relations;
- Personal visitors;
- Political activities;
- Professional organizations; and
- Stealing/Embezzling.

The employee Code of Conduct is a code of ethical conduct and prescribed behavior. It should clearly specify types of prohibited conduct and indicate that disciplinary action will be taken for violations. You should consistently follow and enforce the policy. How individuals act typically depends on how the people in top management act. Your Code of Conduct policy should be well-communicated and reinforced to all staff. Policy 11.04 is an example of an employee Code of Conduct.

## Summary

There is more to employee performance than just conducting annual performance evaluations. Individual performance goals and objectives should be established for each employee. Ensure that your medical practice has a leading-edge performance management system that adequately measures and tracks employee performance. Your medical practice should also have current policies on employee promotion and transfers.

Recognition and reward programs help retain top talent and motivate employees to improve performance. Therefore, it is recommended that medical practices develop policies about recognition and reward programs for all employees.

## Sample Policies

**Policy 11.01**   <u>**Performance Evaluation**</u>

This is an example of a performance evaluation policy.

---

Policy 11.01          **PERFORMANCE EVALUATION**

<u>Purpose:</u> To establish and maintain guidelines regarding performance evaluations.

<u>Applies to:</u> All *[Practice]* employees.

<u>Policy:</u> The policy of *[Practice]* is to plan, review, and evaluate each employee's performance periodically in an objective, consistent, and uniform manner. The plan and evaluations consist of a written performance plan according to a standard format, with discussion of the plan and evaluations with employees.

<u>Procedures:</u>
1. At the beginning of the performance period, the supervisor and employee establish and document performance objectives and standards.
2. During the performance period, the supervisor provides continual feedback on performance. The employee is responsible for monitoring and improving their performance.
3. The employee's immediate supervisor conducts the performance evaluations, with input from the employee.
4. The performance evaluation is based on the job description, productivity goals, experience, training, and performance of the employee during the performance period.
5. Information derived from performance evaluations is used to determine the employee's eligibility for merit salary increases, promotions, transfers, layoffs, and retention, as well as to identify the employee's training needs.
6. Performance evaluations should be conducted at least annually, and copies of the evaluations are kept by the human resources (HR) department.
7. Performance evaluations should be completed:
   - After the first six months of employment;
   - On each anniversary date of employment thereafter;
   - When the employee is transferred or promoted to a new job;
   - Upon the employee's termination; and
   - Whenever the overall evaluation is below standard, in which case additional evaluations are required every three months until the employee receives an average rating.
8. The employee's performance planning and evaluation are a permanent part of the employee's file.

9. Supervisors are encouraged to keep informal records of significant events and discuss these events with the employee.

10. Performance planning and evaluations should be used to encourage better communication between the employee and the supervisor.

11. After the supervisor completes the performance evaluation, the administrator reviews it to ensure objectivity and fairness before discussing the evaluation with the employee. After the administrator approves the evaluation, the supervisor discusses the evaluation with the employee.

12. During the performance evaluation meeting, the employee has the opportunity to discuss concerns, correct inaccuracies, and provide written comments concerning any aspects of the evaluation. The completed written evaluation is forwarded to the HR department to include in the employee's file.

13. Each supervisor uses the following guidelines to prepare and conduct the performance evaluation:

    • Evaluate each employee's performance on the basis of job-related criteria and productivity goals;

    • Evaluate each employee on the basis of overall performance since the previous evaluation;

    • Make each performance evaluation meeting as positive and constructive as possible, maintaining a balance between praise and criticism;

    • Keep the meeting and evaluation confidential and private;

    • Schedule the meeting far enough in advance with the employee to give him or her time to prepare;

    • Allow enough time so the meeting is not rushed;

    • Use the performance evaluation to establish goals for the next period and to encourage improvement;

    • Note deficiencies and suggest specific, concrete, and practical steps for improvement;

    • Encourage the employee to talk freely about his or her job, then listen attentively and take the employee's comments seriously; and

    • Check the employee's progress, commend improvements made since the previous evaluation, and take appropriate action when improvement has not been made.

14. If the performance evaluation contains ratings that the employee believes are unjustified, and the matter has not been resolved to the employee's satisfaction during the meeting, the employee should contact HR to discuss the matter.

15. Supervisors are encouraged to continually discuss the employee's job performance on an informal basis throughout the year, not just during the formal performance evaluation process.

Approved by: Practice Administrator

Effective date: 1/1/20__

## Policy 11.02       **Promotion and Transfer**

Below is an example of a promotion and transfer policy.

---

**POLICY 11.02**          **PROMOTION AND TRANSFER**

Purpose: To establish and maintain guidelines for promotion and transfer.

Applies to: All *[Practice]* employees.

Policy: The policy of *[Practice]* is to fill vacancies from within whenever possible. *[Practice]* strives to place employees in jobs according to their abilities and the needs of *[Practice]*. To achieve this goal, employees may be transferred from one job to another, either at their own request or as a result of a management decision.

Promotions and transfers may be made on factors such as the basis of current job performance records, performance evaluations, experience, education, knowledge, skills, abilities, and other qualifications. Promotion and transfer decisions will be made without regard to age, disability, race, national origin, color, religion, gender, genetic information, or any other status protected under federal and state law. Seniority is considered only when two or more candidates possess equal qualifications.

Procedures:

1.  Management reserves the right to transfer employees as needed and determined in its sole discretion, considering factors including, but not limited to, fluctuations in workloads, fluctuations in production flow, and more efficient use of employees.

2.  Employees who refuse to transfer on management's order are subject to disciplinary action for insubordination and failure to follow an authorized supervisor's order.

3.  Employees may request a job transfer for the following reasons:
    - Increased career opportunities;
    - Personality conflicts with manager/supervisor or coworkers; and
    - Health and safety reasons.

4.  All transfer requests must be submitted to the supervisor, the HR representative, or the Practice Administrator. The designated person will determine if an appropriate job opening is available and if the employee is qualified for that position.

5.  If there is an open job position for which the requesting employee is qualified, the employee must apply for and submit their résumé and application/job bid form to the HR representative or designated person using the process described in this policy.

6.  If no vacant position exists, the transfer request is held until a suitable job becomes available for which the employee can apply or for three months, whichever comes first. After three months, the employee can resubmit a request for transfer.

7.  All open job positions are posted internally on bulletin boards and on the intranet. In some cases, an open position may be posted internally and externally concurrently. Positions should not be posted only externally. Job openings should be posted for a minimum of five business days.

8. Full-time and part-time employees interested in applying for an open position must submit their résumé and application or job bid form to the HR representative or designated person.

9. Applications will be considered only if the candidate meets the following requirements:

   • Employees are eligible only after completing six months in their current position.

   • Employees' most recent performance evaluations must be a rating of "meets expectations" or "exceeds expectations."

   • Employees must meet attendance requirements.

   • Employees must have the minimum required skills and experience for the position for which they are applying.

   • Employees must not be at any stage of disciplinary action or procedure.

   • If an employee is selected to interview for an open position, the employee must notify their current supervisor prior to being interviewed. Employees shall receive time off with pay to interview for a promotional job opening.

   • An application/job bid for an open position will be considered current and active until the position is filled or, if the position is not filled, for three months. After three months, the candidate must submit a new application/job bid if they would like to continue to be considered for the open position.

10. Hiring managers/supervisors are required to consider all qualified internal candidates.

11. Prior to making a promotion/transfer decision, the hiring manager is required to conduct a reference check with the current supervisor.

12. The hiring manager/supervisor is required to notify the current manager/supervisor prior to an offer being extended to the employee.

13. It is the responsibility of the hiring manager/supervisor to communicate with internally interviewed candidates who are not selected for the position.

14. If the employee meets all of the candidate requirements and the employee accepts the offer, the current manager/supervisor must support the employee's transition.

15. The current manager/supervisor and hiring manager/supervisor will work together to determine the transition date.

16. In the case of significant business impact, the current and hiring manager/supervisor will negotiate an extended transition time that could include job sharing. If appropriate, the current manager/supervisor may allow the employee to move immediately.

17. Employees accepting an offered promotion/transfer must successfully complete a probationary training period not to exceed six months.

18. Any promotional salary increases or wage changes will be effective on the date of transfer.

19. Employees with no break in service between their positions will retain their seniority.

Approved by: Practice Administrator

Effective date: 1/1/20__

## Policy 11.03     <u>Employee Recognition and Rewards</u>

Below is an example of a recognition and rewards policy.

---

POLICY 11.03     **EMPLOYEE RECOGNITION
AND REWARDS**

<u>Purpose:</u> To establish and maintain guidelines for an employee recognition and rewards program.

<u>Applies to:</u> All *[Practice]* employees.

<u>Policy:</u> *[Practice]* has established an Employee Recognition and Rewards Program that is flexible enough to take individual preferences into account. The policy of *[Practice]* is to recognize and/or reward exceptional individual and team performance and achievement through the use of recognition and rewards that are creative and meaningful.

<u>Procedures:</u>
1. The designated human resources (HR) professional is responsible for the management and communication of the recognition and rewards program.
2. Recognition and rewards are given for significant, outstanding performance that advances *[Practice]* goals and are tied to a specific accomplishment.
3. Recognition and rewards should be meaningful to the recipient(s) and given in a timely manner to be most effective.
4. Rewards are not adjustments to base salary, hourly wages, or supplemental compensation.
5. Supervisors/Managers are responsible for recognizing and rewarding their staff.
6. Staff members may nominate a coworker for a reward by submitting a brief description to their immediate supervisor explaining why a reward should be considered. Supervisors will decide whether to grant recognition or a reward to the nominated employee(s).
7. Supervisors must report all recognition and rewards to the designated HR professional so it can be added to the employee's file.
8. Employees may be recognized for exceptional work including but not limited to:
   - Exemplary performance;
   - Developing a new or modified business process, product/service, or other innovation;
   - Completing a special project;
   - Safety;
   - Outstanding teamwork;
   - Exceptional achievements;
   - Productivity;
   - Public service; or
   - Patient care.

9.  Employees may be rewarded with various nonmonetary rewards that could include gifts cards; meal vouchers; theatre, concert, or sporting event tickets; paid time off, and so on.

10. Rewards valued at more than $100 require approval from the designated HR professional.

11. Recognition and rewards are not to be used as a substitute for supplies, support services, or *[Practice]*-required training.

12. One-time cash rewards are administered through payroll and checks are issued during the normal payroll cycle with appropriate taxes withheld from the recipient's paycheck.

13. All recognition and reward activities must be in compliance with applicable federal, state, and local laws including but not limited to anti-discrimination laws.

14. All recognition and reward activities must be in compliance with applicable federal, state, and local tax laws.

Approved by: Practice Administrator

Effective date: 1/1/20__

**Policy 11.04**          <u>**Code of Conduct**</u>

This is an example of an employee Code of Conduct policy.

---

POLICY 11.04          **CODE OF CONDUCT**

<u>Purpose:</u> To establish and maintain guidelines regarding employee behavior.

<u>Applies to:</u> All *[Practice]* employees.

<u>Policy:</u> The policy of *[Practice]* is that rules and regulations regarding employee behavior are necessary to provide high-quality patient care, to promote safety, and to efficiently and effectively operate *[Practice]*. *[Practice]* does not tolerate conduct that interferes with *[Practice]* operations or is offensive to patients, visitors, or fellow employees. *[Practice]* is committed to a business that conducts itself with the highest level of integrity and ethics at all times. The following list is illustrative and not intended to be all-inclusive.

<u>Procedures:</u>
1. Employees should always act in *[Practice's]* best interests, upholding the highest ethical standards.
2. Employees should avoid any activity that may compromise or appear to compromise these interests.
3. If an employee is presented with a situation that is not in line with *[Practice's]* Code of Conduct, he or she should notify the supervisor immediately.
4. Employees must refrain from engaging in any activity or practice that conflicts with the interests of *[Practice]* or its patients. Employees with questions concerning conflicts of interest should contact their supervisor or the administrator.
5. All employees are expected to behave in a manner conducive to efficient patient care and the highest level of safety, including:
   - Reporting to work on time and being at the workstation ready to work at the assigned starting time;
   - Notifying the supervisor when they will be absent from work or are unable to report to work on time;
   - Complying with all safety and health regulations;
   - Performing assigned job duties efficiently;
   - Eating meals only during meal periods and only in designated areas;
   - Maintaining a work area that is clean and orderly;
   - Treating patients and visitors of *[Practice]* courteously and respectfully;
   - Treating patient health records and information confidentially; and
   - Discharging personal financial obligations promptly so creditors will not ask *[Practice]* for assistance in collecting debts.
6. *[Practice]* prohibits the following conduct:
   - Use of alcohol, marijuana, or any illegal substance on *[Practice]* property;
   - Reporting to work under the influence of alcohol or other substances, including behavior- or mood-affecting prescription drugs;
   - Possessing, selling, or using illegal substances while on *[Practice]* property;

- Misusing *[Practice]*, employee, or patient property;
- Stealing;
- Gambling on *[Practice]* property, including professional or organized gambling, sports or other forms of pools, raffles, and friendly wagers; and
- Falsifying health records.

7. Employees who commit any prohibited actions and/or behaviors may be subject to disciplinary action up to and including termination of employment.

<u>Approved by:</u> Practice Administrator

<u>Effective date:</u> 1/1/20__

# Employee Discipline and Separation

One of the more complex problems faced by healthcare providers is establishing and administering an effective and equitable disciplinary system. To be successful, employees must feel that disciplinary actions occur only when they are justified. Employees should view the system as fair, consistent, and free from personal biases. This can only happen when policies are communicated clearly to everyone and when supervisors are properly trained to administer disciplinary actions. Management should review disciplinary actions and how staff members accept them. The perception that the group has an unjust disciplinary system can lead to poor morale, decreased productivity, and vulnerability to union-organizing attempts, grievances, and litigation filings.

Disciplinary systems are complex because they are the confluence of conflicting rights for management and staff. Management expects that employees will professionally perform essential job duties and responsibilities. Employees expect to be treated fairly. Conflict arises whenever the expectations of management and employees do not match. Accommodating both can be challenging.

## Employee Discipline

Discipline has two purposes. First, it is training and learning how to successfully fulfill one's job duties and responsibilities. Second, and more traditionally, it is action taken by the employer against an employee for either poor performance or a violation of the organization's policies and/or rules. The objective of disciplinary action is generally to remedy a problem. To fulfill this objective, management must establish standards of appropriate conduct, a procedure for evaluating behavior, and a system for administering disciplinary action.

There are many disciplinary system approaches. Regardless of the approach, all disciplinary systems and policies should make clear that the employer has a right to immediately terminate an employee at any time, without warning, and for any reason or no reason. Preventive discipline is one approach that seeks to heighten employees' awareness of organization rules and policies to avoid infractions and motivate employees to perform their job effectively. When improper behavior occurs, management stresses the importance of improvement and offers constructive suggestions and training. Other disciplinary systems use penalties appropriate to the specific infraction and circumstances. Such systems usually consist of various potential actions, depending on the seriousness of the problematic conduct or performance and whether it has occurred before, including verbal reprimand, written reprimand, suspension, demotion, and dismissal.

Your disciplinary policy should attempt to meet the following objectives:
- Establish a procedure to inform your employees of below-standard conduct or performance;
- Provide a means by which the employee is given warning and counseling, as appropriate, ensuring that he or she understands what is expected;
- Provide appropriate disciplinary action; and
- Reserve the employer's right to immediately terminate an employee at any time, with or without warning, and with or without reason.

Your practice's supervisors and managers are the keys to a successful disciplinary system. They are responsible for enforcing the rules and taking the appropriate action when violations occur. The designated human resources (HR) professional should approve and monitor all disciplinary actions to ensure consistency because occasionally a supervisor may abuse his or her authority or be unaware of how a disciplinary matter was previously handled. That is one key reason why your employee disciplinary policy should be written. Equally important is training all supervisors and managers about how to implement it.

As indicated previously, it is important to ensure that your disciplinary allows for immediate termination. Employers should not promise "progressive discipline" or a series of progressive steps the employer will follow to discipline employees because there will be situations where an employee should be terminated immediately.

Policy 12.01 at the end of this chapter is an example of a disciplinary policy, and Form 12.1 is a form to record disciplinary actions. Medical practices can adopt this disciplinary policy with appropriate changes to reflect a practice's specific management philosophy, organizational needs, and size, and taking into account current applicable federal, state, and local laws.

### Disciplinary Process Guidelines
Medical practices should attempt to deal constructively with employee performance problems, unsatisfactory behavior, and employee errors. Your disciplinary process approach should be determined by your practice in light of the facts and circumstances of each case. When analyzing the specific situation, consider the following factors:
- The seriousness of the situation;
- The employee's past conduct and length of service; and

- The nature of the employee's previous performance or incidents involving the employee.

Depending on the facts, disciplinary action may include oral or written warnings, probation, suspension with or without pay, or immediate discharge. With employees employed on an at-will basis, a practice and its employees both have the absolute power and authority to terminate the employment relationship at any time without notice and with or without reason or cause.

**Legal Requirements**

Many laws may be implicated when disciplinary measures are being administered. Employees who believe that they have been wrongfully disciplined or discharged, whether due to discrimination or otherwise, increasingly resort to litigation. Given the scope of potential damage awards and the cost of defending claims, healthcare employers are advised to develop discipline and discharge procedures that limit or control exposure to such litigation. When developing disciplinary guidelines, management must be fully committed to implementing the guidelines; otherwise, your disciplinary system could be unsuccessful and costly in terms of time and dollars.

*Civil Rights Act*

Title VII of the Civil Rights Act of 1964 prohibits covered employers from discriminating against individuals on the basis of race, color, gender, national origin, or religion. This extends to hiring, discharge, compensation, and other conditions and privileges of employment. States also have fair employment practice statutes prohibiting employment discrimination that may include additional protected statuses, such as sexual orientation and marital status.

*Age Discrimination in Employment Act*

The Age Discrimination in Employment Act of 1967 (ADEA), as amended, forbids covered employers from discriminating against individuals who are 40 years of age and older. ADEA's prohibitions are similar to those of Title VII and include any form of discrimination based on a person's age.

*Rehabilitation Act and Americans with Disabilities Act*

The Rehabilitation Act of 1973 protects disabled individuals. The act broadly defines *disability* to including physical or mental impairments that substantially limit one or more major life activities. Under Section 504, recipients of federal financial assistance, such as Medicare funds, are prohibited from discriminating against people with disabilities. The Americans with Disabilities Act of 1990, as amended, also protects qualified individuals with disabilities.

*National Labor Relations Act*

The National Labor Relations Act (Wagner Act) prohibits interfering with, restraining, or coercing employees in the exercise of rights relating to organizing, forming, joining, or assisting a labor organization for collective bargaining purposes, or from working together to improve terms and conditions of employment, or refraining from any such activity.

## Supervisory Guidelines for Administering Discipline

Most charges of discrimination and litigation arise from discipline and discharge decisions. Continual performance feedback, consistency in administering disciplinary actions, and good documentation can often make the difference between whether a conflict leads to a charge of discrimination or a lawsuit.

If your practice combines regularly scheduled performance evaluations with effective discipline, it should be able to detect and resolve most employee problems that develop. Ideally, employee discipline should educate employees about deficiencies in behavior, performance, or conduct as well as motivate them to make the necessary improvements to continue working at your practice. It is usually more cost-effective to "rehabilitate" an existing employee than to terminate him or her and then hire a new one. However, there will be circumstances where employee behavior or performance problems are so egregious as to require immediate termination.

In most circumstances, before disciplining an employee, the supervisor or manager should investigate and gather all the important facts related to the infraction. Sometimes this will require interviewing pertinent parties, including the employee, keeping a written record of these interviews, and reviewing documents. Based on the results of the investigation and if there is nothing from the employee's version of events that warrants further investigation, the supervisor and manager should recommend whether or not to discipline the employee. Their recommendation should be discussed with your practice administrator or HR professional to ensure consistency in administering discipline.

A standard procedure for administering disciplinary action is for the supervisor or manager and the designated HR professional to discuss the disciplinary action in private with the employee. The meeting should be held as soon after the offending behavior or conduct as possible. The supervisor or manager should explain why the conduct or performance is unacceptable and the harmful impact it has on your practice, staff, and/or patients. The employee should also be asked to present his or her version of the events while the supervisor takes detailed notes. During this meeting, the employee should also be informed that any subsequent offenses or other violations of the medical practice's rules, policies, or procedures may result in further disciplinary action up to and including termination. If the employee is being disciplined for performance-related issues, typically a performance improvement plan may be helpful to attempt to correct the situation.

Disciplinary action is not always successful in resolving problems. There are times when an employee's performance or conduct is such that the only way to deal with the situation is to end the employment relationship.

## Written Disciplinary Action Guidelines

To justify disciplinary actions and to build a strong case to defend them, certain elements should appear in a written disciplinary form. These include:

- Citing the policy and rule violation;
- Describing in detail the misconduct or unsatisfactory performance including date, time, and place;
- Listing the prior infractions, warnings, or disciplinary action;
- Specifying how the conduct or performance can be corrected and improved; and

- Stating that failure to improve will be cause for further disciplinary action, including dismissal.

To ensure that discipline is administered consistently, medical practices should develop a notice of disciplinary action form. The form should assist with standardizing the disciplinary process throughout your practice. Form 12.1 at the end of this chapter is a template that your practice may consider adopting for this purpose.

## Employee Complaint Policy

The purpose of having or developing an employee complaint policy is to provide employees an orderly process for the prompt and equitable resolution of any concern or complaint. In a unionized practice, this policy is usually termed a *grievance policy and procedure.*

The HR department or person assigned this role is responsible for strengthening the employer/employee relationship. Consequently, this person plays an integral role in receiving, investigating, and resolving employment complaints and concerns. Employee concerns of workplace harassment, unfair treatment by his or her immediate supervisor, working conditions, or other job concerns are just a few of the complaints typically voiced by employees.

Practices want employees to feel comfortable discussing their concerns with a designated representative so their concerns can be immediately addressed and resolved. They should encourage employees to bring forward any concerns or complaints they have regarding their employment as well as provide guidelines with specific steps to follow. It is recommended that practices have or develop a written policy that describes the process for lodging an employee concern or complaint. This policy should be in the employee handbook and included in employee onboarding training as well as other appropriate training updates.

Some employers boast about having an open door policy so their employees believe they have access to everyone from their immediate supervisor to the group administrator or president. Unfortunately, some open door policies aren't as effective as planned. A more effective approach is establishing a formal employee complaint policy and procedure that allows your practice to provide a valve for employee discontent, thereby improving morale and productivity. An effective procedure can serve as a tool to increase communication and rapport between supervisors and employees.

This policy should specifically indicate who employees should file a concern with, and in what order. Generally, the employee complaint policy directs employees to first raise any concern with their immediate supervisor, if appropriate, or with their manager. But if this is not appropriate, or the employee is not satisfied with the outcome, the policy usually directs them to address his or her concern with the HR department or person responsible for these issues. If the employee is still not satisfied, he or she will be directed to address his or her concern with someone in upper-level management. Typically, policies list three or move levels of personnel of progressively higher levels of authority for an employee to potentially approach. Finally, the policy should clarify that any concerns or complaints relating to unlawful discrimination or harassment should be addressed through the specific complaint procedure developed in the practice's discrimination and harassment policy. The employee complaint policy will vary among employers, depending on the size of the practice and the relationship between management and employees.

Since passage of the Sarbanes–Oxley Act of 2002—which requires publicly traded companies to have a confidential, anonymous mechanism for employees to report suspect accounting matters—the number of employers providing telephone hotlines to employees has increased, which is another way for employees to voice concerns and complaints to a neutral third party, often the HR representative. Employer telephone and Web-based hotlines or helplines are integral to the employer's broad communication efforts aimed at generating both positive and negative no-fault feedback. The role of employee helplines generally have an expanded role asking employees to report improper activities or violations or suspected violations of applicable policies, procedures, internal controls, laws, and regulations. This typically includes, but is not limited to, all forms of harassment, discrimination, theft, security breaches, disclosure of individually assigned passwords or combination/access codes, unauthorized disclosure of information, fraud, dishonesty, bribes, kickbacks, illegal activities, and workplace violence. However, some employees may prefer to go to someone they know instead of using a hotline or helpline.

Regardless of which approach is used, all employee concerns should be promptly investigated and management should take appropriate action. In addition, for complete closure of an employee concern, the HR department or designated person should document the complaint and its resolution including a conclusion and/or follow-up with the complainant.

Policy 12.02 provides a sample of an employee complaint policy. It should be modified to fit your practice's size, structure, and philosophy.

## Whistleblowing

Whistleblowing is when an employee or former employee raises concerns about illegal behavior. Whistleblowing is different from other types of complaints. Non-whistleblowing complaints are when an employee raises concerns about the way in which the employer has acted in relation to his or her personal performance or conduct. Whistleblowing is focused on raising concerns about misconduct and/or unethical or illegal behavior or activities occurring in an organization. Although the most famous whistleblowing cases were reported to regulators or other government officials, whistleblowing has also occurred internally in medical practices.

Medical practices should have a culture of openness and establish a procedure for reporting concerns, especially where patient safety may be at risk or when other concerns such as acts of substance abuse, drug diverting, theft, inappropriate relationships, ethics, and/or safety violations surface. Employers should adopt an honest and transparent approach so employees feel comfortable in raising concerns internally to promote the practice's culture of openness.

Physician practices are required to have compliance programs. As part of its compliance program and to achieve open lines of communication, practices should establish a simple procedure for reporting concerns by using telephone hotlines or other anonymous reporting methods as well as nonretaliation policies protecting whistleblowers who report violations in good faith. One effective way to do this is to designate a corporate compliance officer and create a reporting process that allows the employee an open, anonymous, and protected method of communication with the compliance officer. The corporate compliance officer should be a high-level person who reports directly to the highest governing authority, typically the board of directors. This person should provide the governing body with periodic updates on the effectiveness of the compliance program.

There are federal and state laws that offer different types of whistleblower protection according to the subject matter of the complaint, and the type and size of employer. Medical practices should be aware that these laws aim to protect the whistleblower's rights, including protection against retaliation. Your practice should have a policy that addresses how whistleblowers may report misconduct and how their rights will be protected. Regardless of your practice's size, the whistleblower policy is a critical tool for your practice with respect to patient safety, correcting or improving systems and practices, and promoting employee morale, as well as providing a positive culture and preserving the image of your practice in the community.

Policy 12.03 is a sample whistleblowing policy. You can modify it to fit your practice's size and philosophy. You should consult with your legal counsel to ensure that your policy is in compliance with both federal and state laws. Form 12.2 is a template for a Whistleblower Reporting Form, which can be modified to fit your medical practice's needs.

## Termination

Terminating employees can be an uncomfortable and costly experience. Employees may quit, or be laid off or fired. Whatever the reason for termination, it causes disruption in the workplace.

As soon as management learns that the employee is leaving the practice or as soon as an employee is fired, the designed HR professional should begin the recruitment process to fill the vacated position. Some medical practices conduct exit interviews on or before the employee's last day of work. This interview is frequently performed by an HR professional. Exit interviews often review employee concerns or dissatisfaction, which can be helpful in altering your practice's polices or management decisions in the future. The designated HR professional usually processes terminations. Reasons for termination and associated management issues should be forwarded to the administrator or designee.

Up-to-date termination records are useful for analyzing your practice turnover rate, department turnover rate, and reasons why employees leave your practice. This information may indicate widespread departmental job dissatisfaction, poor management, or a faulty selection process.

Establishing an employee termination policy may be helpful for various reasons. It helps to ensure that involuntary termination decisions are consistent and do not involve unlawful discrimination. A termination policy that covers voluntary termination decisions helps document the reasons for employee termination. This information is essential in reports made to various state commissions that are responsible for administering state unemployment compensation insurance programs. Whomever is responsible for your practice's payroll needs this information to prevent salary and insurance benefit overpayments. Finally, capturing information about voluntary termination can provide valuable insight into employee dissatisfaction, which may help reduce turnover. Policy 12.04 at the end of this chapter is a sample termination policy that can be adapted to reflect your medical practice's specific management philosophy and size.

**Types of Employee Termination**

· Voluntary resignation

· Discharge

· Position elimination

· Layoff/Reduction in force

**Employee Discharge**

Employee discharge, or firing, should generally be used when an employee has not corrected his or her behavior in response to disciplinary action or other correction attempts. However, immediate discharge should be used as necessary for breaches such as serious practice policy violations, including but not limited to unlawful harassment, violence, stealing, and embezzlement. Sometimes the only way to deal with poor employee performance or unsatisfactory conduct is to quickly end the employment relationship. Remember the contemporary HR saying, "Fire fast and hire slow."

Discharging an employee is not easy, emotionally or legally. In order to protect your practice from wrongful termination charges or litigation, you should attempt to rectify the situation, if possible, using coaching, counseling, and your practice's disciplinary process. Also, work closely with your practice's legal counsel when making termination decisions.

*General Considerations for All Discharges*

You should consider the following questions when making discharge decisions. A "yes" answer to any of these questions does not mean that you should avoid discharging the employee. Rather, it means that you should carefully consider the risks involved and make an informed decision about termination. These questions are designed to allow you to conduct a risk assessment prior to proceeding with the decision to terminate.

- Were any representations made to the person that he or she was not employed as an "at-will" employee? If so, what were those representations?

- Is there a written offer of employment, a letter confirming the terms of the employment, an employment contract, or a collective bargaining agreement applicable to this employee?

- Will the discharge violate any "public policy"? For example, could the employee argue that the reason for discharge was the exercise of political beliefs, exercise of a statutory right, or the reporting of the employer to a government agency? Or is there an outstanding or settled Workers' Compensation claim?

- Does the individual fit into a protected status (i.e., race, color, ethnicity, gender, national origin, religion, disability, age, veteran status, or other statuses that may be protected by state law such as sexual orientation, marital status, etc.)?

- Has the individual made any protected complaints, such as complaints of unlawful discrimination or harassment, or whistleblowing complaints?

- Has the individual requested a reasonable accommodation for his or her religion or disability?

- Will the termination prevent the employee from vesting in your practice's pension, stock, or other bonuses in the immediate or foreseeable future?

- Has a thorough and proper investigation been conducted so that the decision is based on facts rather than on subjective opinion, perception, hearsay, or speculation?
- Has the employee been given the opportunity to tell his or her side of the story?
- Are there extenuating circumstances or other mitigating factors that might justify disciplinary action rather than termination?
- Should the employee be suspended, pending further investigation?
- Is terminating this particular employee consistent with how your practice has treated other employees with similar behavioral or performance problems?
- Is the decision timely?
- Could this type of termination induce staff to seek union representation?
- Have you consulted with an employment attorney in order to fully assess possible risks and to assist you in making an informed decision?

### *Considerations for Disciplinary Discharges*

In addition to the general considerations mentioned previously, consider the following questions whenever you are contemplating a discharge as a disciplinary action:

- Was the violated rule or policy known to the employee? Was the policy or rule published?
- Has this individual received disciplinary action in the past, such as a verbal warning, written warning, written reprimand, suspension, and so on?
- Did the employee have an opportunity to take corrective action?
- Are the witnesses, if any, credible?
- Was the information regarding the infraction obtained lawfully, such as a drug/alcohol test, private investigator, body or vehicle search, and so on?
- Is there proper documentation to support your decision?
- Does the employee's overall documented record support the decision, such as being consistently tardy, absent, uncooperative, or failing to correct behavior after receiving warnings?
- Is terminating this employee consistent with how you have applied the rule or policy to other employees who have engaged in similar behavior?

### *Considerations for Poor Performance Discharges*

In addition to the general considerations mentioned previously, consider the following questions whenever you are contemplating a discharge for poor performance:

- Do the prior and current performance evaluations support the decision?
- Was the employee not only told of the deficiencies, but also given sufficient time and opportunities to make the necessary improvements to meet expectations?
- Was the employee denied any requested training or other assistance to help him or her improve?
- Is the cited reason for the discharge the real reason?
- Can the deficiency be measured objectively? Are the criticisms specific to the employee's actions rather than to his or her attitude?

- Does the employee's overall documented record support the decision? For example, did the employee just receive an outstanding performance evaluation and a merit raise?

- Was the employee ever told that his or her failure to improve would result in termination?

- Is terminating this employee consistent with how your practice has treated other employees with similar performance deficiencies?

*Method of Discharge*

Once the decision to discharge has been made, your practice needs to consider how the termination will happen. The following questions and suggestions should be considered:

- Where will the meeting be conducted? It should be conducted in private.

- Who will lead the meeting? Usually the supervisor or manager should lead the meeting.

- Should a witness be present? Whenever possible, a witness should be present, preferably an HR professional.

- Has the employee's computer access been discontinued?

- Has a checklist been prepared of what the employee needs to return to the employer, such as identification cards, keys, and so on?

- Has the employer prepared the final paycheck? Have any other payments, such as accrued vacation pay and expense reimbursements, been taken into account and included in the final paycheck in accordance with applicable law?

- Have appropriate steps been taken to protect the confidentiality of proprietary practice information and patients' private health information?

- Has anyone who has knowledge of the reasons for termination been instructed that this information should be treated as confidential? When asked for details about this employee's departure, individuals should state only that he or she is no longer with your practice.

**Voluntary Termination**

Voluntary termination or resignation is when the employee resigns of his or her own free will. This type of termination is the most common. Management should try to determine as precisely as possible the reason for an employee's decision to leave. Typical reasons include securing a better position elsewhere, moving out of town, or experiencing personal dissatisfaction. In the last case, it is critical to find out the nature of the personal dissatisfaction. Turnover in a medical practice is costly. When your practice loses competent employees, it must spend considerable time and money to replace them and train new employees.

The best method for obtaining this information is through an exit interview. The interview can be summarized and this information sent to management for review. Obtaining information concerning voluntary termination can protect your practice from complaints by concerned federal, state, or local government agencies, and it can identify internal problems that are causing employee dissatisfaction. The templates at the end of this chapter include a Resignation Form (Form 12.3), a Termination Evaluation (Form 12.4), and an Exit Interview Questionnaire (Form 12.5), all of which can be modified to fit your medical practice's needs.

### Retirement

Traditionally, retirement has been at the end of a person's career. Today, however, retirement is seen more as a transition to a new stage of life. Prior to 1979, many organizations had retirement polices that made retirement mandatory at age 65. The Age Discrimination in Employment Act (ADEA), as amended, generally prohibits mandatory retirement at a certain age. However, practices can use age 65 as the "normal" retirement age when employees become eligible to retire. The difference is that no employee may be forced to retire at any age.

Some employers offer early retirement packages to encourage employees to retire earlier that they would otherwise. The "buyout" concept is an offer of cash inducements for early retirement. This approach allows employers to downsize in a way that does not discriminate. Compliance with all employment laws, including those covering employee benefits, is critical when a practice offers an early retirement package option.

Some employees want to go into semi-retirement. Under this approach, a person reduces his or her normal working schedule to a predetermined lower number of hours per week. These can be configured as a reduced number of days per week or hours per day.

Another option is full retirement, but with the retired employee continuing to work for the employer as an independent contractor. This arrangement can be beneficial to both the employer and the employee as long as the individual is truly an independent contractor. There are significant risks with misclassifying employees as independent contractors, so you should consult with an attorney before proceeding with such an arrangement.

As discussed in chapter 5, retirement benefits vary greatly from one practice to another. Keep in mind that retirement benefits are regulated by various federal and state laws, including the Employee Retirement Income Security Act (ERISA). Your practice should work with your attorneys and financial professionals to determine which retirement benefits to offer employees. However, when a long-time employee does retire, many employers will recognize his or her contribution to your practice by hosting a retirement party and presenting him or her with a valuable gift or token of appreciation.

### Layoffs

A layoff is a separation from employment, usually due to financial reasons, such as a decline in workload, a lower demand for service, a shortage of operating capital, or other factors over which the employee has no control. Layoffs are frequently referred to as reductions in force or RIFs. The most important element in managing a layoff is developing a contingency plan for processing it. Procedures for identifying candidates for layoff should be established in advance.

In the past, some organizations have used longevity to determine who is laid off. Today, most employers consider factors such as skills, ability, performance, and work history. Employers should use objective criteria to determine who is laid off. Factors related to job performance give practice management more flexibility in retaining the best employees. However, layoff decisions based on performance are more difficult to defend, especially if your practice's performance evaluation tools are subjective, or if performance history is poorly documented. Layoff decisions must not involve unlawful discrimination. In addition, organizations employing more than 100 workers may fall under the Worker Adjustment and Retraining Notification Act of 1988, which requires advanced notification of certain types of layoffs, including mass layoffs and plant closings. Practices should consult with counsel to ensure compliance with all applicable federal and state laws when considering a layoff.

Depending on the type of employee benefits provided, your practice must decide which benefits, if any, will continue after a layoff. This issue is especially important in connection with group life, sickness, and accident insurance plans. Some medical practices continue these group insurance plans in force for a limited period of time (e.g., 30 days) and/or make the conversions with the cost paid by the laid-off employee. Under the Consolidated Omnibus Budget Reconciliation Act of 1985 (COBRA), if an employee is terminated or loses benefits because of a reduction in hours, employers must extend employee health insurance coverage for up to 18 months with the coverage paid for by the employee.

*Staff Reductions*

Reductions in the workforce through layoffs are a fairly standard practice in some industries, especially as economic conditions change. In today's healthcare industry, organizations including medical practices are restructuring or merging together. Mergers often create situations where two people do the same job; one is selected to keep their position while the other person is either transferred to a new position or laid off. Layoffs are never easy and require a great deal of planning and thoughtful decision making and consideration.

Staff reductions through layoffs have serious effects not only on the laid-off employees but also on other employees. These types of situations create stress, and financial and emotional hardship to the laid-off employees and their families. Layoffs tend to decimate employee morale and loyalty to the organization. Consequently, the decision to lay off staff should be a last resort. It is extremely important that the affected employee understands why he or she is being terminated. When a medical practice concludes that a reduction in staff is needed, it usually comes on the heels of a significant business event: dramatic fluctuations in patient census, new medical reimbursement methods or rates, mergers with other organizations, discontinuation of selected services, and other factors that create an adverse impact on profitability.

Many organizations chose to offer laid-off employees a severance package. However, there is no mandatory government requirement that employers must provide a severance package. Severance packages generally include a specific amount of money or months of pay, extended benefits, and/or outplacement benefits. Practices who take this approach should consult with legal counsel to consider obtaining a release of claims in exchange for the severance benefits provided. A written statement of the terms of a severance package should be prepared before the termination meetings and given to employees during this meeting. Most often, severance packages will guarantee a specific lump sum of money or a set number of months of continued salary. In addition, they may extend some benefits such as health insurance until the employee finds new employment or a set number of months, whichever comes first. The packages typically range from two weeks' pay to several months' depending on the employees' years of service. Some packages include outplacement services for laid-off employees to assist them in obtaining other employment.

### Termination Traps to Avoid

Despite adequate preparation, situations may arise that result in the terminating manager becoming flustered or deviating from the planned agenda during the termination meeting. Traps to avoid during termination meetings include:

- Turning the meeting into a performance evaluation;
- Trying to persuade the employee that the action is justified or getting into a discussion about details related to the termination decision;
- Discussing the supervisor's needs, feelings, or problems;
- Discussing alternatives to termination and allowing any bargaining;
- Bringing up past personality clashes, arguments, or situations;
- Reacting, whether agreeing or disagreeing, when the employee criticizes the employer;
- Arguing about anything;
- Shouting or raising the voice even if employee does so;
- Saying, "I know how you feel";
- Using "this is a blessing in disguise" theme during the discussion;
- Saying, "I do not want to do this but…"; and
- Discussing the personal relationship with the employee.

### After-Termination Guidelines

A meeting with remaining staff, if appropriate, should be held immediately following a termination meeting, especially in the event of a reduction in force involving more than one employee. Often, if just one employee is terminated involuntarily, it is appropriate to simply inform employees that the terminated employee is no longer with your practice. Remaining employees often bear the brunt of a staff reduction, whether it is through discharge, resignation, or layoffs. Although immediately relieved that they still have their jobs, employees often express feelings of concern, anger, guilt, sadness, and distrust. They may feel uncertain about their future. A meeting with remaining employees after a reduction in force should focus on alleviating fears; clearing up any misunderstanding of the situation; open communication about reassignment, if any, of the terminated employees' duties; and open discussions about any concerns employees have. The meeting should convey how your practice will continue to move forward.

Outplacement services can be offered to terminated employees to assist them with finding new employment. Outplacement involves the use of career-planning professionals, paid for by the former employer, to help terminated employees:

- Reassess their skill set;
- Explore new job opportunities;
- Identify specific job leads;
- Acquire new job skills;
- Prepare appropriate materials such as a résumé and cover letter;
- Sharpen interviewing skills; and
- Implement a strategic plan of action for their job search.

Because of the sensitive nature of outplacement, to minimize the negative impact on the employer and the employee, most employers outsource these services. The time needed to counsel and assist an individual in his or her job search can be extensive. Outplacement counseling can ease the pain of job loss and enable terminated employees to find new employment in a more timely manner.

### Separation Agreements

Whenever an employer involuntarily terminates an employee, there is a risk of the employee filing a charge of discrimination with the Equal Employment Opportunity Commission, or the equivalent agency, or a lawsuit. One strategy to prevent expensive and time-consuming legal action is to offer the employee a separation agreement that includes a release of claims. By signing it, the employee agrees to release his or her claims in exchange for receiving additional pay or benefits to which they would not otherwise already be entitled to if they did not sign the separation agreement and release. Typically, smaller practices have not used separation agreements, but they can be very helpful to your practice.

A separation agreement may delay an employee's termination, pending negotiation and implementing the terms of the agreement. Additional costs may be associated with using separation agreements, including extra monetary benefits given to the employee and the legal fees for drafting and negotiating such an agreement. A well-drafted, properly executed separation agreement effectively preempts a potential lawsuit. It provides finality to the termination because it prevents the employee from filing a lawsuit years down the road. However, separation agreements may not be feasible for all situations or employees. The employer cannot force the employee to sign the agreement, even after expensive and time-consuming negotiations.

A separation agreement is not valid unless both sides are aware that they are getting something in exchange for something else. Employees should be fully informed and agree that they are not otherwise entitled to the additional consideration, such as severance pay, that they are receiving in exchange for the release of claims. In addition, your practice should advise the employee to consult with an attorney before signing the agreement.

Your medical practice should develop a procedure for preparing and negotiating separation agreements, for persuading terminated employees to execute separation agreements, and for ensuring that such agreements are legally binding. In addition, the Older Workers Benefit Protection Act requires certain additional provisions including, but not limited to, specific periods of time to consider and revoke the agreement, which must be included to have a valid release of ADEA claims.

Your practice should advise the employee of the seriousness of signing a separation agreement and provide him or her adequate time to discuss the matter with an attorney. Informing an employee of the ramifications of signing a separation agreement and allowing the employee reasonable time to consider the agreement and consult an attorney provides additional evidence that the employer did not coerce the employee into signing the agreement. Moreover, every factor illustrating that an employee signed the agreement voluntarily and knowingly supports its legality, including the fact that the agreement is written in basic language that an employee can understand. Further, an employee who was given the option of taking the agreement home, consulting with an attorney, and deciding whether to sign the agreement serves as persuasive evidence that the agreement was signed voluntarily, and without coercion, threats, or duress. This is particularly significant when an employee is not sophisticated, well educated, or fluent in English. Form 12.6 is a template for a Sample Employment Separation Agreement, which can be modified to fit your medical practice's needs.

## Summary

Disciplining employees is usually one of the hardest management responsibilities and one dreaded by most supervisors. Your medical practice should have policies regarding all types of disciplinary actions. Supervisors should be trained on how to deal with discipline in a consistent manner for all employees. When an employee must be discharged, ensure that all disciplinary policies and guidelines have been followed to reduce the risk of potential charges of discrimination or lawsuits.

**Sample Policies**

---

**Policy 12.01**    <u>Discipline</u>

Following is an example of an employee discipline policy.

---

**POLICY 12.01**                    **DISCIPLINE**

<u>Purpose:</u> To establish and maintain guidelines for employee discipline.

<u>Applies to:</u> All *[Practice]* employees.

<u>Policy:</u> Every employee is responsible for observing *[Practice's]* policies, procedures, and standards of conduct. The primary purpose of this disciplinary policy is to ensure conformance with the established rules and regulations of *[Practice]* to promote effective patient care and safety. *[Practice]* has adopted a progressive disciplinary policy to identify and address all employee-related problems.

The level of discipline assessed in a given situation is determined in *[Practice's]* sole discretion. Most often, employee conduct that warrants discipline results from unacceptable behavior, poor performance, or violation of a *[Practice]* policy or procedure. However, any type of discipline, up to and including termination, may be issued in the sole discretion of *[Practice]* for conduct that falls outside those areas. *[Practice]* need not resort to progressive discipline, but may take whatever action it deems necessary to address the issue at hand. *[Practice]* will attempt to deal constructively with employee performance problems, unsatisfactory behavior, and employee errors.

<u>Procedures:</u>
1. The Practice will attempt to deal constructively with employee performance problems, unsatisfactory behavior and employee errors.
2. The disciplinary process used will be determined by *[Practice]* in its sole discretion in light of the facts and circumstances of each case.
3. Each situation will generally be considered in light of a variety of factors including, but not limited to, the seriousness of the situation; the employee's past conduct and length of service; and the nature of the employee's previous performance or incidents involving the employee.
4. Depending on the facts, disciplinary action may include oral or written warnings, probation, suspension with or without pay, or immediate discharge.
5. Because all employees are employed on an at-will basis, *[Practice]* and its employees both have the absolute power and authority to terminate the employment relationship at any time without notice and with or without reason or cause.

<u>Approved by:</u> Practice Administrator

<u>Effective date:</u> 1/1/20__

## Policy 12.02          <u>Employee Complaint Policy</u>

This is an example of a grievance and dispute policy.

---

**POLICY 12.02          EMPLOYEE COMPLAINT**

<u>Purpose:</u> To establish and maintain guidelines regarding grievances and disputes.

<u>Applies to:</u> All *[Practice]* employees.

<u>Policy:</u> The policy of *[Practice]* is to encourage employees to bring concerns or complaints about work-related conditions or problems to the attention of management.

<u>Procedures:</u>

1. *[Practice]* encourages employees to bring forward any concerns or complaints they may have regarding their employment.
2. Initially, employees should raise any concerns with their immediate supervisor or manager, if appropriate, unless the concern is about this person.
3. If an employee is not satisfied with the outcome of any issue, or if the employee is concerned about his or her supervisor or manager, the employee should direct his or her concern to the human resources (HR) department or HR professional.
4. If an employee is still not satisfied with any particular issue, he or she may bring the concern to the Practice Administrator.
5. The Practice Administrator considers the complaint and renders a final decision.
6. Concerns relating to unlawful discrimination or harassment should be addressed through the complaint procedure set forth in *[Practice's]* workplace harassment policy.

<u>Approved by:</u> Practice Administrator

<u>Effective date:</u> 1/1/20__

**Policy 12.03**      **Whistleblowing**

This is an example of a whistleblower policy.

---

POLICY 12.03                    **WHISTLEBLOWING**

Purpose: To establish and maintain guidelines to encourage employee whistleblowing complaints.

Applies to: All *[Practice]* employees.

Policy: *[Practice]* is committed to high standards of ethical, moral, and legal business conduct. In line with this commitment and *[Practice's]* commitment to open communication, this policy aims to provide a process for employees to raise concerns and reassurance that they will be protected from retaliation, reprisals, or victimization for whistleblowing. This whistleblowing policy is designed to encourage employees to report serious or sensitive malpractices or misconduct, to ensure that all allegations are thoroughly investigated, as appropriate, and suitable action is taken when necessary. This policy covers concerns including but not limited to:

- Criminal offenses;
- Use of deception to obtain an unjust or illegal financial advantage, either for *[Practice]* or personally;
- Intentional misrepresentations directly or indirectly affecting financial statements;
- Failure to comply with legal obligations;
- A miscarriage of justice;
- Danger to the health and safety of any individual;
- Damage to the environment;
- A breach of a fundamental internal control; and
- Serious unethical or unprofessional behavior.

Procedures:

1. An employee who has a good faith concern about a violation of a *[Practice]* policy or law is encouraged to report the concern to his or her immediate supervisor or the designated human resources (HR) professional. If the supervisor or a member of management is related to the employee's concern, or the employee is not comfortable reporting to a supervisor, the employee should report the incident to the Practice Administrator. If executive management is accused, the employee should report the incident or concern to the corporate compliance officer.

2. Non-supervisory employees who suspect a violation of *[Practice]* policy or law should not confront any individual directly or investigate the matter personally.

3. All complaints made by whistleblowers are promptly and thoroughly investigated, as appropriate, by the designated HR professional, Practice Administrator, or corporate compliance officer who will take appropriate action.

4. *[Practice]* prohibits any retaliation against individuals who make a good-faith compliant, file a complaint, or who assist or otherwise participate in an investigation. If, at any time, an employee believes that he or she is being retaliated against or that a complaint is not being handled properly, he or she should contact the designated HR professional, Practice Administrator, or corporate compliance officer.

5. Any person who retaliates against any individual who makes a complaint is subject to disciplinary action up to and including termination.

6. *[Practice]* will make all reasonable efforts to keep any investigation as confidential as possible. However, in many cases, it will be necessary to interview the complainant, the accused, members of management, and other possible witnesses. The Practice Administrator or corporate compliance officer will inform the complainant of the completion of the investigation.

Approved by: Practice Administrator

Effective date: 1/1/20__

**Policy 12.04**     <u>Employee Termination</u>

This is an example of an employee termination policy.

---

POLICY 12.04          **EMPLOYEE TERMINATION**

<u>Purpose:</u> To establish and maintain guidelines regarding employee termination.

<u>Applies to:</u> All *[Practice]* employees.

<u>Policy:</u> The policy of *[Practice]* is to recognize that conditions may develop that require *[Practice]* to terminate an employee's employment. These conditions include employee retirement, resignation, discharge, layoff, or reduction in force.

1.  The designated human resources (HR) professional or Practice Administrator must be notified of any employee termination.

2.  All terminated employees must return to the HR professional any identification badges, *[Practice]*-issued uniforms, keys, computers, or any other property of *[Practice]* on or before the last day of work.

3.  The procedure for resignation is as follows:

    •  Employees are encouraged to give written notice of their intention to resign. Supervisory and management employees are encouraged to give three weeks' notice. All other employees are encouraged to give two weeks' notice.

    •  Any employee who is absent from work without notifying his or her immediate supervisor of the reason for the absence is considered to have abandoned the job and to have resigned after the third consecutive day of absence.

    •  Resigning employees are required to complete the Resignation Form prior to the last day of work and submit it to their immediate supervisor. The supervisor completes the form and submits it to the designated HR professional.

    •  Supervisors are required to complete the Termination Evaluation form and forward it to the designated HR professional. This form becomes part of the employee's file.

    •  If possible, the designated HR professional will conduct an exit interview with the resigning employee before the employee's last working day. A written report of the exit interview is prepared and placed in the employee's file. Pertinent information requiring management review may be forwarded to *[Practice]* management.

    •  The final paycheck is given on the next regular payday after the employee's last working day.

4.  The process for retirement is as follows:

    •  Employees are eligible for retirement on the first day after their 65th birthday.

    •  If appropriate, *[Practice]* will recognize retiring employees for their service to *[Practice]*.

5.  The procedure for layoff is as follows:

    * *[Practice]* reserves the right to reduce its current workforce.

    * Layoffs may occur on a departmental basis or throughout *[Practice]*.

    * Supervisors inform the employee of the reason for the layoff, the estimated length of the layoff, and the employee's chances for recall.

    * The designated HR professional is responsible for answering questions concerning layoffs and benefits.

Approved by: Practice Administrator

Effective date: 1/1/20__

## Sample Forms

**Form 12.1**    <u>Notice of Disciplinary Action</u>

This is a Notice of Disciplinary Action sample template. Modify the template to fit your medical practice's needs.

---

**FORM 12.1**                      **NOTICE OF DISCIPLINARY ACTION**

*[Practice]* requires all supervisors to complete this form when any disciplinary action is taken. Submit this form to the designated human resources professional to place in the employee's file. This completed form is part of the employee's official record. This is an official notice of a disciplinary action.

| **Name of Employee** (Last, first, MI) | **Date of Notice** |
|---|---|
| **Department** | **Name of Supervisor** |

**Type of Infraction or Violation:** Mark the following reason(s) for disciplinary action.

| | | |
|---|---|---|
| ☐ Excessive Tardiness | ☐ Quality of Work/Poor Performance | ☐ Carelessness |
| ☐ Absenteeism | ☐ Violation of Safety Regulations | ☐ Negligence |
| ☐ Abuse of Sick Leave | ☐ Abusive or Offensive Language | ☐ Insubordination |
| ☐ Unacceptable Personal Conduct | ☐ Under the Influence of Drugs/Alcohol | ☐ Violation of Practice Policy |
| ☐ Failure to Follow Instructions | ☐ Willful Damage to Practice Property | ☐ Disclosing Confidential Information |
| ☐ Falsifying Documents | ☐ Theft | ☐ Violent Behavior/Threat of Violence |
| ☐ Other (please specify): | | |

**Date of Infraction or Violation**

**Type of Disciplinary Action Taken:** Mark the type of disciplinary action taken at this time.

| | | **Effective Date** | **Return Date** |
|---|---|---|---|
| ☐ Oral Warning (does not require employee signature) | ☐ Suspension without Pay | | |
| ☐ Written Warning | ☐ Discharge | | N/A |

**Description of Incident:** Describe in detail the infraction/violation.

| **Prior Disciplinary Actions:** Mark the prior disciplinary action(s) taken, if any, for this infraction/violation. | **Date of Prior Action** |
|---|---|
| ☐ Oral Warning | |
| ☐ Written Warning | |
| ☐ Suspension without Pay | |

**Corrective Action Plan:** Briefly describe the consequences for failure to correct behavior or improve performance.

By signing this form, I acknowledge receipt of this disciplinary action and that its contents, including the consequences, have been discussed with me. I understand that further misconduct or violation(s) will result in additional disciplinary action, up to and including discharge. I understand that my signature does not necessarily indicate agreement.

| **Employee Signature** | **Date** |
|---|---|
| **Supervisor Signature** | **Date** |

A copy of this form will be placed in the employee's personnel file.

**Form 12.2**       **Whistleblower Reporting Form**

This is a Whistleblower Reporting Form template. Modify the template to fit your medical practice's needs.

---

FORM 12.2              **WHISTLEBLOWER REPORTING FORM**

*[Practice]* is committed to high standards of ethical, moral, and legal business conduct. This form is designed to encourage employees to report serious or sensitive malpractices or misconduct. This form is used by *[Practice]* to initiate an investigation, if appropriate, concerning an incident or incidents for possible unethical or illegal activities. *[Practice]* will make all reasonable efforts to keep this information confidential to the extent possible. Submit the completed and signed form to your immediate supervisor or the designated human resources professional.

| **Name of Complainant** (Optional) | **Date** |
|---|---|

**Relationship to Practice**

☐ Employee                    ☐ Patient                    ☐ Visitor

---

**Name of Individual Who Allegedly Engaged in Improper Conduct** (Last, first, MI)

**Names of Witnesses and/or Others Involved**

**Description of Event(s):** Explain in detail the alleged improper conduct, including the nature of the conduct, when it occurred, where it occurred, how the individual(s) carried out the activity(ies), and how you became aware of the improper activity(ies). Attach additional pages if necessary.

**Evidence and Documentation:** Specifically list any other facts, information, and/or documentation you are aware of that support your allegation(s).

---

*[Practice]* takes every allegation of improper conduct very seriously. You can assist in the investigation of the incident(s) by providing as much information and as many details as possible. *[Practice]* will hold this report and all investigative findings as confidential as possible.

**Certification:** By submitting this form, I hereby certify that all information provided by me in this report is true, complete, and accurate to the best of my knowledge and made in good faith.

## Form 12.3        **Resignation Form**

This is a Resignation Form template. Modify the template to fit your medical practice's needs.

---

FORM 12.3                     **RESIGNATION FORM**

*[Practice]* requires you to complete this form as soon as you decide to leave the practice. This enables prompt processing of your final paycheck. Please notify your immediate supervisor at least two weeks in advance of your expected last day. You may also attach a letter of resignation if desired. Please submit this form to your supervisor before your last day of work.

| **Name of Employee** (Last, first, MI) | **Date** |
|---|---|
| **Department** | **Name of Supervisor** |

I, _____, hereby resign from my position of _____
  (Print Name)                                                        (Insert Position)
with the practice. My resignation is effective on _____ (last working day).
                                        (MM/DD/YYYY)

**Reason(s) for Resignation:** Mark the following reason(s) why you are leaving the practice.

☐ Accepted Other Employment        ☐ Medical/Illness
☐ Furthering Education              ☐ Personal
☐ Moving/Spouse Transfer           ☐ Other (please specify):

**Comments:** Please briefly describe the reason(s) why you are leaving the practice.

Your final paycheck will be mailed to the address listed below. On or before your last day of work, you must return any and all identification badges, keys, equipment, uniforms, and any other *[Practice]* property.

| **Employee Signature** | **Date** |
|---|---|
| Home Address (Number and street name) | Home Phone Number including Area Code |
| City, State, and Zip Code | Mobile Number including Area Code |
| Home E-mail Address | |

| Supervisor Comments | |
|---|---|
| **Supervisor Signature** | **Date** |

A copy of this form will be placed in the employee's personnel file.

**For Official Use Only**

Practice-owned Property Collected: ☐ Identification Badge   ☐ Office Keys   ☐ Uniform   ☐ Other:

---

## Form 12.4 <u>Termination Evaluation</u>

This is a Termination Evaluation template. Modify the template to fit your medical practice's needs.

FORM 12.4                         **TERMINATION EVALUATION**

*[Practice]* requires all supervisors to complete this form when an employee is terminated, whether voluntarily or otherwise. Please submit this form to the designated human resources professional no more than five business days after the employee's last day.

| Name of Employee (Last, first, MI) | Date |
|---|---|
| **Position Title** | **Department** |
| **Name of Supervisor** | **Date of Termination** |

**Reason for Termination:**

☐ Voluntarily Resigned            ☐ Retired

☐ Laid Off                              ☐ Discharged

| Would you recommend this employee to be eligible for rehire?   ☐ Yes   ☐ No, please explain: |
|---|
| **Supervisor Signature**                                                   **Date** |

## Form 12.5     **Exit Interview Questionnaire**

This is an Exit Interview Questionnaire template. Modify the template to fit your medical practice's needs.

---

FORM 12.5         **EXIT INTERVIEW QUESTIONNAIRE**

As an employer, *[Practice]* is committed to building a positive work environment for its employees. This Exit Interview Questionnaire provides a valuable source of information to measure our success in reaching this goal. The data obtained may be used to improve the work environment or processes, including employee retention efforts.

*[Practice]* greatly appreciates your time in completing this questionnaire. We hope that you will be candid with your responses so we may gain as much as possible from your experiences at *[Practice]*.

| Name of Employee (Optional) | | Exit Interview Date |
|---|---|---|
| **Position Title** | **Department** | |
| **Name of Supervisor** | | **Length of Employment** |

**Reason for Termination:** What factors led to your decision to leave the practice? Check all that apply.

| | |
|---|---|
| ☐ Change of career | ☐ Retirement |
| ☐ Opportunity for career advancement | ☐ Lack of recognition |
| ☐ Pursue educational opportunity | ☐ Issues with supervisor/management |
| ☐ Change of residence (moving) | ☐ Salary/wages |
| ☐ Commuting distance | ☐ Benefits |
| ☐ Working conditions | ☐ Family circumstances |
| ☐ Work schedule/load | ☐ Non-work-related personal life |
| ☐ Other (please specify): | |

Before making your decision to leave, did you investigate other options that would enable you to stay?

☐ No     ☐ Yes, please explain:

Did your supervisor...

| | Never | Sometimes | Almost Always | Comments |
|---|---|---|---|---|
| Demonstrate consistent and equitable treatment? | ☐ | ☐ | ☐ | |
| Provide you ample training to do your job? | ☐ | ☐ | ☐ | |
| Establish realistic standards of performance? | ☐ | ☐ | ☐ | |
| Provide consistent, thoughtful feedback on your job performance? | ☐ | ☐ | ☐ | |
| Provide recognition, praise, and encouragement on the job? | ☐ | ☐ | ☐ | |
| Develop team efforts and cooperation among coworkers? | ☐ | ☐ | ☐ | |
| Assign and delegate work fairly and equitably? | ☐ | ☐ | ☐ | |
| Offer opportunities for growth and learning experiences on the job? | ☐ | ☐ | ☐ | |
| Encourage and listen to ideas and suggestions? | ☐ | ☐ | ☐ | |
| Effectively resolve complaints and/or problems? | ☐ | ☐ | ☐ | |
| Follow practice policies and procedures? | ☐ | ☐ | ☐ | |

**Comments:** Please add any notes, and comment on your supervisor's areas of strength and areas needing improvement.

How would you rate the following aspects of your job?

| | Poor | Fair | Good | Excellent | Comments |
|---|---|---|---|---|---|
| Orientation training for your department | ☐ | ☐ | ☐ | ☐ | |
| Cooperation within your department | ☐ | ☐ | ☐ | ☐ | |
| Cooperation with other departments | ☐ | ☐ | ☐ | ☐ | |
| Communications within your department | ☐ | ☐ | ☐ | ☐ | |
| Communications within the practice as a whole | ☐ | ☐ | ☐ | ☐ | |
| Communications between you and your supervisor | ☐ | ☐ | ☐ | ☐ | |
| Morale in your department | ☐ | ☐ | ☐ | ☐ | |

**Comments:** Please add comments about your job conditions.

How do you feel about the following aspects of the practice?

| | Poor | Fair | Good | Excellent | Comments |
|---|---|---|---|---|---|
| Overall work experience | ☐ | ☐ | ☐ | ☐ | |
| Overall job satisfaction | ☐ | ☐ | ☐ | ☐ | |
| Practice as an employer | ☐ | ☐ | ☐ | ☐ | |
| Practice's commitment to patient care | ☐ | ☐ | ☐ | ☐ | |
| Practice's commitment to patient safety | ☐ | ☐ | ☐ | ☐ | |
| Practice's overall communication with employees | ☐ | ☐ | ☐ | ☐ | |
| Practice's management philosophies | ☐ | ☐ | ☐ | ☐ | |
| Practice's commitment to a safe work environment | ☐ | ☐ | ☐ | ☐ | |
| Physical working conditions | ☐ | ☐ | ☐ | ☐ | |
| New employee orientation training | ☐ | ☐ | ☐ | ☐ | |
| Employee morale | ☐ | ☐ | ☐ | ☐ | |
| Opportunities for advancement/growth | ☐ | ☐ | ☐ | ☐ | |
| Training and development programs | ☐ | ☐ | ☐ | ☐ | |
| Salaries/Wages | ☐ | ☐ | ☐ | ☐ | |
| Health insurance plan | ☐ | ☐ | ☐ | ☐ | |
| Dental insurance plan | ☐ | ☐ | ☐ | ☐ | |
| Vision plan | ☐ | ☐ | ☐ | ☐ | |
| Retirement savings plans | ☐ | ☐ | ☐ | ☐ | |
| Paid time off | ☐ | ☐ | ☐ | ☐ | |
| Other employee benefits | ☐ | ☐ | ☐ | ☐ | |

**Comments:** Please add comments about organizational conditions.

Please answer the following questions.

| | | | | | Comments |
|---|---|---|---|---|---|
| Was your workload usually… | ☐ Too light | ☐ About right | ☐ All right | ☐ Too great | |
| Was the job pressure and stress… | ☐ Too light | ☐ About right | ☐ All right | ☐ Too great | |
| Was your job challenging? | ☐ Never | ☐ Rarely | ☐ Sometimes | ☐ Always | |

**What did you like most about your employment at the practice?**

**What did you like least about your employment at the practice?**

**What does your new situation provide that your job with the practice does not?**

**What are your suggestions for how the practice could improve?**

| | | |
|---|---|---|
| **Would you consider working for the practice again in the future?** | ☐ Yes | ☐ No, please explain: |
| **Would you recommend working for the practice to others?** | ☐ Yes | ☐ No, please explain: |

**Additional comments about your job at the practice.**

**Form 12.6** **Sample Employment Separation Agreement**

This is a Sample Employment Separation Agreement template that may not be used without review and revisions by legal counsel to take into account the specific separation and employee, and to ensure compliance with current, applicable law.

---

FORM 12.6 **SAMPLE EMPLOYMENT
SEPARATION AGREEMENT**

This Employment Separation Agreement (herein "Agreement") is made and entered into as of this ____ day of _____, 20____, by and between {*PRACTICE*} (herein "Company"), a {*CITY, STATE*} {*CORPORATION, PC, LLC, LLP*} and _____ (herein "Employee").

RECITALS:

   A. Employee has been employed by Company, and Employee's employment relationship with Company ended on {*DATE OF TERMINATION*}.

   B. Employee and Company have reached agreement on the terms of Employee's departure to clarify and resolve any disputes that may exist between them arising out of the employment relationship and its termination, and any continuing obligation of the parties to one another following the end of the employment relationship.

NOW, THEREFORE, in consideration of the promises and covenants contained in this Agreement, the parties hereto, intending to be legally bound, agree as follows:

1. RECITALS. The above recitals are true and correct and are made a part hereof.

2. TERMINATION OF EMPLOYMENT AGREEMENT. Company and Employee hereby agree that, except as specifically provided in this Agreement, the Employment Agreement dated {*DATE OF EMPLOYMENT AGREEMENT*}, and except as set forth in Section 5 below and except as otherwise specifically provided in this Agreement, neither Company nor Employee shall have any further rights, obligations, or duties under the Employment Agreement as of {*DATE OF TERMINATION*}. During the period between the execution of this Agreement and {*DATE OF TERMINATION*}, Employee will continue to be available for consultation, guidance, project completion, and travel to any of the Company locations, if necessary, and as directed by the Administrator.

3. SEPARATION PAYMENTS. In consideration of Employee's agreement to the terms of this Agreement, Company will provide Employee the following payments and benefits (herein "Separation Payments"):

   a. Company shall pay to Employee the earned salary, accrued, unused vacation time, and all other amounts Company owes Employee through {*DATE OF TERMINATION*}.

   b. Employee shall be covered under Company's group medical, dental, vision, and life insurance programs until {*DATE OF TERMINATION OF BENEFITS*}, which expense shall be covered by Company and Employee at the same proportional rate as are being paid on the {*DATE OF TERMINATION*}. Thereafter, if Employee so elects, Employee may be covered under Company's group health insurance program, at Employee's expense, for a period of eighteen (18) months (or such longer period as may be required by law), or until Employee becomes covered by any other group health plan, whichever occurs first, in accordance with the Consolidated Omnibus Budget Reconciliation Act (COBRA). This continued coverage is subject to and in accordance with Company's terms and conditions of policies and procedures governing the program and in accordance with applicable law.

    c.   If Employee executes this Agreement, on the seventh (7th) day following the date Employee executes this Agreement, Company shall provide Employee with the following consideration:

        i.   A lump sum payment to Employee in the amount of {*XX*} dollars and 00/100 ($ {*XX.00*}), less applicable tax withholdings; and

        ii.   The letter of recommendation to potential employers, attached hereto (collectively, the "Consideration").

4.   COMPANY PROPERTY. Employee will immediately return to Company any and all building or office keys, security passes, or other access identification cards or badges including business cards, and any and all Company property that is currently in Employee's possession, including, but not limited to, any and all documents, records, credit cards, mobile phones, computer equipment, and any and all information about Company's practices, procedures, policies, trade secrets, patient lists, or patient information. All items must be returned prior to leaving the premises on {*DATE OF TERMINATION*}.

5.   WAIVER AND RELEASE. In exchange for the Consideration provided by the Company set forth herein, Employee agrees as follows to release the following claims set forth in subsections a, b, and c below (collectively, the "Released Claims"):

    a.   Employee hereby knowingly and voluntarily waives, releases, and forever discharges Company as well as any entity related to Company in the present or past (including, without limitation, its predecessors, parents, subsidiaries, shareholders, affiliates, and divisions), and any successors of Company and their present and past officers, directors, members, committees, shareholders (together with any officers, partners, managers, members, employees, agents and affiliates of any such shareholder), agents, employees, accountants and attorneys (collectively the "Released Parties") from any and all claims, demands, damages, lawsuits, obligations, promises, and causes of action, both known and unknown, at law or in equity, relating to or arising out of Employee's employment with Company, the Employment Agreement, or separation of Employee's employment from Company. However, nothing contained herein shall be interpreted to (i) limit Employee's or Company's right to enforce this Agreement through legal process, (ii) prevent Employee from filing a charge of discrimination with or participate in an investigation by the Equal Employment Opportunity Commission.

    b.   Employee agrees to release and forever discharge by this Agreement the Released Parties from all liabilities, causes of action, charges, complaints, suits, claims, obligations, costs, losses, damages, injuries, rights, judgments, attorneys' fees, expenses, bonds, bills, penalties, fines, and all other legal responsibilities of any form whatsoever, whether known or unknown, whether suspected or unsuspected, whether fixed or contingent, whether in law or in equity, including but not limited to those arising from any acts or omissions occurring prior to the effective date of this Agreement, including those arising by reason of any and all matters from the beginning of time to the present, arising out of Employee's employment with Company and the separation of Employee's employment from Company.

    c.   Employee specifically releases the Released Parties from any and all claims, known or unknown, under all applicable local, state, and federal laws, including but not limited to Title VII of the Civil Rights Act of 1964, the Rehabilitation Act, the Family and Medical Leave Act, the Employee Retirement Income Security Act, the Consolidated Omnibus Budget Reconciliation Act, the Americans with Disabilities Act, the Equal Pay Act, the Age Discrimination in Employment Act, the Genetic Information Nondiscrimination Act, the Worker Adjustment and Retraining Notification Act, Uniformed Services Employment and Reemployment Rights Act, and the Fair Credit Reporting Act, as well as all common law claims.

    d.   The Released Claims do not include any claims that cannot be waived as a matter of law, including but not limited to future claims that arise after the date of execution of this Agreement, and claims for unemployment compensation benefits.

6.   CONFIDENTIALITY. Employee shall not disclose, either directly or indirectly, any information whatsoever regarding any of the terms or the existence of this Agreement to any person or organization. The only exceptions

to Employee's promise of confidentiality herein is that Employee may reveal such terms of this Agreement (i) as is necessary to comply with a request made by the Internal Revenue Service; (ii) as otherwise compelled by a court or agency of competent jurisdiction; (iii) as required by law; (iv) as is necessary to comply with requests from Employee's accountants, attorneys, financial advisors, or other professional advisors for legitimate business purposes or personal financial planning; and (v) to Employee's spouse, if any (provided that such spouse agrees to maintain the complete confidentiality of this Agreement).

7. EMPLOYMENT RECOMMENDATIONS; NON-DISPARAGEMENT.

   a. Company hereby agrees that, in the event a future prospective employer of Employee seeks information from Company regarding the competence, experience, or abilities of Employee, Company shall follow its standard human resources guidelines, policies, and practices with respect to such inquiry and provide Employee's dates of employment and last job title only.

   b. In addition, Employee shall refrain from making any written, oral, or electronic statement or taking any action, directly or indirectly, that Employee knows or reasonably should know to be disparaging or negative concerning Company or any of Company's partners, officers, directors, or employees, except as required by law. Employee shall also refrain from suggesting to anyone that any written, oral, or electronic statements be made that Employee knows or reasonably should know to be disparaging or negative concerning Company, or any of Company's partners, officers, directors, or employees or from urging or influencing any person to make such statement. Employee's promises in this subsection, however, shall not apply to any judicial or administrative proceeding by which Employee is a party or in which Employee has been subpoenaed to testify under oath by a government agency or by any third party.

8. EMPLOYEE'S REPRESENTATIONS.

   a. Employee understands and acknowledges that the Consideration is in addition to anything of value that Employee would be entitled to receive from Company if Employee did not sign this Release.

   b. In exchange for the Consideration, Employee understands and acknowledges that Employee is giving up and releasing all of the Released Claims.

   c. Employee will not make any demands or claims against the Company for compensation or damages relating to the Released Claims.

   d. The Consideration that Employee is receiving is a fair compromise for the release of the Released Claims.

   e. Employee is legally able and entitled to receive the Consideration being provided in settlement of the Released Claims.

   f. Employee has not been involved in any personal bankruptcy or other insolvency proceedings at any time since Employee began employment with the Company.

   g. No child support orders, garnishment orders, or other orders requiring that money owed to Employee by Company be paid to any other person are now in effect.

   h. Employee represents and confirms that Employee has been fully paid for all wages, overtime, commissions, bonuses, vacation pay, and other compensation that Employee earned during Employee's employment with Company or that were due to Employee in connection with the termination of that employment.

   i. Employee has read this Agreement carefully and understands all of its terms.

   j. In signing this Agreement, Employee has not relied on any statements or explanations made by the Company except as specifically set forth in this Agreement.

   k. Employee is voluntarily releasing the Released Claims against the Company.

   l. Employee intends for this Agreement to be legally binding.

9.  MISCELLANEOUS.

    a.  In the event any provision of this Agreement is found to be unenforceable, void, invalid, or unreasonable in scope, such provision shall be modified to the extent necessary to make it enforceable, and as so modified, this Agreement shall remain in full force and effect.

    b.  The paragraph headings in this Agreement are for convenience only and do not form any part of or affect the interpretation of this Agreement.

    c.  The waiver by any party of a breach of any condition of this Agreement by the other party shall not be construed as a waiver of any subsequent breach. No waiver of any right hereunder shall be effective unless in writing and signed by the party against whom the waiver is sought to be enforced.

    d.  The rights and obligations of the parties under this Agreement shall inure to the benefit of, and shall be binding upon, their respective heirs, executors, administrators, successors, assigns, subsidiaries, affiliates, directors, officers, partners, employees, representatives, and agents, as applicable.

    e.  This Agreement constitutes the entire agreement of the parties with respect to the subject matter hereof and supersedes any previous employment agreements or contracts, whether written or oral, between Company and Employee.

    f.  This Agreement shall be construed under, and governed by, the laws of the State of {STATE}.

    g.  Employee and Company acknowledge that each has had the opportunity to read, study, consider, and deliberate upon this Agreement, and to consult with legal counsel, and both parties fully understand and are in complete agreement with all the terms of this Agreement.

IN WITNESS THEREOF, the parties have executed this Agreement as of the day and year first written above.

COMPANY:                                              EMPLOYEE:

{NAME OF PRACTICE}

By: _____         By: _____

Name: _____         Name: _____

Title: _____

Date: _____         Date: _____

CHAPTER 13

# Employee Handbook

All of the policies and procedures that your practice develops should be contained in your practice's policies and procedures manual. These policies provide supervisors and managers with the tools necessary to make sound and consistent employment decisions. However, the medical practice needs to communicate its policies, procedures, employee benefits, management and employee responsibilities, and other essential information to all employees. A good way to provide this information is by creating an employee handbook. An employee handbook typically provides a brief overview of a practice's management philosophy, contains your practice's policies, and is distributed to all employees through a printed copy or on the intranet. In contrast, a policies and procedures manual is primarily used by supervisors and managers to make sound, consistent, and legal human resources (HR) decisions. Together with your practice's policies and procedures manual, the employee handbook contributes to organizational productivity, a competent workforce, and high employee morale. When revisions or additions are made to the policies and procedures, the employee handbook should be updated as necessary so the two reflect the same information.

The primary purpose of an employee handbook is to help employees perform effectively by explaining a medical practice's policies, benefits, and rules as well as the employees' roles and responsibilities. The employee handbook may also have a code of conduct that outlines management and employee responsibilities. It is usually more formal, personal, and conversational than the policies and procedures manual.

## Benefits of an Employee Handbook

The employee handbook is one of the most important communication tools for the employer and its employees. It can be used as a marketing and branding tool for current and prospective employees. It is an important management tool and resource document as well as contains employment legal information. Key benefits of developing an employee handbook for your practice include:

1. Serves as a management tool to communicate your practice's policies to employees;
2. Allows your practice to highlight its mission, goals, and objectives;

3. Provides a marketing opportunity to publicize the practice's accomplishments;

4. Aids employees to follow established rules; and

5. Ensures that all employees receive the same information and that this information is easily accessible.

## Legal Considerations for an Employee Handbook

Employee handbooks may sometimes be considered an enforceable contract although handbooks should have disclaimers stating they are not a contract. Lawsuits regarding employee handbooks commonly involve breach of contract charges in which the employee claims that language in the handbook constituted an offer that the employee "accepted." From the charging employee's perspective, this offer and acceptance creates a binding contract between the employer and the employee, which the employer allegedly breached.

One may think that by not having an employee handbook, a practice will have no contractual obligations. However developing an employee handbook is advisable in today's litigious environment. It is recommended that your practice carefully craft, continuously review, and revise its employee handbook to guard against the most troublesome areas that cause the majority of handbook-related litigation.

Medical practice managers should have every employee sign a disclaimer emphasizing two critical points:

1. Employees are at-will workers who can be terminated at any time, for any reason or no reason; and

2. The employee handbook is not a contract.

> **An Employee Handbook:**
>
> - Serves as a communication tool;
> - States the practice's goals and objectives;
> - Highlights the practice's accomplishments; and
> - Informs employees about rules and policies.

> **Employee Handbook Legal Vulnerabilities**
>
> - Employment-At-Will Statement
> - Disciplinary Policies
> - Complaint Procedures

Check with your legal counsel to ensure that your practice is in an "at-will" state.

Every employee should sign a disclaimer, either during employee orientation or on their first day of work, acknowledging they received and read the employee handbook. The signed acknowledgment statement provides essential legal protection for your practice stating that the employee has read, understood, and agreed to comply with the handbook. A copy of the signed acknowledgment statement should be given to employees for their records, and the original should be placed in employees' files.

The employment-at-will statement should be one of the first elements in the employee handbook. The acknowledgment statement usually appears as one of the last pages, which helps ensure that employees do actually read the handbook. If a practice has physical printed copies of the employee handbook, they should be returned to your practice when employment has been terminated. Form 13.1 at the end of this chapter is a Sample Employment-At-Will Disclaimer, and Form 13.2 is a Sample Employee Handbook Acknowledgment statement, both of which should be modified for your practice.

## Key Elements of an Employee Handbook

The employee handbook should begin with a brief history of the medical practice, its organizational structure, accomplishments, mission, vision, values, and objectives. It is advisable to have an HR professional help your practice develop your employee handbook to ensure that employment policies, practices, pay practices, performance evaluations, benefits, and other HR-related issues are appropriately addressed. Your practice's legal counsel should review the handbook before it is distributed to employees in addition to every time a new policy is created or updated to ensure it complies with all applicable laws. As mentioned previously, the designated HR professional should be responsible for periodically updating and revising the handbook as well as informing employees about new changes.

The employee handbook should include:

- Table of contents (see Form 13.3);
- Welcome letter to employees (see Form 13.4);
- Introduction (see Form 13.5);
- Employment-At-Will statement in states where allowable; (see Form 13.1);
- Employee Handbook Acknowledgment statement (see Form 13.2);
- Practice's goals and objectives;
- General working hours and calendar of paid holidays;
- Dress code, customer service, and safety rules;
- Vacation, sick, personal, and other leaves;
- Salary and performance reviews;
- Overtime for nonexempt employees;
- Employee benefits;
- Employee code of conduct and ethics; and
- Termination and discipline procedures.

The employee handbook should have an effective date and contain language that, if revised, the handbook supersedes all previous handbooks a well as a description of the terms and conditions of employment.

Many medical practices choose to begin with a welcome letter from the administrator or chief executive officer. This letter should make employees feel important and encourage them to contribute to practice goals. It should not state how generous, fair, and excellent the employment package is or how employees can expect a long and happy relationship with the medical practice. Form 13.4 at the end of this chapter is an example of a welcome letter to adopt.

The introduction to the employee handbook should give employees an idea of what it is like to work for your practice and describe the types of medical services your practice provides. It presents the medical practice's mission, vision, values, and history. You may wish to include your code of ethics in this section or present it separately. The introduction should explain that one purpose of the employee handbook is to ensure consistent treatment of employees. It should also explain how to use the employee handbook. You should encourage your employees to read the handbook, become familiar with its contents, and ask questions. Form 13.5 at the end of the chapter is a sample introduction.

As with all information presented in the employee handbook, your policies on sexual harassment, workplace violence, and nondiscriminatory practices should be expressed simply and briefly. It is not necessary to have the entire policy as it appears in the policies and procedures manual. However, it is imperative when you have both a handbook and a policies and procedures manual that the two documents do not contain any inconsistent or contradictory statements.

The employee benefits section of the employee handbook should briefly describe the benefits offered and include a statement that you retain the right to terminate any benefits plan at any time. You should avoid language that might imply that benefits are entitlements. In addition, you should state that all coverage is subject to terms, restrictions, and other eligibility requirements stated in your plan documents. The employee handbook should indicate how leaves of absence affect leave accrual and the exercise of benefits.

## Developing an Employee Handbook

Before you begin developing your employee handbook, you should consider the following factors.

1. **The Audience.** The audience is usually your employees. The handbook is one of the first impressions employees will have of your practice. It reflects your practice's image, and it provides an excellent opportunity to establish clear communications among employees and your practice. The handbook should be easily understandable by all employees. Technical, complex language or legal jargon should be avoided; rather, the writing should be simple, conversational, and gender neutral.

2. **Diction.** Your word choice is critical. Employers must pay particular attention to verbs. Using mandatory verbs, such as *must*, *will*, and *shall*, to describe the employer's responsibilities, particularly when coupled with specific descriptions of management's responsibilities or actions, could make the statement be interpreted as a legally binding contract. Courts frequently rule that such language is clear and definite for an employee to believe an offer had been made. Permissive verbs and/or qualified phrases should always be used. These include *may*, *should*, *will*, *attempt*, and *seeks*. Permissive verbs alone can often defeat an employee's claim that a handbook is a contract. The diction should be short and to the point.

3. **Design.** Regardless of whether your practice chooses to print employee handbooks or have them accessible online, the visual appearance can be important. It should be appealing to the eye and complement your practice's branding. When possible, use color on the cover page while the body of the handbook could be black and white. Consider using pictures or photographs of your physicians and/or your practice facility. Do not place too much print on a single page. A page with lots of white space is more appealing to the eye and is more inviting to read. Both physical and electronic versions of the handbook should be well organized and specific policies easy to find. For example, your electronic version should utilize hyperlinks to easily move to a certain policy or rule.

4. **Schedule.** A realistic timeline for writing and producing your employee handbook is four to six months. Avoiding establishing a realistic timeline can jeopardize its quality and accuracy. Refrain from assigning an arbitrary date and having everyone rush to meet it. Allow ample time for all parties to fulfill their responsibilities. The employee benefits statements in the handbook generally take the longest to prepare. Allow eight to twelve weeks to complete that section. Also, do not forget to allow time for a legal review by an experienced attorney to ensure that your handbook complies with all applicable laws.

5. **Budget.** The cost estimate for developing the employee handbook should include charges for writing it, desktop publishing, editing, proofreading, design, layout, artwork, and either printing costs or IT development costs.

To accommodate changing conditions, always include a statement that *the medical practice reserves the right to alter, change, or delete any policy, procedure, or guideline at any time and without notice.*

## Guidelines for Writing an Employee Handbook

Below are recommended guidelines to use when developing your practice's employee handbook.

1. Begin with a disclaimer stating that your employee handbook is not a legal document.

2. Keep sentences short and simple.

3. Avoid legal or complex terminology, and use language that can be easily understood by most employees.

4. Write in the second person using "you."

5. Use pictures, charts, and graphics where possible.

6. Check for spelling and grammatical errors.

7. Use gender-neutral language.

## Common Mistakes to Avoid

As mentioned previously, developing an employee handbook can be difficult and tricky. Try to avoid these common mistakes to ensure your employee handbook is as complete, effective, and mistake-free as possible:

1. Failing to include disclaimer clauses describing the limitations of the employee handbook, including statements saying it is not a binding contract, it is intended only to offer guidance, the employer retains the right to change the terms at any time without notice, and the employment relationship is at-will and therefore the employee may be terminated at any time with or without cause;

2. Failing to update and revise it and have legal counsel review it at least annually;

3. Failing to require all employees to acknowledge they received the employee handbook or were given access to it;

4. Using marketing language or virtuous statements about how generous and excellent working for your practice can be to protect your practice from charges of unfair employment practices;

5.  Including the words "permanent employment," which negates the employment-at-will statement affirming that employees can be terminated at any time with or without cause;

6.  Including detailed employment and management procedures that can create an obstacle to your practice's ability to make decisions that should be made on a case-by-case basis;

7.  Including privacy statements, which creates problems if you need to search the office or locker of an employee who is suspected of theft or drug use; rather your practice should specifically retain the right to search lockers, offices, and vehicles on practice property to the extent allowed by applicable law;

8.  Failing to include the right to amend written policies, which may prohibit your practice from changing the conditions of employment;

9.  Including statements of the job security of employees such as guaranteeing employment as long as employees are doing their job or indicating that employees are joining a "family" on a permanent basis;

10. Failing to define the employee category that your employee handbook covers, as top managers and practice administrators are usually covered by a slightly different set of policies and procedures;

11. Committing to giving pay raises every year rather than stating that salaries may be increased from time to time as determined by management; and

12. Stating that discipline occurs for just cause can cause legal problems rather than outlining examples of disciplinary actions that may occur in different situations or generally describing your disciplinary policy, stating that it should be considered a guide and does not entitle employees to any particular disciplinary procedure or progressive discipline.

## Employee Handbook Checklist

An employee handbook can be a shield or sword depending on its content. To determine the relevance of your handbook and how well it has stood the test of time, answer the following questions and use them as a guide to determine whether revisions in your handbook are warranted.

1.  **Does the employee handbook contain any statements indicating that the handbook is a contract?** Eliminate any statements indicating that the handbook is a contract. There should be statements throughout your handbook explaining to staff that your handbook only provides information on current policies and procedures. It is not a contract of employment.

2.  **Is the employment relationship defined as being "at-will"?** The employee handbook should specifically and conspicuously state that the employment relationship is "at-will" and subject to termination by either party at any time, without stated cause. Such language should appear on the first page and throughout the handbook where appropriate. Review your handbook to ensure that it does not contain language that is inconsistent with that position.

3.  **Does the handbook contain a policy regarding workplace harassment that includes a specific complaint procedure?** Every employee handbook should state that sexual and other forms of workplace harassment are not tolerated; and retaliation against an employee for making a complaint of discrimination or harassment is strictly prohibited. The statement should list prohibited conduct and outline the procedure for reporting alleged harassment.

4. **Does the handbook contain the words** *probationary* **or** *permanent* **when describing employment?** Eliminate the words *probationary* and *permanent*. Those words are usually considered to imply that an employee who completes his or her initial period is granted permanent employment and associated benefits. Consequently, you may encounter problems when terminating that employee. Insert language that states that no employee is guaranteed employment for any period of time. Consider words such as *provisionary, orientation*, or *introductory period* instead of *probationary period*.

5. **Does the handbook describe your practice's disciplinary policy?** Eliminate or drastically change any required disciplinary steps that may look like progressive discipline is required prior to termination. Any list of inappropriate behaviors or conduct should state that it is not exhaustive. Although it is imperative that you treat all employees consistently, you need the flexibility to terminate an employee on the spot for any reason. Promising to progress through a series of four steps could invite a lawsuit if you fail to follow your own policy.

6. **Does the handbook contain a section on equal employment opportunity, which includes mention of people in all protected statuses under federal, state, and local laws applicable to your practice?** Be sure that the handbook contains language that the medical practice does not discriminate on the basis of any protected class.

7. **Does the handbook contain language in which fringe "benefits" could be considered fringe "entitlements"?** The description of benefits should be accompanied by a statement that your practice retains the right to end any benefits plan at any time. In addition, state that all coverage is subject to the terms, restrictions, and other eligibility requirements stated in your plan documents. Include provisions about how leaves of absence affect leave accrual and the exercise of benefits.

8. **Does the handbook contain an effective date?** The employee handbook should contain language that the revised handbook supersedes all previous handbooks and it supersedes any oral and written description of the terms and conditions of employment.

9. **Does your practice require each employee to sign a statement indicating they have access to and read the employee handbook and understand all of its provisions?** Ensure that your medical practice uses a form to this effect, have employees sign it, give them a copy, and keep one in the employee's file.

10. **Does the handbook state that you have the right to discharge an employee who fails to cooperate with an investigation?** Such a statement gives you the right to terminate an employee who refuses to cooperate with an investigation.

## Summary

Your medical practice's employee handbook should be developed carefully and thoughtfully so it cannot be construed as a contract. The objectives of the employee handbook are two-fold. First, you want encourage employees to become familiar with practice policies and rules, and you want employees to ask questions at any time about areas unclear to them. Second, you want employees to feel welcome and part of the team that provides quality healthcare to patients. A well-written employee handbook that is promoted by management can do much to help employees feel proud to be a part of the medical practice. Form 13.3 is a sample employee handbook table of contents that practices may use as a quick checklist to get some ideas about the types of policies a practice may consider including in its employee handbook.

## Sample Forms

**Form 13.1**        <u>**Sample Employment-At-Will Disclaimer**</u>

This is a sample Employment-At-Will Disclaimer.

---

FORM 13.1              **SAMPLE EMPLOYMENT-
AT-WILL DISCLAIMER**

This Handbook will familiarize you with *[Practice's]* practices, policies, plans, programs, and procedures relating to your work, pay, and benefits.

This Handbook applies to all employees.

It is your responsibility to read this Handbook carefully, be familiar with its contents, and keep it handy for future reference. Please be sure to address any questions or issues you may have with either your supervisor or human resources personnel as soon as they arise.

This Handbook supersedes all previous employee handbooks, memoranda, e-mails, or other communications dealing with the subject matter. The statements made in this Handbook are not intended to, nor do they, constitute a contractual agreement. Your practice reserves the right to amend, suspend, terminate, deviate from, add to, or supersede any practice, policy, plan, program, or procedure at any time with or without notice.

**Employment with *[Practice]* is at will, which means that *[Practice]* retains the right to end employment of any individual at any time, for any reason, with or without cause or notice. Statements in the Handbook or in any other *[Practice]* publication are not to be construed as affecting or modifying in any way the at-will status of *[Practice]* employees. No statement, written or oral, or other communication establishing employment for a specific period or under particular terms or conditions, or otherwise altering the at-will status of a *[Practice]* employee, will be enforceable unless it is in writing signed by the Practice Administrator of *[Practice]*.**

This Handbook is the property of *[Practice]* and must be returned upon request or upon termination with *[Practice]*.

**Form 13.2**          **Sample Employee Handbook Acknowledgment**

This is a Sample Employee Handbook Acknowledgment page.

---

FORM 13.2          **SAMPLE EMPLOYEE
HANDBOOK
ACKNOWLEDGMENT**

I have received a copy of the Employee Handbook ("Handbook"), which outlines current practices, policies, plans, programs, and procedures of *[Practice]*.

I understand that it is my responsibility to read and become familiar with the information contained in this Handbook and any revisions made to it. I understand that the Handbook is intended as a reference document containing general employment guidelines and does not necessarily represent all guidelines and practices of *[Practice]*. I further understand that the language contained in this Handbook and other guidelines or policy statements of *[Practice]* do not create a contract of employment. I am aware that the information in the Handbook is subject to change from time to time without prior notice, that this Handbook and its contents revoke and supersede any and all previous statements on similar subjects, and that *[Practice]* may deviate from the policies in individual circumstances in its discretion.

**I understand that my employment is at will, which means that neither I nor *[Practice]* is bound to continue the employment relationship, and that either I or *[Practice]* may end the relationship at any time for any reason without notice. I further understand that nothing in this Handbook modifies the at-will employment relationship between me and *[Practice]*.**

I agree, in accepting or continuing employment with *[Practice]*, to abide by its policies, procedures, and practices and understand that failure to comply with *[Practice's]* policies, procedures, and practices may result in my dismissal.

I understand that this Handbook is *[Practice's]* property and must be returned upon request by *[Practice]* or separation.

_____          _____
Employee Signature                       Date


_____
Printed Name


Please sign and return to *[designated HR professional]*.

---

**Form 13.3**       <u>**Sample Employee Handbook Table of Contents**</u>

This is a sample employee handbook table of contents.

---

FORM 13.3            **SAMPLE**
**TABLE OF CONTENTS**

Employment At-Will Disclaimer
Welcome
Introduction
Organization History
Practice Goals and Objectives
Equal Opportunity Statement
Workplace Harassment
Employment
     Attendance and Punctuality
     Work Hours and Scheduling
     Meals Periods and Breaks
     Employee Status
     Performance Evaluations
     Outside Employment
     Employee Files and Inquiries
     Resignation
     Layoffs
     Employment Separation Procedure
     Re-employment
     Promotions and Transfers
Compensation
     Pay Period and Payday
     Payroll Deductions
     Recording Your Hours Worked
     Overtime
     Pay Increases
     Expense Reimbursement
     Incentive Pay
Standards and Expectations of the Workplace
     Patient Safety and Confidentiality
     Care of Equipment and Supplies
     Violence-Free Workplace
     Drug-Free Workplace

**Form 13.4**      <u>**Sample Employee Handbook Welcome**</u>

This is a sample Employee Handbook Welcome page.

---

FORM 13.4                **SAMPLE EMPLOYEE
HANDBOOK WELCOME**

Welcome!

We are pleased that you have joined our medical practice. As you begin your employment, we want you to know how important our employees' contributions are to *[Practice]*'s mission – to offer our patients the highest quality medical services.

This Employee Handbook is one tool designed to contribute to your effectiveness. We encourage you to read it in its entirety and to become familiar with the policies and procedures as outlined.

If you have any questions or need additional information about a particular topic, your supervisor is available to assist you as is the Human Resources Department.

FORM 13.5 **SAMPLE EMPLOYEE HANDBOOK INTRODUCTION**

Welcome to *[Practice]*! Since our founding in 1987 as a two-physician practice, we have grown to include 20 physicians, 50 care providers, and more than 100 support staff at two office locations. The mission of the practice is to provide high-quality medical services to our patients. Our vision is to exemplify the best in medical practice by promoting the best healthcare and treatments of our patients. Our values are to treat patients and employees with the highest ethical standards.

Our code of ethics serves to inform employees and the public about our guidelines for ethical conduct in the delivery of care and service. We have a strong commitment to:

- Inform patients of their rights and respect these rights;
- Ensure quality of care as defined by the patient, physician, and outcomes;
- Focus on prevention and education as well as the treatment of illness or injury; and
- Treat all patients and employees with respect.

*[Practice]* has prepared this Employee Handbook to provide you with an overview of *[Practice's]* policies, benefits, and rules. It is intended to familiarize you with important information about *[Practice]* as well as provide guidelines for your employment experience with us in an effort to foster a safe and healthy work environment. Please understand that the Employee Handbook only highlights *[Practice]* policies, practices, and benefits for your personal understanding and cannot be construed as a legal document. The guidelines are not intended to be a substitute for sound management, judgment, and discretion.

It is our belief that we must all work together to make *[Practice]* a viable, healthy, and profitable organization. This is the only way we can provide a satisfactory working environment that promotes genuine concern and respect for others including all employees, our patients, and their families. If any statement in this Employee Handbook is not clear to you, please contact your supervisor for clarification. This Handbook supersedes any and all prior policies, procedures, and handbooks of *[Practice]*.

Our commitment to the highest quality care has been our focus from day one, and it continues to this day. *[Practice]* has achieved its present position in the community because of the quality of care we provide. We expect to continue to evolve and expand in the years ahead.

It is the policy of *[Practice]* to provide equal employment opportunities to all employees and applicants for employment and not to discriminate on any basis prohibited by law, including race, color, creed, sex, age, religion, national origin, sexual orientation, disability, and veteran or marital status. It is our intent and desire to provide equal employment opportunities in employment, recruitment, selection, compensation, benefits, promotion, transfer, layoff, termination, and all other terms and conditions of employment.

We strive to fill positions with the most qualified individuals available. Employees are to be considered for promotion or transfer upon consideration of present performance, specialized backgrounds, and potential, among other factors.

# The Bigger Picture

This manual was designed to help practices consider the types of policies and procedures to use to help a practice's leaders manage employees for peak performance and productivity. When developing or updating your policies and procedures manual, think about the bigger picture and how you can help your supervisors and leaders become better managers and perform to the best of their abilities. Unless the managers couple these policies with a wide repertoire of managerial skills, the medical practice will not develop as an entity or change appropriately with the times and trends.

The policies in this manual also affect managers and supervisors as employees of the medical practice. The designated human resources (HR) professional has the added responsibility to enhance the skills of his or her supervisors and managers so your practice can continue to be successful. In their role as employees, managers and supervisors need to know your practice's policies on vacation, holidays, benefits, health, safety, and so on. In their role as managers, they must also be aware of policies related to employee hiring and performance management. However, few policies relate directly to the managers' role in handling external relationships or dealing with mergers and acquisitions.

Medical practices' governing policies typically concentrate on guidelines for the board of directors. Some of these policies may provide guidance on higher-level management responsibilities but they rarely spell out the expectations as clearly as the employment policies contained in this manual. Some of the skills most appropriate for management and governing responsibilities include knowing how to:

- Fulfill the Body of Knowledge for medical practice management domain of professional responsibility with an emphasis on accountability;
- Interact effectively with payers, community partners, industry peers, partners, and even competitors through appropriate communication channels;
- Deal with a merger or an acquisition with proper attention not only to the business aspects but also to the people factors; and
- Handle change management and corporate culture situations effectively.

There are several ways in which the designated HR professional can help managers and supervisors better understand and deal effectively with the bigger picture. Ensuring that your medical practice's professional development activities cover organizational strategy, professional and leadership development, professional responsibility, and accountability is a good start.

## Strategic Direction

The HR department's role in helping to develop an organizational strategy is visible through job classifications, analysis, and job descriptions. As a medical practice grows and changes, its future depends on having the right talent doing the right things by developing and steering the organization to achieve its strategic goals and objectives identified in its strategic plan.

Practice managers and supervisors should be encouraged to learn more about the medical practice's strategic plan and initiatives. Better yet, they should be involved in the strategic plan development process to build ownership and accountability in achieving the goals. Successful supervisors live and work by your practice's mission, vision, values, and strategic direction. Supervisors should develop their team around these guidelines, ensuring that they are constantly working toward achieving the same goals.

### Organizational Development

Achieving the strategic goals and objectives of the medical practice depends on how successfully the organization's board of directors and leaders develop, change, and move the organization forward. Organizational development shifts the emphasis from technical skills and organizational structure to organizational purpose, human interactions, and organizational culture. Organizational development also switches the typical sequence of how change naturally occurs as a reactive event to a proactive process of planning, driving, and leading change. This fundamental shift in philosophy must start with changing the personal values of employees from valuing individual success to organizational success, followed by valuing positive, effective human interactions. Once the organization is working toward the same goals, practice leaders can begin to maximize organizational effectiveness and build its culture.

### Change Management

Managers and supervisors direct the change process based on the medical practice's strategic direction. Therefore, the strategic direction of your practice must be communicated to all employees, whether it is organic growth (e.g., hiring more physicians, adding new specialties, opening new offices/clinics) or growth through a merger or acquisition. In successful organizations, all employees are working toward the strategic direction regardless of the end goal.

Change management involves change agents, change champions, and change implementers. Managers and supervisors direct the transformation outlined in your practice's strategic plan. They help the medical practice spot trends, predict and deal with the constant change occurring in the health field, and find the most successful path for maneuvering through areas requiring extreme caution.

### Attitude Change

Managers and supervisors are tasked with converting the attitudes and habits of their employees to match the strategies of the medical practice. In other words, they must set an example of how the medical practice and its employees should treat other people. Attitude changes might involve a new approach of developing a patient treatment plan. For example, traditionally, a hierarchical structure is in place where the physician instructs the nurse what to do, and the nurse then gives instructions to a medical assistant. The attitude change could occur when a practice changes this process to try to provide higher-quality care by requiring the physician, nurse, and medical assistant to collaborate as equals on a team to determine the best treatment plan. This change in both attitude and behavior in a medical practice requires lots of help and support from all levels of management as well as effective communication.

Before a practice can implement an attitude change, the leaders need to know where to start. Managers and supervisors can survey their employees to determine how open to change they are. Such employee surveys can help managers and supervisors assess and measure employee attitudes. Practice leaders and supervisors need to know that resistance is a natural response to change. They will need to be prepared for both attitudinal positive and negative phases. These ups and downs are also natural when anyone faces a situation that will require changes in habitual behaviors. Practice leaders should help managers and supervisors identify the rewards related to change and help employees see the "big picture." They need to point out that change is a reality and that the medical practice must have a change strategy to survive and succeed in an uncertain future. Practice leaders should strive to build employee ownership in the change by engaging them in the strategic planning process. This will also help them see their part in shaping your practice's future.

### Corporate Culture

Practice leaders, managers, and supervisors all help reshape your practice's climate or culture, that is, how the organization behaves and what it values. Organizational culture, commonly known as corporate culture, is the personality of the medical practice; its character; and how it feels to employees, job applicants, and patients. Clues to the culture can be seen in the mission statement and other statements of medical practice philosophy, beliefs, and values about "who we are" and "how we do it here."

Your practice's managers and supervisors are the embodiment of your practice's culture. The desired culture should be mirrored in the physical environment of the medical practice, its branding, its employment policies, its turnover rate, the administrator's leadership style, the supervisors' communication methods, and its image in the community. Consider whether your medical practice's culture matches its mission and values statements as well as all other communication pieces about respect for each patient and employee.

There is no one right or correct organizational culture. However, the medical practice's leadership defines its practice culture, and if and when it should be modified. Often a change in culture is part of a major new strategic direction, such as fast growth or a merger. Keep in mind the corporate culture is very difficult to change.

Because of the recent, and most likely continuing, changes to the healthcare industry, such as increasing regulations and reductions in Medicare payments, medical practices are merging with other practices more often. In addition to mergers, many physicians are leaving private practice to work for hospitals as employed physicians. Mergers can sometimes create a classic culture clash when two organizations with different cultures join together. Crafting a new common culture can be difficult for the leadership team, but it can be done through the comprehensive preparation of strong strategies, tactics, and communication. Conversely, if the leadership does not plan for or address a possible culture clash, the results could mean organizational failure.

## Organizational Structure

Leaders and managers should develop new or modified organizational structures to accommodate changes in economic conditionals, new types of patient care, different employee roles, and collaborative systems for allocating resources and sharing authority. Task forces and committees can help managers smooth the way for structural change by stimulating participation and improving coordination.

For example, organizations that are reorganizing need to take coordination to a higher level. Having separate and independent silos is not effective or sustainable. A reorganization is a good time to integrate finance and marketing, administrative and clinical, physicians and support staff, the board of directors, and the senior management team. Coordinating each department's plans and activities can vastly improve the chances for developing a structure that only fits planned changes but allows the medical practice to thrive.

## Professional Responsibility and Accountability

Professional responsibility and accountability are two areas that frequently appear in a manager's job description and which certainly affect a manager's compensation. Significant strategic, fiscal, and supervisory responsibilities translate into higher pay because of the accountability expected of managers. The more responsibility and accountability, the more their actions, or nonactions, powerfully impact the organization – meaning, the higher the risk and responsibility, the higher the pay.

MGMA's Body of Knowledge specifies that one of the four general competencies for medical practice management is professionalism. This is demonstrated through continuous learning; effective management of stress and information generated by diverse situations; ethical decision making; and service activities that support the development of colleagues, profession, and the community. Professional responsibility is now part of the human resource management domain, specifically under Task 8:* provide personal commitment to enhance knowledge, skills, and abilities in healthcare administration.

Managers are expected to bring professionalism and accountability to life by being answerable for one's acts. It is an acceptance of the obligation and willingness to accept personal responsibility. Managers are also obligated to take this value and translate it into corporate accountability and responsibility by helping the medical practice develop policies on ethical management and provide oversight on clinical, personnel, and business matters. They should also help develop a code of ethics for your practice and model the expected behaviors.

---

* *Body of Knowledge for Medical Practice Management*, 2nd edition (ACMPE, 2011.)

## Coaching and Mentoring

Coaching and mentoring have some similarities but are fundamentally different. Coaching is short term, task oriented, performance driven, and focused on specific issues such as how to manage more effectively or think more strategically. Coaches help individuals learn the required attitude, behavior, and skills needed to perform their job successfully within agreed-upon success parameters. Coaching sessions are well defined and with a clear focus and specific timeline. Often supervisors or managers and the coach will identify the areas that need to be improved, and the coach will provide feedback on progress. Coaching is one of the best ways to stimulate, establish, and improve employee performance.

Coaches can give managers advice on how to deal with an employee conflict or how to improve a relationship with a peer. Most importantly, coaches help managers plan ahead and develop a game plan before tackling a challenging situation. A coach can also observe a manager's behavior and provide immediate feedback, helping the manager see how he or she could have handled the situation differently and more effectively. Consider coaching when a manager:

- Is not meeting performance expectations;
- Needs to develop specific competencies; or
- Needs assistance in acquiring a new skill as an additional responsibility.

Mentoring, on the other hand, is more developmental, long term, and relationship oriented where the mentee shares personal issues that affect his or her personal success. These issues can be related to work–life balance, self-confidence, self-perception, and influencing others. Mentoring focuses on the mentee and conversations often extend beyond work into broader issues, such as work–life balance. Mentoring discussions are not so much focused on specific skills but rather on the person's attitudes and behaviors. Effective mentors act as a sounding board and influence the other person. Mentors share their knowledge and experiences, help identify developmental opportunities, and can have a positive influence on the mentee. Instead of working to achieve predetermined goals, mentors offer advice, suggestions, and opinions. Consider mentoring when your practice:

- Needs to develop its leaders as part of succession planning;
- Seeks to assist diverse employees; or
- Seeks to develop its talent pool by equipping them with new skills and competencies.

The designated HR professional can help spur increased performance by promoting coaching and mentoring as part of professional development activities and offering seminars on coaching and mentoring for supervisors and managers. Managers may find it appropriate to be a coach in some circumstances and a mentor in others.

## External Relationships

Successful managers and supervisors develop effective communication and marketing messages for both internal and external relationships. They must keep in mind that their customers and stakeholders are more than just their patients and their coworkers. Other stakeholders with whom they frequently communicate include external colleagues, payers, regulators, outside consultants, attorneys, accountants, and competitors. Medical practices can help managers and supervisors develop their communication and marketing skills by offering seminars or workshops on these topics. Once managers and supervisors understand that communication methods and styles can profoundly impact internal and external relationships, they should be willing to strengthen these skills through workshops and/or coaching.

For example, one medical practice decided to extend the hours of its Pediatrics Department to accommodate the needs of working parents and to fulfill the requirements of a payer's contract. Your practice needs to first consider the plan for communicating this change to the staff, the patients, and the payer. Secondly, your practice should determine which communication methods will be used to successfully implement this change. Lastly, managers must consider the impact of the plan, including how staff will react and how parents can provide feedback on the change.

## Summary

This manual is designed to help medical practices develop and use appropriate employment policies and procedures to evolve their practices into highly effective organizations. However, these policies will only be as effective as the managers who use them to guide the medical practice and its workers. Helping managers to focus on the bigger picture and the skills necessary to operate in this wider arena is a critical function of the designated HR professional. His or her role has expanded from a protector and screener to a strategic planner and change agent helping managers and supervisors attract, retain, and develop top talent.

The Medical Group Management Association has several resources, such as publications and conferences, that address these bigger-picture topics. Consult the Website (www.mgma.com) or make contact toll-free at 877.ASK.MGMA (275.6462).

# Index

# Accessing the Files

As a purchaser of this book, all forms, policies and procedures
are available for you to download as a Microsoft® Word document.
**Visit mgma.org/HRManual and complete the form to
access the file.**